Welcome to

THE

— Family Guides —

THESE HANDY, PORTABLE BOOKS are designed to be the perfect traveling companions. Whether you're traveling within a tight family budget or feeling the urge to splurge, you will find all you need to create a memorable family vacation.

Use these books to plan your trips, and then take them along with you for easy reference. Does Jimmy want to go sailing? Or maybe Jane wants to go to the local hobby shop. *The Everything® Family Guides* offer many ways to entertain kids of all ages while also ensuring you get the most out of your time away from home.

Review this book cover to cover to give you great ideas before you travel, and stick it in your backpack or diaper bag to use as a quick reference guide for activities, attractions, and excursions you want to experience. Let *The Everything® Family Guides* help you travel the world, and you'll discover that vacationing with the whole family can be filled with fun and exciting adventures.

 TRAVEL TIP

Quick, handy tips

 **RAINY DAY FUN**

Plan ahead for fun without sun

≡**FAST FACT**

Details to make your trip more enjoyable

 JUST FOR PARENTS

Appealing information for moms and dads

THE EVERYTHING

— Family Guides —

The Disneyland Resort, California Adventure, Universal Studios, and the Anaheim Area,

2nd Edition

Dear Reader,

For many of you, your Disneyland trip is a dream vacation. For many years, it was my vacation dream, too, but the first time I visited Disneyland, I was disappointed. In the years since Walt Disney first realized his dream, the park he created has grown so popular that long lines can sour even the sweetest temperament. It took me more than a half-dozen visits to learn how to put the "happy" back into the "Happiest Place on Earth," but once I did, I found the Disneyland of my dreams. After ten years writing about California and exploring its nooks and crannies, the Disney theme parks remain among my favorite destinations.

In this book, I share my best tips and secrets: how to save money, stay out of line, keep your energy up, find the best place to watch the parades, and much more. I hope you can apply my experience to make your trip the best ever.

One of the biggest Disneyland myths is that you have to spend many days to see and do it all. Using this book's timesaving tips, you can enjoy all of Disneyland and California Adventure in three days, leaving time to explore the surrounding area. You'll find a cornucopia of ideas for other things to do in Chapters 15 through 20.

Relax and enjoy your trip. Planning will help you make the most of it, but don't overdo it. Be flexible if an unexpected pleasure arises. Have fun. When you get home, e-mail me at *gocalifornia.guide@about.com* to let me know how it went.

Betsy Malloy

THE

EVERYTHING®

FAMILY GUIDE TO
THE DISNEYLAND®
RESORT, CALIFORNIA
ADVENTURE®,
UNIVERSAL STUDIOS®,
AND THE
ANAHEIM AREA

2nd Edition

A complete guide to the best hotels,
restaurants, parks, and must-see attractions

Aadamsmedia
Avon, Massachusetts

To Walt Disney, who (in my child's mind) appeared in my living room every week just to tell me about his Disneyland, the stuff that childhood dreams of travel were made of. It took me almost forty years to see it in person, but it was all that he promised.

• • •

Innovation Director: Paula Munier
Editorial Director: Laura M. Daly
Associate Copy Chief: Sheila Zwiebel
Acquisitions Editor: Lisa Laing
Development Editor: Brett Palana-Shanahan
Production Editor: Casey Ebert

Director of Manufacturing: Susan Beale
Production Project Manager:
Michelle Roy Kelly
Prepress: Erick DaCosta, Matt LeBlanc
Interior Layout: Heather Barrett,
Brewster Brownville, Colleen
Cunningham, Jennifer Oliveira

• • •

An Everything® Series Book.
Everything® and everything.com® are registered trademarks of F+W Publications, Inc.

Published by Adams Media, an F+W Publications Company
57 Littlefield Street, Avon, MA 02322 U.S.A.
www.adamsmedia.com

ISBN-10: 1-59869-389-1
ISBN-13: 978-1-59869-389-8

Printed in Canada.

J I H G F E D C B A

Library of Congress Cataloging-in-Publication Data
available from the publisher

This publication is designed to provide accurate and authoritative information with regard to the subject matter covered. It is sold with the understanding that the publisher is not engaged in rendering legal, accounting, or other professional advice. If legal advice or other expert assistance is required, the services of a competent professional person should be sought.
—From a *Declaration of Principles* jointly adopted by a Committee of the American Bar Association and a Committee of Publishers and Associations

Many of the designations used by manufacturers and sellers to distinguish their products are claimed as trademarks. Where those designations appear in this book and Adams Media was aware of a trademark claim, the designations have been printed with initial capital letters.

Although the author has taken care to ensure that this book accurately sets forth information as of the time it was prepared, prices, practices, and policies at Anaheim attractions may change at any time and may be different from the information provided here.
The following are registered trademarks of The Walt Disney Company: Adventureland®, Audio-Animatronics®, California Adventure®, Disneyland Resort®, Fantasyland®, Frontierland®, Indiana Jones Adventure®, Main Street, U.S.A.®, Mickey Mouse®, Tomorrowland®, The Twilight Zone: Tower of Terror®, Walt Disney World®.
Universal Studios® is a registered trademark of Universal Studios, Inc.

*This book is available at quantity discounts for bulk purchases.
For information, please call 1-800-289-0963.*

Contents

The Top Ten Best Things about Disneyland and Disney's California Adventure

1. Watching a little girl dressed like Snow White getting a hug from a grown-up Cinderella

2. Riding Space Mountain, the ultimate "dark" ride that feels like flying through the stars

3. Buying a pair of Mickey Mouse ears and wearing them all day long without feeling silly—no matter what your age

4. Riding Haunted Mansion October through December, when the 999 ghosts have special guests

5. Watching the fireworks show from just behind the ropes in front of Sleeping Beauty Castle

6. Taking the "Walk in Walt's Footsteps" Tour and learning how it all began

7. Soarin' Over California, smelling the orange trees and salt air, and flying into the Disneyland fireworks at the end

8. Sitting in the Courtyard at Disney Animation, watching scenes from classic Disney cartoons

9. Picking up a birthday button, and having cast members wish you happy birthday all day long

10. Watching Disney's Electrical Parade, an experience so beloved Disney couldn't put its lights out

Acknowledgments

To Peat, who taught me how to write, to Prasad for supporting a difficult but rewarding midlife career change, and to Walt Disney, who followed his dream to create Disneyland.

Introduction

This book describes the major attractions and theme parks in Anaheim, California, where the Disneyland Resort is located, in surrounding Orange County, and in neighboring Los Angeles and San Diego Counties. As you'll quickly discover, there's a lot to see and do, enough to provide anyone with a memorable vacation adventure.

Every year, millions of people visit Southern California and have a wonderful time. However, unless you're planning to spend several weeks (and a small fortune), there's no possible way to experience everything this area has to offer. Once you look over all that's available, you'll have to make some tough decisions about what you have time and money to enjoy.

This book is designed to help you make those decisions. It includes descriptions of all the attractions and activities at Disneyland, Disney's California Adventure, Downtown Disney, Knott's Southern California Resort, Six Flags Magic Mountain, and Universal Studios Hollywood, along with other things to do in Orange County and Los Angeles County, plus San Diego's SeaWorld, San Diego Zoo, San Diego Wild Animal Park, LEGOLAND, and more. You'll also find lots of suggestions and tips for saving time and money while making the most of your vacation.

To help you choose which rides, shows, and attractions are most worth experiencing while visiting the Disneyland resort and California Adventure, this book offers a star-based ratings system. The ratings are based on the age group that will find each attraction most appealing. For each ride, you'll see a chart listing several age groups, plus a one- to three-star rating for that attraction.

These ratings are only recommendations. If you have a mature nine-year-old, he or she may very well enjoy a ride, show, or attraction that's more suitable for an eleven- to fifteen-year-old. As a parent, that's a judgment call you'll need to make based on the information provided within this book and after seeing the ride, show, or attraction for yourself once you get to the theme park.

This book is 100 percent "unofficial," which means that it is in no way authorized or sanctioned by the Walt Disney Company, Universal Studios Hollywood, Six Flags Magic Mountain, Knott's Southern California Resort, SeaWorld, the San Diego Zoo and Wild Animal Park, LEGOLAND, or any other theme park, attraction, travel agency, hotel chain, restaurant, or airline. As a result, the author can tell you about things frankly and offer money-saving advice that you may not find in any other travel guide or vacation-planning book.

As you begin planning your Southern California vacation, keep in mind that a little time spent planning can go a long way to improve your enjoyment and save your money. Make your reservations early, plan your time realistically so you know how much you can really do, and make sure everyone gets a say in the schedule. You'll be off to a great start for an even greater vacation.

Greater Anaheim Metro Area

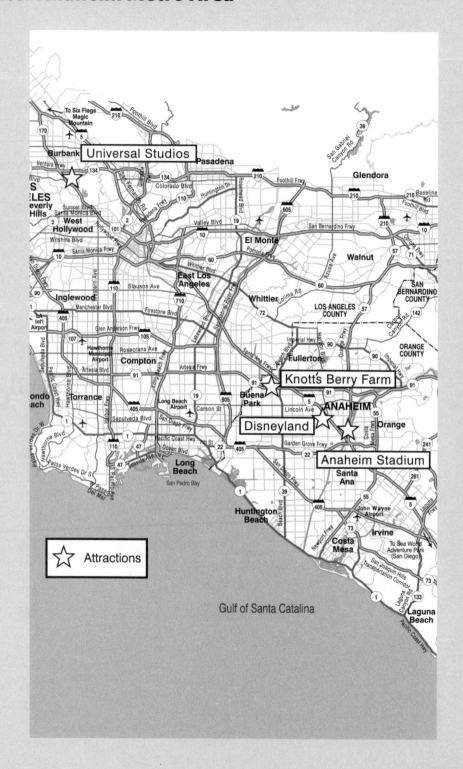

Disneyland Theme Park

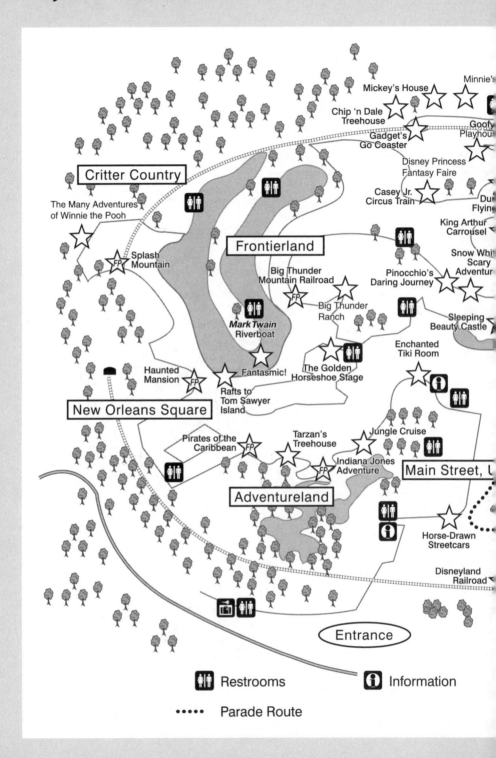

Mickey's House

Minnie'

Chip 'n Dale
Treehouse

Goofy
Playhou

Gadget's
Go Coaster

Disney Princess
Fantasy Faire

Casey Jr.
Circus Train

Dur
Flyin

King Arthur
Carrousel

Critter Country

Snow Whi
Scary
Adventur

The Many Adventures
of Winnie the Pooh

Frontierland

Big Thunder
Mountain Railroad

Pinocchio's
Daring Journey

Splash
FP Mountain

Big Thunder
Ranch

Sleeping
Beauty Castle

Mark Twain
Riverboat

Enchanted
Tiki Room

Haunted
Mansion

Fantasmic!

The Golden
Horseshoe Stage

FP

Rafts to
Tom Sawyer
Island

New Orleans Square

Tarzan's
Treehouse

Jungle Cruise

Pirates of the
Caribbean

FP

Indiana Jones
Adventure

FP

Main Street, U

Adventureland

Horse-Drawn
Streetcars

Disneyland
Railroad

Entrance

†∮† Restrooms   **ⓘ** Information

••••• Parade Route

2

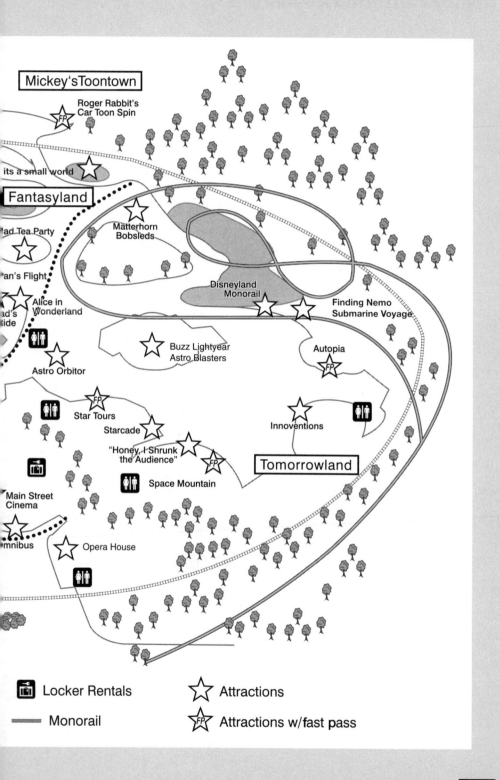

Mickey's Toontown

Roger Rabbit's
Car Toon Spin
FP

its a small world

Fantasyland

ad Tea Party

an's Flight

Alice in
Wonderland
ad's
ide

Astro Orbitor

Matterhorn
Bobsleds

Disneyland
Monorail

Finding Nemo
Submarine Voyage

Buzz Lightyear
Astro Blasters

Autopia
FP

Star Tours
FP

Innoventions

Starcade

"Honey, I Shrunk
the Audience"
FP

Tomorrowland

Space Mountain

Main Street
Cinema

mnibus

Opera House

Locker Rentals   Attractions

Monorail   FP Attractions w/fast pass

Disney California Adventure

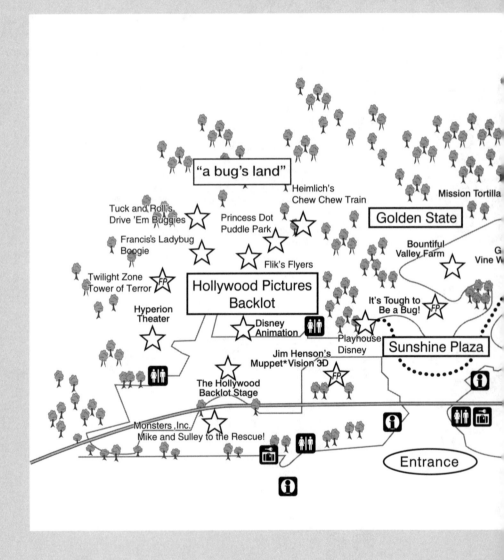

"a bug's land"

Heimlich's Chew Chew Train

Mission Tortilla

Tuck and Roll's Drive 'Em Buggies

Princess Dot Puddle Park

Golden State

Francis's Ladybug Boogie

Bountiful Valley Farm

G Vine W

Twilight Zone Tower of Terror

FP

Flik's Flyers

Hyperion Theater

Hollywood Pictures Backlot

Disney Animation

It's Tough to Be a Bug!

FP

Playhouse Disney

Sunshine Plaza

Jim Henson's Muppet*Vision 3D

The Hollywood Backlot Stage

FP

Monsters, Inc. Mike and Sulley to the Rescue!

Entrance

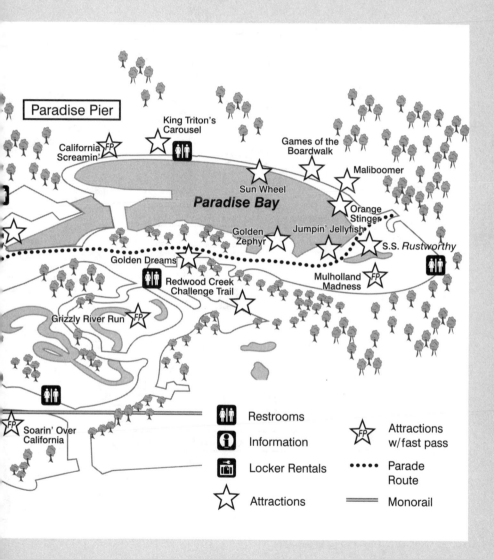

Paradise Pier

King Triton's Carousel

California Screamin' FP

Games of the Boardwalk

Maliboomer

Sun Wheel

Paradise Bay

Orange Stinger

Golden Zephyr

Jumpin' Jellyfish

S.S. Rustworthy

Golden Dreams

Redwood Creek Challenge Trail

Mulholland Madness FP

Grizzly River Run FP

Soarin' Over California FP

	Restrooms		Attractions w/fast pass FP
	Information		Parade Route
	Locker Rentals		Monorail
	Attractions		

Knott's Berry Farm

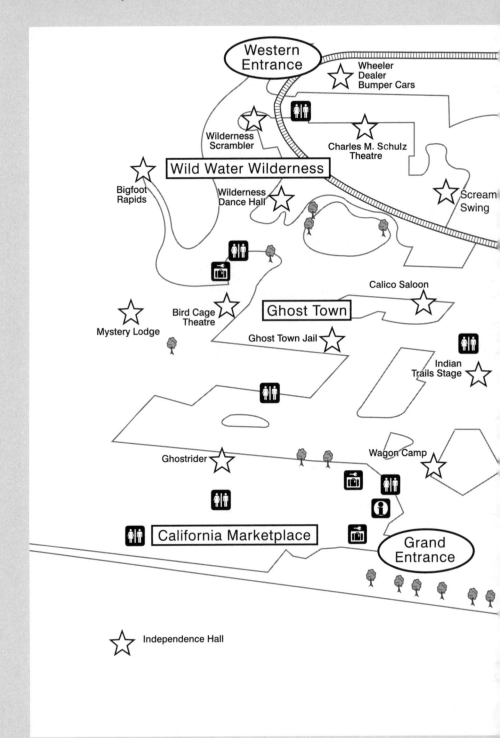

Western Entrance

Wheeler Dealer Bumper Cars

Wilderness Scrambler

Charles M. Schulz Theatre

Wild Water Wilderness

Bigfoot Rapids

Wilderness Dance Hall

Scream Swing

Calico Saloon

Bird Cage Theatre

Ghost Town

Mystery Lodge

Ghost Town Jail

Indian Trails Stage

Ghostrider

Wagon Camp

California Marketplace

Grand Entrance

Independence Hall

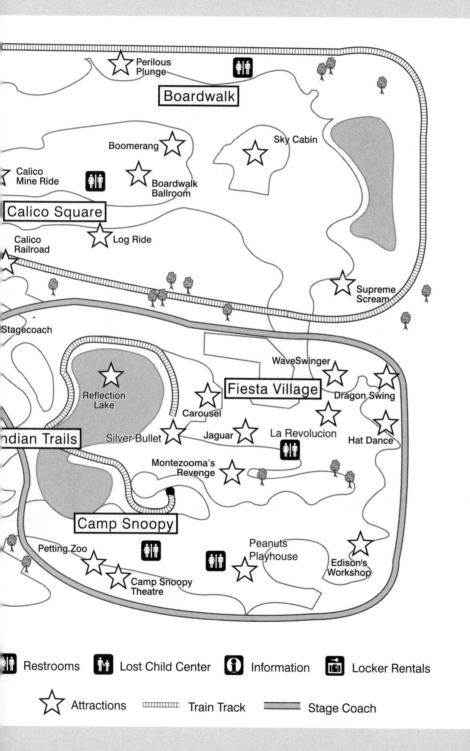

Perilous Plunge

Boardwalk

Boomerang

Sky Cabin

Calico Mine Ride

Boardwalk Ballroom

Calico Square

Calico Railroad

Log Ride

Supreme Scream

Stagecoach

Reflection Lake

WaveSwinger

Fiesta Village

Dragon Swing

Carousel

ndian Trails

Silver Bullet

Jaguar

La Revolucion

Hat Dance

Montezooma's Revenge

Camp Snoopy

Petting Zoo

Peanuts Playhouse

Edison's Workshop

Camp Snoopy Theatre

Restrooms Lost Child Center Information Locker Rentals

☆ Attractions Train Track Stage Coach

Six Flags Magic Mountain

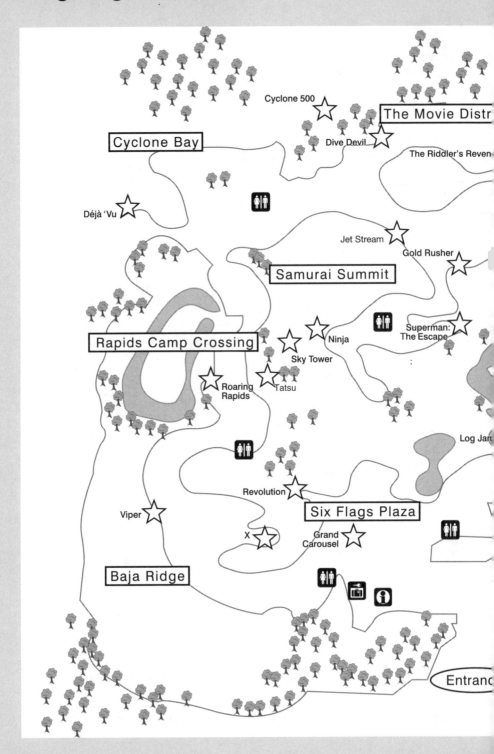

Cyclone 500

The Movie Distr

Cyclone Bay

Dive Devil

The Riddler's Reven

Déjà 'Vu

Jet Stream

Gold Rusher

Samurai Summit

Ninja

Superman:
The Escape

Rapids Camp Crossing

Sky Tower

Roaring
Rapids

Tatsu

Log Jan

Revolution

Six Flags Plaza

Viper

X

Grand
Carousel

Baja Ridge

Entranc

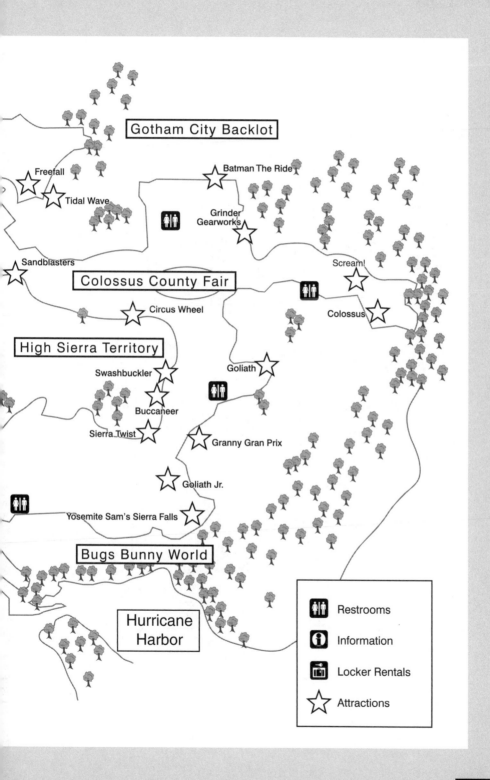

Gotham City Backlot

Freefall

Tidal Wave

Batman The Ride

Grinder Gearworks

Sandblasters

Scream!

Colossus County Fair

Circus Wheel

Colossus

High Sierra Territory

Swashbuckler

Goliath

Buccaneer

Sierra Twist

Granny Gran Prix

Goliath Jr.

Yosemite Sam's Sierra Falls

Bugs Bunny World

Hurricane Harbor

Restrooms

Information

Locker Rentals

Attractions

9

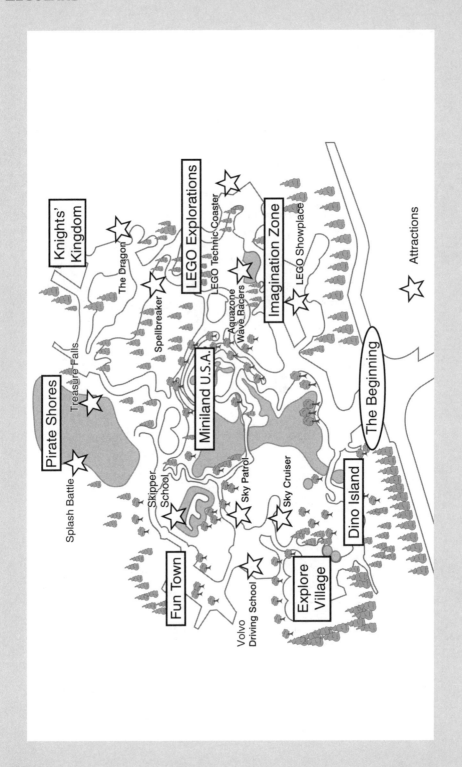

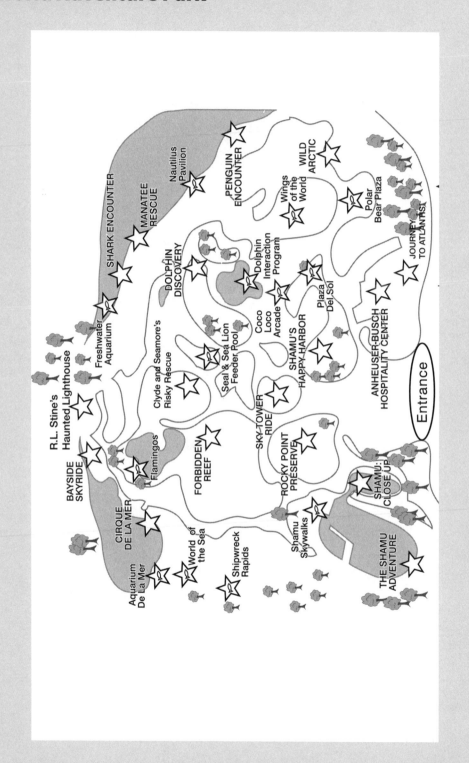

CHAPTER 1

Disneyland: Yesterday, Today, and Tomorrow

AMONG THE HUNDREDS OF tourist attractions in Southern California, none is more popular than Disneyland, especially among young people. In Walt Disney's "happy place," you can interact with favorite Disney characters, experience rides and attractions based on classic Disney movies and television programs, and watch shows, parades, and other spectacles that offer an entertainment experience only Disney can provide.

The Man and the Mouse

When Walt Disney first conceived of Disneyland, the phrase *theme park* did not exist. In fact, at that time, amusement parks tended to be seedy affairs, and the idea that adults and children could enjoy the same recreational experience together was inconceivable. In those days, parents stood and watched while their offspring rode carousels or ponies.

After pioneering a number of firsts, including the world's first sound-on-film cartoon—*Steamboat Willie*, 1928—and the first feature-length cartoon—*Snow White*, 1937—Walt Disney built his Burbank, California, studio in 1940. Soon, Disney started getting requests from children who wanted to see where Snow White and Mickey Mouse "lived." Rejecting the idea of a studio tour because he thought it would be boring just to watch people working, Disney started thinking about creating a character display on land surrounding the studio. At the same time, he was raising two young daughters and growing dissatisfied with the lack of places where parents could have fun with their kids.

Disney was also a lifetime fan of circuses, carnivals, and fairs, and he was enchanted with trains and railroading. Slowly, his interests and thoughts began to coalesce; an idea took shape for something new, something so revolutionary that he had trouble finding words to explain it to potential investors.

By 1948, Disney's idea began to crystallize. He circulated a memo about his "kiddie park" that included the seeds of Main Street, U.S.A. and Frontierland. By 1952, he presented a plan to the Burbank City Council, but it wasn't until 1955 that Disneyland became a reality, by then relocated to Anaheim.

On opening day, July 17, 1955, an estimated 90 million people watched the park's grand opening on television. By 1959, Disneyland became so popular that an international incident almost ensued when the first Soviet premier Nikita Khrushchev was denied entrance (on grounds that the park could not guarantee his safety). Within two and a half years, 10 million guests, famous and ordinary, had passed through its gates.

Disneyland was a new concept, an amusement park that offered state-of-the-art attractions, parades, and other forms of entertainment—all based on Walt Disney's most beloved characters. Shortly after it opened, Will Jones wrote in the *Minneapolis Tribune*: "If it's an amusement park, it's the gosh-darndest, most happily inspired, most carefully planned, most adventure-filled park ever conceived. No ride or concession in it is like anything in any other amusement park anywhere." Since then, Disneyland has been called a "creative experiment in urban design" in *Architectural Forum* magazine, "the most important single piece of construction in the West in the past several decades" by *Yale Architectural Digest*, and a whole lot of fun by the guests who have visited it.

Disneyland innovations include the first tubular steel roller coaster (Matterhorn Bobsleds), the first simulator-based ride (Star Tours), and the first daily operating monorail in the western hemisphere.

Disneyland retains dozens of classic rides and attractions created by Walt and his team of "Imagineers", but it also continues to add exciting new features designed for the entire family. Today's Disneyland theme park offers more than sixty rides, shows, and attractions. They are described in detail in Chapter 9.

Walt Disney's Dream Lives On

Walt Disney originally conceived of and built the Disneyland theme park. Although much larger than when it began, it still holds true to Disney's dream. As you plan your own trip, you're about to experience what hundreds of millions of people already have—the magic of Disneyland. No matter how many people pass through the gates of this incredible place, each one takes away a unique experience and set of memories.

Walt Disney, with his team of Imagineers and animators, created Mickey Mouse and all the Disney animated characters. Walt and his brother Roy founded Disney Brothers Studios in 1923. Soon thereafter, they became the force behind dozens of full-length animated and live-action movies, television programs, and, of course, the theme parks.

≡FAST FACT

When asked how he came up with the idea for Disneyland, Walt Disney is quoted: "Well, it came about when my daughters were very young and Saturday was always Daddy's day with the two daughters. I'd take them to the merry-go-round and as I'd sit there, sat on a bench, you know, eating peanuts, I felt that there should be some kind of an amusement enterprise built where the parents and the children could have fun together. So that's how Disneyland started."

Dubbed "the Happiest Place on Earth," Disneyland is the original Disney theme park. Located in Anaheim, California, it opened to the public on July 17, 1955, with eighteen major attractions. Today, the Disneyland Resort includes two major theme parks, three resort hotels, and dozens of shops and restaurants in Downtown Disney. Disneyland alone now contains more than sixty major attractions.

Since Disneyland's opening, the magical experience has touched more than 500 million people of all ages and nationalities. On a peak-season day, more than 65,000 guests pass through the park's main entrance. Back in the 1940s and early 1950s, when Walt and his team dreamed up this theme park, who could have imagined that a 180-acre orange grove in Anaheim would become a tourist destination to be enjoyed for generations?

The Hidden Mickeys

"It all started with the mouse!" Walt Disney Company employees say. Mickey Mouse is, without a doubt, the best-known cartoon character on the planet. He's also the corporate icon for one of the most powerful entertainment companies in the world, as well as the face behind the world's most popular theme parks.

In fact, you'll see this famous mouse everywhere you look. Throughout the park, countless "Hidden Mickeys" show up in the rides, attractions, landscaping, and other structures, an ongoing tribute to the rodent that started it all.

A Hidden Mickey is an image or outline of Mickey Mouse concealed in a Disney attraction's design. According to the unofficial Hidden Mickey Web site *www.hiddenmickeys.org/disneyland*, these Hidden Mickeys started out as inside jokes among Walt Disney Imagineers. As you explore the Disneyland Resort, keep your eyes peeled for Hidden Mickeys; they're everywhere! The whole family can have fun looking for them. Who can spot the most Hidden Mickeys each day?

Guided Disneyland Tours

If all the rides and shows aren't enough for you, Disneyland offers special tours to enhance your experience. Knowledgeable Disneyland cast members give these tours daily. To avoid disappointment, call (714) 781-4400 to reserve up to thirty days in advance. Tour prices do not include park admission.

≡FAST FACT

At Disneyland's grand opening in 1955, Walt Disney said: "To all who come to this happy place: welcome. Disneyland is your land. Here age relives fond memories of the past…and here youth may savor the challenge and promise of the future. Disneyland is dedicated to the ideals, the dreams and the hard facts which have created America…with the hope that it will be a source of joy and inspiration to all the world."

If you're a Walt Disney fan or interested in Disneyland's rich history, "A Walk in Walt's Footsteps" Tour is for you. This three-and-a-half-hour guided walking tour takes you on a journey into the past, through the life and times of Walter Elias Disney.

Along the way, you'll learn about Walt's original vision and discover how he brought his dream to life. You'll also get a peek at areas of the park most guests aren't allowed to explore, including the Club 33 lobby. This enjoyable tour is something adult Disney fans will appreciate, but kids may find boring. Cost is $59 per person, which includes a private lunch on the Disney Gallery patio.

The three-and-a-half-hour Welcome to Disneyland tour takes small groups for a detailed look at the landmarks and history. The price of the tour is $24 per person. Your guide will teach you how to use the fastpass system, and you'll get two bonus passes as well as priority seating at selected restaurants.

Families will enjoy the three-hour Discover the Magic Tour as they hunt for hidden treasure and avoid villains with the help of Disney characters. It includes lunch and a souvenir and is designed for children between the ages of five and nine. Strollers are not recommended, and an adult must accompany kids under eighteen. Cost is $59 for the first two tickets, $49 for each additional ticket.

Club 33

Just behind the Disney Gallery, around the corner from the Pirates of the Caribbean entrance, you'll find a door next to the Blue Bayou restaurant marked "33" for its address at 33 Royal Street. Behind this door is a private, members-only club known as Club 33. When Walt Disney entertained dignitaries, celebrities, and other special guests at Disneyland, he wanted a quiet, upscale, secure place where he could offer them a fine-dining experience. He and his wife, Lillian, traveled to New Orleans and handpicked all of the art still on display in Club 33.

═FAST FACT

As a regular Disneyland guest, you can't see inside Club 33 firsthand, but if you happen to be in New Orleans Square when someone enters or exits, you might catch a glimpse. You can also get a peek inside the lobby if you take "A Walk in Walt's Footsteps" Tour.

A few months after Walt's death, in May 1967, his private dining room reopened as Club 33. Today, some of the world's best chefs showcase their talents for Club 33 members.

Membership in this club is exclusive and expensive. A Club 33 representative says people often wait several years (the most recent estimate was seven to ten years) to become a member.

Commemorate Your Visit

Thousands of ten-inch hexagonal bricks pave the main Disneyland entry plaza, some imprinted with names of guests who wanted to commemorate their visit to Disneyland in a lasting way. They form the Walk of Magical Memories.

For $150, you can add your own brick, personalized with up to three lines of text (sixteen characters per line). Use special symbols to commemorate weddings and anniversaries, or imprint Mickey's head or hands along with your text.

You'll get a certificate to commemorate your purchase, a map, and a special number so you can find your brick in person. Since the brick you sponsor stays at the park (for at least ten years), you can buy a replica made of wood or acrylic to display at home for $35.

To sponsor a brick, drop by the newsstand near the Disneyland entrance or call Disneyland Resort Merchandise Services at (800) 760-3566 to order it.

In the Works: What's Coming at Disneyland

The old 20,000 Leagues under the Sea ride, closed since 1998, gets a new life in summer 2007. The theme is the same, an undersea submarine voyage, but now it's based on the popular film *Finding Nemo*. You'll find Nemo's friends Dory, Marlin, Crush, and Bruce swimming past, and you can listen to them through sonar headphones.

Opening at California Adventure in 2008 will be Toy Story Mania! This new ride is based on the characters from the Disney-Pixar films *Toy Story* and *Toy Story 2*. Riders will wear 3-D glasses and be "shrunk" down to toy size, hop on ride vehicles, and then travel along a carnival midway route where they will play games using an onboard cannon, and be cheered on by *Toy Story* characters.

Rumors are spreading about a new land to be called Carland (based on the Disney-Pixar movie *Cars*). This new land will have several car-related rides including a version of Disney's Test Track from Walt Disney World. This plan is not confirmed by the Disney Company.

CHAPTER 2

Preparing for Your Vacation

A BIT OF PREPARATION will help make your Southern California vacation the best it can possibly be. This chapter will help you make travel plans, and you might even save money in the process. This chapter also discusses some Disneyland basics you'll need to know so you can pack accordingly and be ready for whatever weather California throws your way.

Vacation-Planning Strategies

As you plan your California vacation, keep these travel tips in mind:

- **Set a budget and stick to it.** When they're having fun, people tend to make spontaneous purchases. Set aside money in your budget to purchase extras and souvenirs. It may also help to give your kids a spending limit for the day.
- **Get input from everyone.** Ask them about the kinds of activities they want to enjoy. Make sure they all have at least some say in how to spend your vacation, so everyone has a great time.
- **Be flexible about dates.** Take a look at "When to Experience the Magic" in Chapter 5 to find the best times to visit Disneyland. Even if the time of year for your trip is fixed, you can still save money, especially on airfare, by changing your trip just a day or two or flying in and out of a different airport.

- **Make reservations early.** Hotels and restaurants fill up quickly and frequent-flyer tickets sell out months in advance. If you wait until you arrive in Anaheim, you'll also find Disneyland tours, dining experiences, and special Fantasmic! viewings sold out as well. For Disneyland and California Adventure dining and Fantasmic! viewing, call (714) 781-4400 from thirty days to at least two weeks ahead to avoid disappointment.

Don't be shortsighted. Evaluate the total cost of any strategy you consider. For example, the $20 you save on airfare by flying into LAX could be wiped out by shuttle costs to and from your destination.

Using a Travel Agent

If you're busy, using a full-service travel agency to plan your trip and make your reservations will save you a lot of time. However, many hotel companies guarantee their best rates when reserved directly online and most travel agents earn their income by taking a commission on the total price of the trip they coordinate for you, so they're not always motivated to find you the lowest possible rates. Of course, there are plenty of exceptions.

When choosing a travel agent, find someone who is highly recommended by someone you trust, who specializes in planning family vacations, and who is familiar with Southern California and Anaheim. AAA and American Express both have highly reputable travel agencies that offer their services to members either in person or by telephone.

Booking Your Vacation Online

If you have some time to plan your vacation and you have access to the Internet, you can save money by making your own travel arrangements online.

When using the Internet, you have three primary options:

1. **Book direct.** Visit the airline, hotel chain, and rental-car company Web sites. Some guarantee that you'll get the lowest prices by reserving directly through their Web sites, and they may offer Internet-only specials. However, ferreting out the best deals and comparison-shopping can be very time-consuming.

2. **Use a one-stop, online travel service.** Sites such as Travelocity (✍*www.travelocity.com*), Expedia (✍*www.expedia.com*), Orbitz (✍*www.orbitz.com*), and Yahoo! Travel (✍*http:// travel.yahoo.com*) allow you to search quickly for the best flights, fares, and hotel and rental-car rates, and they may also offer travel packages.

3. **Try auction and deep-discount Web sites.** If you have a somewhat flexible travel schedule and can tolerate some uncertainty, you can save on airfares, hotels, and rental cars using services such as Priceline (✍*www.priceline.com*), Sky Auction (✍*www.skyauction.com*), Last Minute Travel's "Off the Record" (✍*www.lastminutetravel.com*), or Hotwire (✍*www .hotwire.com*).

Name-brand companies use these services to sell excess inventory at bargain-basement prices. However, if everyone knows that a specific hotel is offering discounted rooms for $50 a night, no one will want to pay their regular price of $100 a night. To avoid this problem, these services shield the seller's identity. They tell you when and where you'll be flying (but not the name of the airline), or they reveal the quality level and general location of a hotel (but not its name). You don't know exactly what you've reserved until after you pay for it, and then you're locked in, with no changes or cancellations allowed. It's less risky than it might seem because the reputable Web sites work only with well-known companies.

If you're willing to make these concessions, advertisements say you can name your own price, but that doesn't mean you can offer $10 for a four-star hotel in high season and expect to have your bid accepted.

🧳 TRAVEL TIP

If you want to try using Priceline, the Web site *✍www.biddingfor travel.com* can be a big help. Not only can you see what price others have gotten and where they're staying, but if you do a little research and post your particulars, a moderator will suggest a bidding strategy for you. If you're planning to buy your airfare, hotel, and rental car through Priceline, buy your airfare first because the company may then offer special "Insider Rates" for hotels and rental cars.

Priceline and other auction sites work more or less the same. You do a little research, submit a bid, and it's either accepted or rejected. Under certain circumstances, you can bid again, but you may have to wait to do so.

Other sites such as Hotwire are a little different. You submit your request, and they quote a firm price but will not reveal the details until after you've made your purchase.

═FAST FACT

Priceline and other auction sites can save you a lot of money, but you can't make changes or cancel your reservation, and you will not accrue frequent flyer miles or hotel points. If your travel plans are apt to change because of family or work situations, this may not be the best solution.

Most California residents already know how to get to Disneyland. It's just off the I-5 in Orange County and the exit is labeled "Disneyland." Many come in their own automobiles, but if you're getting to Southern California from farther away, you have several options.

Flying to Southern California

As a rule, book your flight as far in advance as possible. You'll get the best prices if you buy your tickets twenty-one days in advance, with reasonable savings up to fourteen days ahead. Ticket prices rise significantly if bought less than seven days before you travel. If your schedule permits staying a Saturday night, you'll usually get a better airfare.

Be sure to arrive at the airport at least ninety minutes before your scheduled departure time and have your driver's license, military ID, or passport ready to show multiple times at various security checkpoints.

The items allowed past the security checkpoint or in a carryon bag change frequently. To find out the current regulations, check with the Transportation Safety Administration (TSA) at *www.tsa.gov* or (866) 289-9673.

The airports most commonly used by Southern California visitors are Los Angeles (LAX) and Orange County's John Wayne Airport (SNA). Other options, depending on your exact travel plans, include Long Beach (LGB), Burbank (BUR), or even San Diego (SAN).

Los Angeles International Airport (LAX)

Los Angeles International Airport (LAX), ranked third in the world for number of passengers handled, offers the most frequent flights and airline choices. However, it's busy, noisy, sometimes confusing, and thirty-five miles from Anaheim.

 TRAVEL TIP

So-called red-eye flights that leave between 10 P.M. and midnight and return to the East Coast the following morning are usually the cheapest flights available. Although some people hate flying all night, others find it's the easiest way to conquer jetlag, and they can save up to several hundred dollars.

To learn more about LAX and the airlines that service it, visit the Los Angeles World Airports' Web site at *www.lawa.org* and click on the LAX link. The following table lists the domestic airlines that fly into LAX; these airlines are subject to change, so be sure to check the Web site whenever booking flights into Los Angeles.

DOMESTIC AIRLINES THAT FLY INTO LAX

Air Canada: (800) 247-2262 or *www.aircanada.ca*

AirTran Airways: (800) 247-8726 or *www.airtran.com*

Alaska Air/Horizon Air: (800) 547-9308 or *www.alaskaair.com*

American Airlines/American Eagle: (800) 433-7300 or *www.aa.com*

ATA Airlines: (800) 435-9282 or *www.ata.com*

Continental: (800) 525-0280 or *www.continental.com*

Delta Airlines: (800) 221-1212 or *www.delta-air.com*

Frontier Airlines: (800) 432-1359 or *www.frontierairlines.com*

Hawaiian Air: (800) 367-5320 or *www.hawaiianair.com*

Miami Air: (305) 871-8001 or *www.miamiair.com*

Midwest Express: (800) 452-2022 or *www.midwestexpress.com*

Northwest Airlines: (800) 225-2525 or *www.nwa.com*

Southwest: (800) I-FLY-SWA or *www.southwest.com*

Spirit Airlines: (800) 772-7117 or *www.spiritair.com*

Sun Country Airlines: (800) 359-6786 or *www.suncountry.com*

United/TED: (800) 241-6522 or *www.united.com*

US Airways/America West: (800) 428-4322 or *www.usairways.com*

Virgin Atlantic: (800) 862-8621 or *www.virgin-atlantic.com*

 **TRAVEL TIP**

If your travel plans are subject to change, consider using Southwest Airlines. You may have to pay a fare difference when you change your flight, but you won't have to shell out up to $100 for a "change fee."

All rental car lots at LAX are located outside the airport. Look for the purple Car Shuttle signs on the lower level outside baggage claim to get a ride to their lots. Only these car-rental companies can pick you up and drop you off inside the airport:

CAR RENTAL COMPANIES AT LOS ANGELES INTERNATIONAL AIRPORT

Advantage Rent-A-Car: ✆(800) 777-5500 or ✉www.arac.com

Alamo Rent-A-Car: ✆(800) 327-9633 or ✉www.alamo.com

Avis Rent-A-Car: ✆(800) 230-4898 or ✉www.avis.com

Budget Rent-A-Car: ✆(800) 527-0700 or ✉www.budget.com

Dollar Rent-A-Car: ✆(800) 800-3665 or ✉www.dollar.com

Enterprise Rent-A-Car: ✆(800) 736-8222 or ✉www.enterprise.com

Fox Rent-A-Car: ✆(800) 225-4369 or ✉www.foxrentacar.com

Hertz: ✆(800) 654-3131 or ✉www.hertz.com

National Car Rental: ✆(800) 227-7368 or ✉www.nationalcar.com

Thrifty Car Rental: ✆(800) 847-4389 or ✉www.thrifty.com

John Wayne Airport, Orange County (SNA)

Located in Irvine, California, about fifteen miles from the Disneyland Resort, John Wayne Airport, (949) 252-5200 or *www.ocair.com*, is smaller than LAX and is serviced by fewer airlines. However, if you're only going to the Disneyland Resort (Anaheim), it's a more convenient airport to fly into and out of, and it's quieter and easier to navigate. Again, remember that these airlines are subject to change, so be sure to check the Web site first.

DOMESTIC AIRLINES THAT FLY INTO JOHN WAYNE AIRPORT

Alaska Airlines: ✆(800) 547-9308 or ✉www.alaskaair.com

Aloha Airlines: ✆(800) 367-5250 or ✉www.alohaairlines.com

American Airlines: ✆(800) 433-7300 or ✉www.aa.com

Continental: ✆(800) 525-0280 or ✉www.continental.com

Delta Airlines: ✆(800) 221-1212 or ✉www.delta-air.com

Frontier Airlines: ✆(800) 432-1359 or ✉www.frontierairlines.com

Northwest Airlines: ☏(800) 225-2525 or ✎www.nwa.com

Southwest: ☏(800) I-FLY-SWA or ✎www.southwest.com

United Airlines: ☏(800) 241-6522 or ✎www.united.com

US Airways/America West: ☏(800) 428-4322 or ✎www.usairways.com

These car-rental companies operate at John Wayne Airport.

CAR RENTAL COMPANIES AT JOHN WAYNE AIRPORT

Avis Rent-A-Car: ☏(800) 230-4898 or ✎www.avis.com

Budget Rent-A-Car: ☏(800) 527-0700 or ✎www.budget.com

Enterprise Rent-A-Car: ☏(800) 736-8222 or ✎www.enterprise.com

Hertz: ☏(800) 654-3131 or ✎www.hertz.com

National Car Rental: ☏(800) 227-7368 or ✎www.nationalcar.com

Thrifty Car Rental: ☏(800) 847-4389 or ✎www.thrifty.com

A number of other car-rental companies have off-airport locations, and some of them may offer lower rates. They include Advantage Rent-A-Car, Beverly Hills Rent-A-Car, Fox Rent-A-Car, Rent 4 Less, United Auto Rental, and U-Save Auto Rental.

Airport Shuttles

Several nonstop shuttle van services go from LAX to the Disneyland area. Super Shuttle, (800) 554-3146 or *www.supershuttle.com*, and Prime Time Shuttle, (800) 733-8267 or *www.primetimeshuttle .com*, both pick up at LAX and offer online reservations. They charge $15 per person to take you from LAX to Disneyland. You can also simply look for the Share Ride Vans stop when you arrive and ask the coordinator to help you get a shuttle to Anaheim.

Shuttle services are usually more convenient than using a scheduled bus service and cheaper than taking a taxi or limo if only a few people are traveling. However, in a shared van, you may ride with up to three other parties and can make multiple stops before reaching your hotel. If you're traveling with four or more adults, a town car, taxi, or private van service may be more cost-effective and convenient.

The Disneyland Resort Express bus, (714) 978-8855 or *http://ana heimsightseeing.com*, offers service from all LAX terminals directly to Disneyland and Anaheim-area hotels. Cost one way is $19 for adults and $16 for children three to eleven. Round-trip fares are $28 for adults, $20 for kids. Check their Web site for discount coupons.

Both Super Shuttle ($10 per person) and Prime Time Shuttle ($12 per person) operate from John Wayne Airport to Disneyland. The Disneyland Resort Express bus (714) 978-8855 or *http://anaheim sightseeing.com*, also offers service from John Wayne Airport directly to Disneyland and Anaheim-area hotels. Cost one way is $14 for adults and $12 for children three to eleven. Round-trip fares are $24 for adults, $16 for kids. Check their Web site for discount coupons.

Door-to-door taxi service is also available from several licensed companies; however, this mode of transportation is costly. Expect to pay about $35 or more each way between John Wayne Airport and Disneyland and $75 or more each way between LAX and Disneyland.

Taking the Train

The closest Amtrak stop is the Anaheim station, located about two miles from the Disneyland Resort at 2150 E. Katella Avenue, served by the Pacific Surfliner route. To get information about taking an Amtrak train from anywhere in the country to Disneyland, call (800) USA-RAIL or go online at *www.amtrak.com*.

Amtrak offers travel discounts to students, veterans, and AAA and AARP members who present their ID or membership card when purchasing a ticket. You can buy Amtrak tickets online, from many travel agents, by visiting any Amtrak ticket office, or by calling Amtrak.

Busing to Anaheim

Greyhound's Anaheim bus depot (100 West Winston Road) is about a mile from the Disneyland Resort. From this bus stop, you can get a taxi to Disneyland. Direct bus service to Disneyland is also available from downtown Los Angeles and San Diego, although these buses make multiple stops along the way. For bus schedules or additional information, contact Greyhound at (800) 231-2222 or *www.greyhound.com.*

The Truth about California Sunshine

There's a reason Southern California has a reputation for good weather. Most of the year, it's as nice as you imagined it to be, but there are exceptions. Summer days can get quite hot at mid day and cool off to sweater weather after dark. June often brings "June gloom," days when a low-lying layer of clouds never clears. The rainy season can start as early as October and last through April or May, but it's usually wettest from November through February. The rest of the year, there's little precipitation, no matter how gray the sky looks.

AVERAGE TEMPERATURES AT DISNEYLAND		
Month	Average High (°F)	Average Low (°F)
January	65	44
February	67	45
March	68	46
April	70	50
May	72	53
June	77	56
July	82	61
August	83	60
September	81	59
October	77	55
November	73	50
December	67	46

Theme Park Attire

Comfort and protection from the sun are the most important criteria when choosing your theme park wardrobe. Any time of year, it's best to dress in lightweight, comfortable layers.

Comfortable shoes are very important, especially if you're going to Disneyland, which is a big park that spreads over a large area. Your best bet is a pair of nicely broken-in running or walking shoes. This is not the place to wear new shoes for the first time, and leave the high heels at home.

You'll have to stow everything when you go on a ride. If you can stick everything you're carrying into your pockets, it's the best way to go. If you have more, bring a bag large enough to stuff a couple of those layers of clothing into, but don't fill it with heavy items you'll have to carry around all day. If you think you need to bring more than you can easily carry, you can rent a locker at the park.

A waist pack works well, as long as it's easy to shift around to the front when you get onto a ride. Glasses, hats, and other loose items are liable to fall off on a fast ride, so be sure you have a case or other place to stow them. Don't count on putting your glasses in your shirt pocket. They'll probably fall out. Wear a hat or visor and sunglasses, even if the skies are overcast.

If you plan to take rides that get you wet (especially Splash Mountain or Grizzly River Run), wear clothing that dries quickly, choosing lightweight synthetic fabric instead of heavy cotton. Bring along a change of socks if you have room to carry them.

JUST FOR PARENTS

Many young children, especially girls, enjoy dressing like a Disney character when they visit Disneyland, and a picture of your little princess hugging her favorite Disney character is a great souvenir. Avoid a tearful scene at the front gate by knowing that anyone wearing a costume must be less than nine years old.

On rainy days, many people are inclined to bring an umbrella to the theme parks, but it makes navigating crowds and going on rides particularly difficult. Instead, wear a waterproof hat or hooded raincoat.

In an emergency, the parks sell plastic rain ponchos for about $5 each.

Other Things to Bring with You

Besides the proper attire, these things will help you stay comfortable during your theme park visit:

- **Water bottle:** You can save a lot of money by carrying a water bottle into the park and filling it from a water fountain.
- **Waterproof sunscreen:** Even on overcast days, California sun can cause serious sunburn.
- **Motion sickness medication:** If you or anyone in your party suffer from motion sickness and want to go on the faster rides, bring your favorite remedy.
- **Time-killers:** If you don't use RideMax to shorten the time you spend in line, bring something to keep the kids (and yourself) amused while you wait.
- **Earplugs:** If noise bothers you, buy a pair for the airplane ride.

You may also want to bring along a blanket or something else to sit on while watching the fireworks or Fantasmic! Don't carry it around all day. Leave it in the car and take the tram back to get it, or use one of the lockers.

Use the Packing Checklist in Appendix D to help make sure you're taking everything you need.

CHAPTER 3

Cost Control for Your Vacation

FOR MANY, A TRIP to Disneyland and Southern California is the trip of a lifetime, but it shouldn't cost your life savings to take it. Planning your itinerary before you leave and setting budgetary spending limits will help you enjoy your vacation without going into debt.

Your Budget

As you plan your trip, it's important to establish a basic travel budget and stick to it. Once you reach your destination, you'll no doubt be tempted to dine at fancy restaurants, buy souvenirs, and participate in other potentially costly activities. When you create your budget, set aside some money for these splurges.

Use the following checklist to estimate the cost of your trip to the Disneyland Resort and Southern California.

BUDGET CHECKLIST		
Expense	Calculation	Totals
Adult airfare	$_____ per ticket × _____ (# of adults)	$_____
Child airfare	$_____ per ticket × _____ (# of children)	$_____
Rental car	$_____ per day/week × _____ (# of days/weeks)	$_____
Insurance/gas	$_____ per day × _____ (# of days)	$_____
Taxi, bus, etc.	_____ (# of people) × _____ (# of trips)	$_____
Hotel/motel	$_____ per night × _____ (# of rooms) × _____ (# of nights)	$_____
Adult Disney ticket	$_____ per ticket × _____ (# of people) × _____ (# of days)	$_____
Child Disney ticket	$_____ per ticket × _____ (# of people) × _____ (# of days)	$_____
Adult Universal Studios ticket	$_____ per ticket × _____ (# of people) × _____ (# of days)	$_____
Child Universal Studios ticket	$_____ per ticket × _____ (# of people) × _____ (# of days)	$_____
Other attraction	$_____ per ticket × _____ (# of people) × _____ (# of days)	$_____

BUDGET CHECKLIST		
Expense	**Calculation**	**Totals**
Other attraction	$_____ per ticket × _____ (# of people) × _____ (# of days)	$_____
Adult nighttime entertainment	$_____ per person × _____ (# of nights)	$_____
Child nighttime entertainment	$_____ per person × _____ (# of nights)	$_____
Show/movie	$_____ per person × _____ (# of shows)	$_____
Total meal budget	$_____ per person × _____ (# of meals) × _____ (# of days)	$_____
Snack/drink budget	$_____ per person × _____ (# of days)	$_____
Souvenir budget	$_____ per person	$_____
Child care	$_____ per hour × _____ (# of hours) × _____ (# of children)	$_____
Kennel costs	$_____ per day × _____ (# of days) × _____ (# of pets)	$_____
Airport parking	$_____ per day × _____ (# of days)	$_____
Other	_____	$_____
Other	_____	$_____
Other	_____	$_____
Approximate Vacation Expenses Total:		$_____

It's quite possible that your first estimate will be more than your planned budget. The cost-saving tips in Chapter 2 and in the rest of this chapter will help you reduce the total.

TRAVEL TIP

If your vacation includes other Southern California attractions besides the Disney parks, you can save a lot of money with a City-Pass ✐*www.citypass.com*. It bundles a three-day Disney Park Hopper pass with tickets to SeaWorld, Universal Studios, and your choice of a ticket to either the San Diego Wild Animal Park or the San Diego Zoo. The pass costs $235 for adults and $189 for children. If you're planning to visit all the attractions, you'll save $60 to $80 per person.

Vacation Packages and Other Discounts

Discounts and travel packages to the Disneyland Resort and Southern California abound. A travel package may include airfare, lodging, meals, car rental, and admission to one or more theme parks. They're easy, but these packages may not be the cheapest way to go, especially if they include things you won't use. Use the budget checklist in this chapter to calculate the lowest cost you can manage on your own and compare it to the packages. You may be surprised.

The Walt Disney Travel Company, (800) 225-2024 or *www .disneyland.com*, offers its own travel packages, which may include early park admissions and other bonuses. This is a convenient option for busy travel planners and offers perks you can't get elsewhere, but don't assume that their packages are cheaper than making the same reservations separately.

Some airlines offer travel packages, as do the one-stop online travel services listed in Chapter 2.

Number of Days

If you've heard about the long waits (ninety minutes or more) at the popular theme park rides, it may seem as though you'll have to spend four or five days just to experience all Disneyland and California Adventure have to offer, but you don't. With ticket costs counting for a large part of your Disney travel budget, reducing the number of days you spend there is one of the easiest ways to cut your trip costs.

You can cut your wait time (and visit time) in half, and you don't have to sacrifice a minute of Disney magic to do it. Using a software program called RideMax, you can create customized touring plans that take you to each ride when the lines are shortest. You can read more about how RideMax works in Chapter 7, but if you use this $15 tool, you can easily enjoy every Disneyland ride and attraction in two days. Add one more day for California Adventure and you're done.

A family of four with one child over ten years old can save more than $100 by buying three-day tickets instead of five-day ones. Stay longer to enjoy Southern California's beautiful beaches and other attractions if you want, or shorten your whole trip and save even more on hotels and other costs.

Minimizing Hotel Costs

The tips under "Booking Your Vacation Online" in Chapter 2 will help you reduce your hotel costs, but these ideas may also help:

- Big hotel chains frequently offer the best rates for people who reserve directly through their Web site.
- For small hotel chains and independent hotels, you may do better using one of the Web sites listed in Chapter 2.
- Don't forget to check for AAA, AARP, corporate, military, senior citizen, or other discounts.
- It never hurts to call the hotel directly, which actually delivers the lowest published rate almost half the time.

- Auction sites such as Priceline.com or hidden seller sites such as Hotwire.com often deliver the lowest rates, but be sure you understand how they work and their limitations.
- Compare all the costs. Free breakfast or free Internet access (if you need it) makes a hotel a better deal, but parking fees and resort fees effectively raise your daily rate.
- Don't forget to consider total cost. Saving $20 a night at a hotel so far away from the park that you have to rent a car and drive there may not seem like such a bargain when you consider the car rental, gasoline, parking fees, and traffic.

As a final cost-saving check, call your hotel on the day you plan to arrive and ask if they have lowered their rates. It happens more often than you might think.

Saving Money on Food

Buy granola bars, fruit, or other nonperishable food to eat for breakfast if your hotel doesn't offer one. You'll save time as well as money; all the local restaurants are packed first thing in the morning. Carry a few snacks into the park with you, too.

JUST FOR PARENTS

There's something very special (particularly for kids) about Disney's character meals, and everyone seems to enjoy eating Mickey Mouse–shaped waffles while Disney characters roam the dining room and meet guests. However, you don't have to stay in a Disney-owned hotel to do it. If you are staying in the Disney hotel, it doesn't need to be experienced every morning, so do it once and go somewhere else the rest of the time.

COST CONTROL FOR YOUR VACATION

The Blue Bayou is probably the best-known restaurant inside Disneyland, but it's expensive and its food quality is mediocre at best. You may enjoy a meal at a Downtown Disney restaurant more, and pay a lower price. For the least-expensive meals inside Disneyland, go to the Carnation Café, Plaza Inn, River Belle Terrace, or Village Haus. At California Adventure, try the Cocina Cucamonga Mexican Grill, Pacific Wharf Café, or Award Wieners.

The Denny's restaurant across the street from the Disneyland Resort offers inexpensive meals, twenty-four hours a day. It's a great place to stop for lunch or dinner. Because of its location, however, this restaurant tends to be very crowded during peak breakfast time, so be prepared to wait thirty minutes or longer.

Do You Need to Rent a Car?

It's entirely possible that you can visit the Disneyland Resort without a rental car, which will save money as well as driving and parking hassles. You may be able to skip the rental if, for example:

- You plan to spend all of your time at Disneyland, California Adventure, and Downtown Disney.
- You stay at a Disney hotel or one of the hotels within walking distance of Disneyland (see a list of these hotels in Chapter 4).
- You stay at a hotel on the Anaheim Resort Transit route *www.rideart.org*. The cost of a trolley ticket will be less than car-rental costs, but be sure to add the trolley tickets into your budget.

If you decide to forgo the car rental, don't forget to budget for an airport shuttle. If your stay will be short (one or two days) and your group large (four or five people), compare shuttle costs to car-rental costs to find the best deal.

Reserving a Rental Car

Many travelers think the best-known companies are the most expensive, but that isn't always the case. You'll often be pleasantly surprised to discover that majors like Hertz, Avis, and National offer highly competitive rates once you take advantage of their special promotional deals, airline frequent flier discounts, and AAA member discounts.

Taxes and airport fees will make your total bill higher than the base rate quoted. Be sure you know the total cost for your rental before you choose.

TRAVEL TIP

If you're a member of any airline's frequent flier program, you can often receive a rental-car discount or a free upgrade from that airline's promotional partners. Check your monthly frequent flier statement for special offers.

Car-Rental Checklist

Ask these questions to be sure you understand all the costs of your rental:

- ✔ Is there a limit on miles? Extremely low rental rates often limit mileage, and once you travel over the allowed miles, you're charged a hefty fee per mile.
- ✔ What is the company's policy for additional drivers? Only the person whose name appears on the rental agreement can legally drive the car unless you fill out extra paperwork. Some rental companies charge to add additional drivers, but if you are the renter's employer or regular fellow employee on company business, or the renter's spouse/mate/life companion/significant other, there may be no charge.

✔ What about a child safety seat? According to the California Highway Patrol ✎*www.chp.ca.gov*, children under six years old or weighing less than sixty pounds must be secured in an appropriate child passenger restraint (safety seat or booster seat). Most rental-car companies provide child safety seats, but they must be reserved in advance and there may be a small daily fee. Using this service will save you the hassle of having to bring your own seat(s) with you.

✔ Are there vehicles for nonsmokers? If you don't smoke, be sure to address this issue when you make your reservation.

It's easy to spend hours trying to wring every penny out of your daily rental-car rate, but frankly, this may not be a good use of your time. If you've done some research and found a low rate from a good company, it may be time to stop. In fact, you may save more by doing your homework about insurance coverage than continuing to search for a few dollars' lower daily rental rate.

Rental Car Insurance: What You Need to Know

Optional insurance can almost double your daily rental rate, and many travelers don't realize that they may not really need it. You may already have more than adequate protection, but you need to understand the plans and check your coverage.

Rental Insurance Plans: Alphabet Soup

A renter's financial responsibility for loss of or damage to a rental car varies by state, but you could end up responsible for the full value of the car in some circumstances. Rental-car companies offer a variety of optional insurance plans, each identified by an acronym. They're based on what might happen:

- **You damage the car:** Collision Damage Waiver (CDW) or Loss Damage Waiver (LDW), while not technically "insurance," waives or reduces your liability, provided the car is used according to all terms and conditions of the rental agreement.

- You injure someone or damage something while driving: A Liability Insurance Supplement (LIS) can increase liability protection limits to as much as $1,000,000.
- You are injured or killed while driving: Personal Accident Insurance (PAI) covers accidental death and medical expenses resulting from bodily injury, with limits on how much it will pay.
- Something happens to your belongings: Personal Effects Coverage (PEC) provides protection for loss of or damage to covered property of the renter and of the immediate family traveling with them. Dollar limits for this coverage are quite low.

Some companies offer combined coverage for a single daily fee. Check with the rental-car company you choose for details about the options offered and their cost.

 **TRAVEL TIP**

If you rely on your existing insurance and you're forced to make a claim because of an accident in the rental car, your regular insurance rates could go up. One benefit of purchasing the optional insurance from the rental companies is that your existing policies won't be affected if you have to make a claim (assuming any damage or injury claims are under the limit of the insurance you purchase).

Do your homework before you show up at the rental counter. Ask your automobile, medical, and homeowners' insurance agents if any of the abovementioned incidents are covered and what the limits are. Also find out if your credit card automatically provides rental-car insurance if you use the card to pay for the rental. American Express,

Diner's Club, and virtually all Visa and MasterCard credit cards issued as part of an airline's frequent flier program automatically offer this insurance. Being prepared to decline unneeded insurance when you reach the rental counter can save a bundle.

Avoid Expensive Surprises

Every year, many startled renters end up with unexpected charges on their final bill. Use these tips to be sure you aren't one of them:

- **Check the car.** Before you leave the rental company's parking lot, make sure there is nothing obviously wrong with the vehicle. Walk around it, looking for damage. If there's a problem, report it immediately, and be sure to get someone to sign off on it before you leave. Take a picture of it if you can, just in case.
- **Gas up.** If you're required to return the car with a full tank of gas and you fail to do so (which many people do), you'll pay for a fill-up at up to three times the going rate per gallon. If you paid for a full tank when you took the car out, try to return it with as little gas as possible (without running out). Near LAX, you'll find gas stations along Century Boulevard, with the ones nearer the I-405 freeway being slightly less expensive. At John Wayne Airport, you'll find them on MacArthur Boulevard, or Bristol Street.
- **Know what a "day" means.** Car-rental days usually start when you pick up the car and end twenty-four hours later. If you pick up a car at 3 P.M., you usually must return it before 3 P.M. on the day your rental agreement ends, or you'll be billed for additional hours at a high rate.

If you have questions about any aspect of your rental, ask them before you take the car off the lot. At the very least, write down the name of the person who answered them; even better, get the person to sign a note verifying what he or she told you.

■ TRAVEL TIP

If you get stuck on the road, call the rental company and report your situation. They'll often provide free assistance, including towing services, and give you a replacement rental car right away.

If your vacation includes a few days at the theme parks and a few days doing something else, think about renting a car for only the days you need it. Alamo, Budget, Dollar, Enterprise, Hertz, National, and Thrifty all have city offices within a mile or so of Disneyland.

CHAPTER 4

Choosing Your Hotel Accommodations

ALTHOUGH YOU PROBABLY WON'T spend much time in your hotel room while on your Southern California vacation, you'll still want comfortable accommodations that offer the amenities you need and like, at a price that suits your budget. In the Anaheim area and the Disneyland Resort, hundreds of hotels, motels, and inns cater to vacationing families.

If you know what you need, it will help pare down the list of possible hotels quickly and let you focus on the places that are right for you.

Defining Your Needs

By now, you know what your lodging budget per night is, but before you start looking for a hotel, answer these questions:

- How many beds do you need and what size (twin, queen, or king)? How many bedrooms and bathrooms?
- Do you need a rollaway bed? What about a crib?
- Should the hotel have a swimming pool, hot tub, fitness center, tennis courts, or an onsite restaurant? Do you need self-service laundry facilities?
- Do you want a place within walking distance of the Disneyland main gate? If the hotel is not within walking distance, do you want to be on the Anaheim Resort Transit route? Is it

okay if your hotel only offers a twice-daily shuttle to and from the Disneyland Resort? Will you have a car, and are you willing to drive to the park each day?

- You're supposed to be on vacation, but sometimes it's hard to disconnect from the office. What do you need to stay in touch?
- Do you want a refrigerator or microwave in your room?
- Do you want an in-room safe where you can store your valuables?
- Are you traveling with a pet?
- Does anyone in your group have any special needs?
- Do you plan to make phone calls from your hotel room? Some hotels charge a dollar or more every time you pick up the phone to make an outgoing call, even if you're calling locally or using a toll-free number, and charges can mount up.

 TRAVEL TIP

During peak travel times, finding a last-minute vacancy at an Anaheim hotel or motel can be a challenge. If you're having trouble finding accommodations, try calling the Anaheim/Orange County Visitor & Convention Bureau at ☎(714) 765-8888 or visit their Web site at ✐www.anaheimoc.org.

Spend a few minutes to think through what you'll be doing in your room to see if you have any other requirements.

Do Your Homework

The tips for minimizing your hotel costs in Chapter 3 will help you find the best-quoted rate for a room. Unfortunately, in an area like the Anaheim Resort, some hotels, especially the lower-priced ones, drop their guard on customer service and cleanliness. How can you figure out whether a property is a clean, comfortable place that offers good value for money or a dirty, noisy nightmare? The hotels listed in this chapter are all well reviewed within their price ranges, but it may help your search if you read other travelers' reviews at Tripadvisor, *www.tripadvisor.com*, keeping in mind that even the best hotel can have a bad day, and some people wouldn't be happy no matter what the hotel staff does.

Avoid Hidden Fees

Hidden extras can run up your hotel bill when you might not expect it. Asking these questions when you make a reservation will help you avoid many of the common cost-inflating traps.

- Most quoted rates are for double occupancy. Is there an extra charge per person for children or others staying in the room?
- Does the hotel charge for rollaway beds or cribs?
- Does the hotel charge for parking? If they do, how much is it?
- Does the hotel charge for local phone calls or for calling toll-free numbers? If so, how much?
- If you need any business services such as Internet access, fax service, and the like, does the hotel provide it? How much do they charge?
- Can the hotel guarantee you a nonsmoking room if you request one when you make your reservation?
- Is there an extra charge if you have your pet with you? Is it a one-time charge, or per day?

When comparing prices, be realistic. Paying extra for a hotel with a tennis court won't make much sense if you don't have time to take out your racket.

If you want to experience the ultimate Disney vacation and the superior service and hospitality Disney is known for, and you can afford it, stay at one of the Disneyland Resort hotels.

All of the Disney-owned hotels (the Disneyland Hotel, Paradise Pier, and Grand Californian) offer two basic levels of accommodations: standard rooms and suites, and concierge suites, which offer priority check-in, complimentary breakfast, evening wine and cheese reception, DVD players, and complimentary movies. All three hotels are 100 percent nonsmoking. The Disney hotels have a seventy-two-hour reservation cancellation or change policy.

All guests staying at the Disney hotels pay a resort fee of $11.50 per night, which includes parking, local telephone calls, Internet access, and use of the fitness center. For valet parking, add $14 per night.

Guests staying at these hotels sometimes get into the theme parks as much as ninety minutes before they open to the general public. On busy days, guests are also guaranteed admission even if the parks are at capacity.

The Disney hotels offer special promotional rates, package rates, and other discounts throughout the year, based on availability. To learn more, call the reservation number or check their Web site.

The Disneyland Hotel

✉1150 Magic Way, Anaheim 92802
✆(714) 956-6425 TTY ✆(714) 956-6494
✑www.disneyland.com

This Disneyland landmark has been here since the beginning, and it boasts a tropical, sandy beach and fine restaurants. Its 990 rooms are at the end of Downtown Disney, a short walk from the Disney theme parks. The sixty-five-acre hotel complex offers convention and meeting facilities but also caters to families traveling with kids and teens.

The Disneyland Hotel offers a wide range of amenities and activities: three swimming pools, including the Never Land pool (which features tropical landscaping, a 110-foot water slide, a pirate ship, and the "mermaid lagoon" spa). You'll also find several souvenir gift shops, clothing boutiques, and a fitness center.

Disneyland Hotel Dining

Popular fine-dining options, ideal for romantic dinners or for celebrating special occasions, include Granville's Steak House (steaks, prime rib, poultry, and fresh Maine lobsters) and Hook's Pointe (mesquite-grilled American cuisine served in an upscale atmosphere, with a wine list that includes more than twenty-five acclaimed California wines).

 JUST FOR PARENTS

You don't have to stay at a Disney-owned hotel for your kids to enjoy one of the famous character breakfasts. Anyone can walk into any of the hotel restaurants and dine there, and you can also have the same experience (and for less money) inside the parks at Ariel's Grotto in California Adventure or Disneyland's Plaza Inn.

While the upscale restaurants have kids' menus, younger people and their parents may prefer less-formal Goofy's Kitchen, which offers a popular all-you-can-eat buffet and serves breakfast with Disney characters.

For a light snack or cup of coffee, try the Coffee House, Captain's Galley, or Croc Bits 'n' Bites.

Disneyland Hotel Guest Rooms and Rates

Rates vary by season and the room's view, but for one or two people in a room, rates start at $250 to $350 per night for a standard room.

The Disneyland Hotel is the only Disney property that provides rollaway beds, and there's no additional charge for them.

Fans of the Disney film *Pirates of the Caribbean* may enjoy the Disneyland Hotel's special Pirates of the Caribbean suite, if they have a big enough budget.

Guest Services and Perks at the Disneyland Hotel

Optional guest services include child-care services, self-service laundry facilities, and a fully equipped business center.

Disney's Paradise Pier Hotel

✉1717 Disneyland Drive, Anaheim 92802

✆(714) 956-6425

✐*www.disneyland.com*

This California-themed hotel connects directly to Disney's California Adventure. Its two multistory towers contain 502 rooms, including twelve suites and poolside cabana rooms.

Here you'll find a lovely rooftop swimming pool that features California Streamin', a roller coaster–inspired waterslide, a whirlpool spa, two restaurants, a fitness center, and the Paradise Theater where kids can enjoy Disney television shows and films.

Paradise Pier Hotel Dining

For mid-priced dining, the PCH Grill serves wood-fired specialty pizzas, sea bass, baby back ribs, and a selection of other entrées. They also serve the popular Lilo & Stitch Aloha Breakfast, a meal with some of Disney's most popular characters.

If you're in the mood for a somewhat upscale and utterly delicious Japanese dining experience, the hotel's Yamabuki restaurant serves fresh sushi, tempura, and other entrées.

Paradise Pier Hotel Guest Rooms and Rates

Rooms have contemporary Disney- and California-themed furnishings, one king-size bed (or two extra-long double beds), plus a foldout twin sofa bed in the sitting area.

Rates vary by season and the room's view, but for one or two people in a room, rates start at $250 and $350 per night for a standard room.

Cribs are available, but they don't have rollaway beds.

Guest Services and Perks at the Paradise Pier Hotel

The Paradise Pier is less than a one-minute walk from Disney's California Adventure theme park.

Disney's Grand Californian Hotel

✉1600 South Disneyland Drive, Anaheim 92802

✆(714) 956-6425

✐*www.disneyland.com*

Located next to Disney's California Adventure theme park and Downtown Disney, the Grand Californian is the most upscale Disney-owned hotel. This 750-room, low-rise hotel is surrounded by trees and boasts an early twentieth century Arts and Crafts–style design featuring lovely wood paneling inside and out and a dramatic lobby that brings to mind the classic national park lodges of that era.

 TRAVEL TIP

The Disney-owned hotels often fill up far in advance, and you may need to make your reservations more than a year ahead to get a room during the busiest seasons. If your heart is set on staying in one of these properties, but you find the "no vacancy" sign out when you try to make your reservation, keep trying. People cancel often, and you might get lucky.

The hotel boasts an outdoor pool, two whirlpool spas, a children's pool, a dry and steam sauna, a business center, and a fully equipped workout facility. It's also the only Disney hotel with a full-service spa offering massages, facials, manicures, and other pampering treatments.

Grand Californian Hotel Dining

When you get hungry, dining options include the Napa Rose (a top-rated, fine-dining restaurant serving California Wine Country cuisine), Storytellers Café (family dining and Chip 'n Dale's Critter Breakfast), the Hearthstone Lounge (coffee and homemade baked goods), and White Water Snacks (a poolside snack area).

Grand Californian Hotel Guest Rooms and Rates

Rooms have a king-size bed, two queen-size beds, or one queen-size bed and bunk beds. You can get cribs, sleeping bags, and extra cushions on request, but they don't have rollaway beds.

Rates vary by season and the room's view, but for one or two people in a room, rates start at $400 to $450 per night.

Guest Services and Perks at the Grand Californian Hotel

Located in Disney's Grand Californian Hotel is Pinocchio's Workshop, an activity center for kids aged five to twelve that's open every evening, giving parents time to enjoy a quiet dinner alone or to explore Downtown Disney's nightlife. Space is limited, especially during peak season, so be sure to make reservations in advance by calling (714) 956-6755.

The Grand Californian also offers direct entry into California Adventure without having to go through the main gate.

Anaheim-Area Accommodations

Located just outside the Disney property are dozens of hotels, motels, and restaurants that give you a vast choice of places to sleep and eat. The prices vary greatly, but some are affordable even for families traveling on a tight budget.

≡FAST FACT

There are now more than 20,000 hotel rooms available in Anaheim at more than 150 different hotels and motels. Throughout the year (not just during peak seasons), average occupancy is around 77 percent.

KEY TO RATES
$: $80 to $99 per night
$$: $100 to $129 per night
$$$: $130 to $159 per night
$$$$: Over $160 per night

Anaheim hotel tax is 15 percent and is not included in the rates listed. These are average rates based on double occupancy, which you can get by reserving either directly through the hotel or through Web sites such as Travelocity or Expedia.

Chapter 2 discusses how to use hidden-seller sites such as Priceline or Hotwire to get these same hotels or similar ones for much less than "list" price. Using these techniques, you may be able to reserve a very nice hotel for the price of a moderate one or you can get the moderate one for much less money.

All of the listed hotels have swimming pools and other standard amenities.

Hotels Within Walking Distance of Disneyland

Many vacationers find it convenient to stay at a hotel that's a short walk from the Disneyland Resort, so it's easy to leave the park during the day and go to the room to change clothing or take a nap. These properties are all within two blocks of the park:

- Alpine Inn, ☎(714) 535-2186, ☎(800) 772-4422, ✉*www.alpine innanaheim.com*, $, 1 block
- Anaheim Camelot Inn, ☎(714) 635-7275, ☎(800) 670-7275, ✉*www.camelotinn-anaheim.com*, $$$, ½ block
- Anaheim Desert Inn, ☎(714) 772-5050, ☎(800) 433-5270, ✉*www.anaheimdesertinn.com*, $$, 1 block
- Best Western Park Place Inn, ☎(714) 776-4800, ☎(800) 854-8175, ✉*www.bestwestern.com*, $$$, 1 block
- Best Western Raffles Inn and Suites, ☎(714) 750-6100, ☎(800) 654-0196, ✉*www.bestwestern.com*, $, 2 blocks
- Candy Cane Inn, ☎(714) 774-5284, ☎(800) 345-5284, ✉*www .candycaneinn.net*, $, 1 block
- Carousel Inn and Suites, ☎(714) 758-0444, ☎(800) 854-6767, ✉*www.carouselinnandsuites.com*, $, 1 block
- Howard Johnson Plaza, ☎(714) 776-6120, ☎(800) 422-4228, ✉*www.hojoanaheim.com*, $$, 1 block
- Islander Inn and Suites, ☎(714) 778-6565, ☎(800) 882-8819, ✉*www.anaheimislander.com*, $, 2 blocks
- Park Vue Inn, ☎(714) 772-3691, ☎(800) 334-7011, ✉*www .parkvueinn.com*, $$, 1 block
- Tropicana Inn, ☎(714) 635-4082, ☎(800) 828-4898, ✉*www .tropicanainn-anaheim.com*, $$$, 1 block

Hotels on the Anaheim Resort Transit Route

These hotels are a little too far away from the Disneyland entrance to make walking practical, especially when you're tired after a busy day, but they're all on the Anaheim Resort Transit route, making it easy enough to get to and from the park. A trolley pass costs $3 for one day, $6 for two days, and $8 for three days. Kids under ten ride free with a pass-holding adult. Order the pass online at *www.rideart .org* or buy it when you get there, and don't forget to include pass costs when comparing hotel prices.

- America's Best Value Astoria Inn & Suites, ☎(714) 229-0101, ☎(888) 315-2378, *www.bestvalueinn.com*, $, 6 miles
- Best Western Pavilions, ☎(714) 776-0140, ☎(800) 854-8175, *www.bestwestern.com*, $$, 1.5 miles
- Desert Palms, ☎(714) 535-1133, ☎(888) 677-0466, *www.desertpalmshotel.com*, $$, 0.5 mile
- Dolphin's Cove Resort, ☎(888) 438-6493, *www.dolphinscove-resort.com*, $$$, 1.3 miles
- Doubletree Guest Suites Anaheim Resort, ☎(714) 750-3000, ☎(800) 222-TREE, *www.doubletree.com*, $$$, 1 mile
- Embassy Suites Anaheim South, ☎(714) 539-3300, ☎(800) 362-2779, *www1.hilton.com*, $$$, 1.5 miles
- Holiday Inn–Anaheim, ☎(714) 748-7777, *www.hianaheimresort.com*, $$, 1.4 miles
- Holiday Inn Express Anaheim Maingate, ☎(714) 772-7755, ☎(800) 423-0908, *www.ichotelsgroup.com*, $, 1 mile
- Marriott Anaheim Suites, ☎(714) 750-1000, ☎(800) 228-9290, *http://marriott.com*, $$$, 1.7 miles
- Marriott Residence Inn Anaheim, ☎(714) 591-4000, ☎(800) 308-5440, *http://marriott.com*, $$$, 1.6 miles
- Marriott Residence Inn Anaheim Maingate, ☎(714) 533-3555, ☎(888) 236-2427, *http://marriott.com*, $$$, 0.2 miles
- Sheraton Park Hotel, ☎(714) 750-1811, ☎(800) 716-6199, *www.starwoodhotels.com*, $$$, 0.7 miles
- Staybridge Suites, ☎(714) 748-7700, ☎(888) 697-5292, *www.ichotelsgroup.com*, $$$, 1.6 miles

Hotels Worth a Drive

If you're driving to Disneyland in your own car or have decided to rent one when you arrive, you'll find some very nice hotels a little farther from the park. Some are good enough bargains to make them worth the extra travel. If you're staying at one of these hotels, Disneyland parking is $11 and adds to your total trip cost.

- America's Best Value Astoria Inn & Suites, ☎(714) 229-0101, ☎(888) 315-2378, ✉*www.bestvalueinn.com*, $, 6 miles
- Ayres Country Suites, ☎(714) 634-2106, ☎(800) 595-5692, ✉*www.countrysuites.com*, $$, 2.8 miles
- Best Western Pavilions, ☎(714) 776-0140, ☎(800) 854-8175, ✉*www.bestwestern.com*, $$, 1.5 miles
- Best Western Raffles Inn and Suites, ☎(714) 750-6100, ☎(800) 654-0196, ✉*www.bestwestern.com*, $, 2 blocks
- Dolphin's Cove Resort, ☎(888) 438-6493, ✉*www.dolphins cove-resort.com*, $$$, 1.3 miles
- Doubletree Guest Suites Anaheim Resort, ☎(714) 750-3000, ☎(800) 222-TREE, ✉*www.doubletree.com*, $$$, 1.1 miles
- Embassy Suites Anaheim South, ☎(714) 539-3300, ☎(800) 362-2779, ✉*www1.hilton.com*, $$$, 1.5 miles
- Fairfield Inn Anaheim Disneyland Resort, ☎(714) 772-6777, ☎(800) 403-3818, ✉*http://marriott.com*, $$, 1 mile
- Holiday Inn–Anaheim, ☎(714) 748-7777, ✉*www.hianaheim resort.com*, $$, 1.4 miles
- Holiday Inn Express Anaheim Maingate, ☎(714) 772-7755, ☎(800) 423-0908, ✉*www.ichotelsgroup.com*, $, 1 mile
- Hotel Pepper Tree, ☎(714) 774-7370, ☎(877) 888-5656, ✉*www.peppertree.biz*, $, 4.3 miles
- Hyatt Regency Orange County, ☎(714) 750-1234, ☎(800) 633-7313, ✉*www.orangecounty.hyatt.com*, $$$, 1.7 miles
- Islander Inn and Suites, ☎(714) 778-6565, ☎(800) 882-8819, ✉*www.anaheimislander.com*, $, 2 blocks
- Lemon Tree Hotel, ☎(714) 772-0200, ☎(866) 311-5595, ✉*www.lemontree.ws*, $, 3 miles
- Marriott Anaheim Suites, ☎(714) 750-1000, ☎(800) 228-9290, ✉*http://marriott.com*, $$$, 1.7 miles
- Marriott Residence Inn Anaheim, ☎(714) 591-4000, ☎(800) 308-5440, ✉*http://marriott.com*, $$$, 1.6 miles
- Sheraton Anaheim Hotel, ☎(714) 778-1700, ☎(800) 325-3535, ✉*www.starwoodhotels.com*, $$$, 3 blocks

- Staybridge Suites, ✆(714) 748-7700, ✆(888) 697-5292, ✐www.ichotelsgroup.com, $$$, 1.6 miles
- TownePlace Suites, ✆(714) 939-9700, ✆(800) 257-3000, ✐http://marriott.com, $$, 2.3 miles

All-Suites Hotels

These hotels are great for families or others who may be able to rent one room instead of two, given the extra space and privacy these properties offer. Each one has all (or mostly all) suites.

- Ayres Country Suites, ✆(714) 634-2106, ✆(800) 595-5692, ✐www.countrysuites.com, $$, 2.8 miles
- Best Western Raffles Inn and Suites, ✆(714) 750-6100, ✆(800) 654-0196, ✐www.bestwestern.com, $, 2 blocks
- Carousel Inn and Suites, ✆(714) 758-0444, ✆(800) 854-6767, ✐www.carouselinnandsuites.com, $, 1 block
- Desert Palms, ✆(714) 535-1133, ✆(888) 677-0466, ✐www.desertpalmshotel.com, $$, 0.5 miles
- Embassy Suites Anaheim South, ✆(714) 539-3300, ✆(800) 362-2779, ✐www1.hilton.com, $$$, 1.5 miles
- Howard Johnson Plaza, ✆(714) 776-6120, ✆(800) 422-4228, ✐www.hojoanaheim.com, $$, 1 block
- Hyatt Regency Orange County, ✆(714) 750-1234, ✆(800) 633-7313, ✐www.orangecounty.hyatt.com, $$$, 1.7 miles
- Islander Inn and Suites, ✆(714) 778-6565, ✆(800) 882-8819, ✐www.anaheimislander.com, $, 2 blocks
- Lemon Tree Hotel, ✆(714) 772-0200, ✆(866) 311-5595, ✐www.lemontree.ws, $, 3 miles
- Marriott Anaheim Suites, ✆(714) 750-1000, ✆(800) 228-9290, ✐http://marriott.com, $$$, 1.7 miles
- Marriott Residence Inn Anaheim, ✆(714) 591-4000, ✆(800) 308-5440, ✐ http://marriott.com, $$$, 1.6 miles
- Marriott Residence Inn Anaheim Maingate, ✆(714) 533-3555, ✆(888) 236-2427, ✐ http://marriott.com, $$$, 0.2 miles

- Sheraton Anaheim Hotel, ☎(714) 778-1700, ☎(800) 325-3535, ✐*www.starwoodhotels.com*, $$$, three blocks
- Staybridge Suites, ☎(714) 748-7700, ☎(888) 697-5292, ✐*www.ichotelsgroup.com*, $$$, 1.6 miles
- TownePlace Suites, ☎(714) 939-9700, ☎(800) 257-3000, ✐ *http://marriott.com*, $$, 2.3 miles

Camping

If you're traveling in an RV or pitching a tent, these RV parks are the closest ones to the Disneyland Resort:

- Anaheim Resort RV Park (✉200 W. Midway Drive, Anaheim, ☎(714) 774-3860, ✐*www.anaheimresortrvpark.com*) offers 150 landscaped sites with full hookups, wireless Internet, swimming pool, and a free Disneyland shuttle. Rates are $44 to $60 per night for two people and $2 per extra person over three years old.
- Orangeland (✉1600 W. Struck Ave., Orange, ☎(714) 633-0414, ✐*www.orangeland.com*) is a five-minute drive from Disneyland and has 204 paved RV sites with full hookups, wireless Internet access, and a swimming pool. Leashed pets are welcome. Rates are $55 to $70 per day.

CHAPTER 5

Planning Your Travel Itinerary

VISITING SOUTHERN CALIFORNIA THEME parks and tourist attractions is expensive. Chapter 3 will help you add up the cost of theme park admission, lodging, food, rental car, souvenirs, snacks, and other expenses, but no matter how well you plan or how many bargains you find, you're about to make a significant investment in your vacation.

Spending a little time planning your activities will help you make sure your money and time are well spent.

It's Your Vacation

If you're like many Anaheim visitors, you'll be spending a lot of time at the Disneyland Resort. This chapter will help you create a day-to-day plan for how to spend your time there.

When planning your daily itinerary, leave some flexibility in your schedule, or if you feel compelled to plan every minute, know what's most and least important to you so you can find time to enjoy unexpected activities.

TRAVEL TIP

Theme parks and resorts change every year. New rides, attractions, shows, parades, and activities are added, updated, or somehow changed, and old attractions retire. When you visit Southern California, don't be surprised if you encounter something new that's not described in this book.

This book provides an overview of the rides, shows, attractions, shops, and dining options you'll find in the Anaheim area (and beyond), but only you know what you will enjoy the most once you arrive at the Disneyland Resort or one of the other destinations.

Use the Daily Itinerary planner in Appendix E to record your choices as you start to plan your trip in detail.

Itinerary Planning Strategies

As a rule, begin your days bright and early. In fact, getting into the park as soon as the gates open is one of the keys to shorter waits. If you're staying at one of the Disney-owned hotels, take advantage of the early admission days they offer.

≡ **FAST FACT**

Based on the time of year, each park's operating hours vary. To find out what the hours will be when you visit, call ℡ (714) 781-4565 or visit the Disneyland Web site at ✍ *www.disneyland.com*.

When you add up all the time it may take you to get to the gate, this means you'll be getting up early, especially if you want to have a sit-down breakfast before you go and find yourself standing in line with everyone else who wants to do the same thing.

When you're making your plans, don't forget to also allow extra time for that special Character Breakfast if you plan to do one.

Divide Your Days

Visiting a theme park requires a lot of walking, so you may want to schedule several breaks throughout the day, especially if anyone in your group tires easily.

 **TRAVEL TIP**

If you're visiting the Disneyland Resort for one day, there's no way to see and do everything in both parks. If you only have one day, you can either buy a Hopper ticket that allows you to visit both parks and take in the top attractions in each one, or get a single-park ticket and use it to see as much of one park as you can.

An easy plan is to divide your theme park day into three- or four-hour blocks: a morning excursion, afternoon excursion, and evening excursion. For example, you could arrive at the park early in the morning, break for lunch at noon when it's most crowded, and take time to relax at the hotel for a few hours, taking a nap or a dip in the pool. Once everyone is rested, go back to the theme park again for a few hours before breaking for dinner. After dinner, you can experience the nighttime shows and attractions such as Disneyland's fireworks and Fantasmic! or California Adventure's Electrical Parade and go on the rides until the park closes.

The Contrarian's Plan

This plan goes against the crowds. Sleep late in the morning or have a leisurely breakfast in a local restaurant after everyone else has rushed off to the entrance gate, arrive at the theme park around 10 A.M. or noon and stay late into the night.

≡ FAST FACT

You can ride almost every ride in Disneyland in a single day if you use RideMax, get in when the gates open, stay late, and occasionally hustle to stay on schedule. Adopt a slightly more leisurely pace and buy a Hopper pass, and using RideMax, you can take in all of Disneyland and California Adventure in two days. See Chapter 7 to find out how.

During summer, the parks are open quite late, and if you have enough energy left, the nightlife at Downtown Disney goes on until midnight or even 2 A.M. during the busy season.

Pace Yourself

You're on vacation to have fun, not to see Disneyland in an exhaustion-tinged haze. If your child is old enough to walk, think twice before pushing him or her around in a stroller all day. You're likely to tire yourself out while your child remains full of energy late into the evening.

JUST FOR PARENTS

No matter how tempting it is to keep going all day long, you'll have more fun if you take a few breaks. If you just can't bear to leave, the Pirates of the Caribbean ride gives your feet thirteen minutes of rest. You can also sit down in air-conditioned comfort for the Enchanted Tiki Room and other shows. Also, when you're making your plans, allow enough time for the kids to see the characters, including the time you may have to wait in line to do so.

Another way to get a break from the theme park without going too far away is to have a meal in Downtown Disney. Crowds are less dense there, and the food may be better. Take the monorail to the Downtown Disney exit, go to the Rainforest Café and the kids may be so busy watching the animated critters rage and bellow during the fake rainstorm that they won't even realize they're outside the park.

When Time Is on Your Side

If you spend several days at the theme park, you have more options. Use the first day to experience the rides, shows, parades, and attractions you're most excited to see. Use subsequent days to do everything else.

The stores along Main Street, U.S.A. in Disneyland open about thirty minutes earlier and stay open about one hour later than the rides and attractions. They're crowded in the evening, so use the morning of your second day for shopping. Don't lug your acquisitions around all day, though. Instead, leave them at the Newsstand near the Main Entrance, Star Trader in Tomorrowland, or Pioneer Mercantile in Frontierland and pick them up on the way out. At California Adventure, you can leave your packages at Engine Ears Toys. Find a way to remember to pick them up on your way out, such as wrapping the receipt around your car key or hotel room key.

Dividing Your Days

The number of days you should (or can afford) to spend at the Disneyland parks is discussed in Chapter 3.

If you have two days at the Disneyland Resort and buy a Hopper ticket, you can spend a day and a half at Disneyland and half a day at California Adventure. You may also want to allow a few hours to explore Downtown Disney, especially if anyone in your group likes to shop.

If you have a Park Hopper pass, plan to spend at least three to four hours in one theme park at a stretch. Running back and forth will waste a lot of valuable time because you have to wait at the gate every time you change parks.

═FAST FACT

The shows and parades are extremely popular in both parks. To get the best seating, allow time to arrive at the viewing area (or theater) from twenty minutes to an hour or more early. The cast members at Guest Services or the schedule boards can tell you how early you'll need to be there.

Other Attractions in Southern California

If you have more time, take in the other theme parks and major Southern California family attractions: Universal Studios Hollywood, Knott's Berry Farm, Soak City, and Six Flags Magic Mountain take a full day each, and so do San Diego's LEGOLAND, SeaWorld, the San Diego Zoo, and the San Diego Wild Animal Park.

Allow a half-day to visit Hollywood Boulevard or to have some fun at one of the local beaches.

When to Experience the Magic

During the Disneyland Resort's peak periods, you could be sharing your day in the park with up to 65,000 other visitors. There's a reason they're all there at the same time, which may be driven by school schedules or a special event, but it's up to you to decide whether to join them.

Best of Times

Every year, Disney adds more seasonal events and promotions, and the "off season" grows shorter. If someone tells you they visited the park when it wasn't busy, ask how many years ago they went and find out if new features have been added that might have increased attendance since then.

The parks are busiest during Presidents' Week, the weeks before and after Easter Sunday, any time a lot of kids are on spring break (which varies by their school calendar), Memorial Day through Labor Day, early October when the Halloween decorations go up, Thanksgiving weekend, and mid-December through New Year's Day. All of that doesn't leave much slack time, but here are your best bets:

- Early January through President's Week
- The end of Presidents' Week through early March
- Two weeks after Easter Sunday through the week before Memorial Day
- Labor Day through the week before Columbus Day
- The first two weeks of December

🧳 TRAVEL TIP

If you're planning your Disney vacation during one of the busy periods, make your reservations as early as possible, especially if you want to stay at one of the Disney-owned hotels. If your first choice for accommodations is already booked, make alternate reservations that you can cancel if you need to and keep checking back with your first choice. Last-minute cancellations are common.

If your work or kids' vacation schedule forces you to visit during one of the busier periods, see the tips for how to stay out of line in Chapter 7. You'll need them.

Best of Days

Year-round, Saturday is the theme park's busiest day of the week, and it's most crowded at noon any day. Sundays are usually less crowded, unless the next day is a holiday. Weekdays bring smaller crowds, but parades and shows happen less frequently and rides are more likely to be closed for maintenance.

RAINY DAY FUN

If it's raining, you can count on much smaller crowds than usual. Bring along rain gear (avoid umbrellas), or if you're unprepared, buy one of the plastic Mickey Mouse rain ponchos sold throughout the park on rainy days. Parades, outdoor shows, and even a few outdoor rides may be canceled or closed. On the positive side, much of the park (including most of the attractions) will be open and the lines will be far shorter.

Any time of year, the parks close earlier on weekdays than on weekends, and in general, park hours are shorter in winter when the days are shorter.

Annual Events at Disneyland

If there's a special occasion or holiday, the Disneyland Resort will celebrate it in style. The biggest annual events are the Disneyland Halloween and Christmas holiday celebrations, which you can read more about in Chapter 10.

Disneyland also sponsors a half marathon, held each year in September. The flat, loop course runs through Disneyland, out through Anaheim, and back through California Adventure. You have to be fourteen years old to participate, and you must finish the race in three and a half hours or less, a pace of sixteen minutes per mile. Race registration opens in November of the previous year, and it's best to register early.

Celebrating Birthdays

If someone you're traveling with is celebrating a birthday when you're at Disneyland, go to City Hall in Disneyland or Guest Services in California Adventure and tell a cast member. The celebrant gets a special button to wear, and cast members will wish him or her happy birthday throughout the day. People of any age can pick up a birthday button, and kids get a special phone greeting from Mickey.

Elsewhere, you can arrange for a special Disneyland Birthday Party at the Plaza Inn, complete with special guest appearance by Mickey and Minnie. At full-service restaurants, the birthday boy or girl gets a Sorcerer Mickey or Princess Birthday Bucket, topped with a mini-cake and filled with a cloisonné pin and other treats, and Goofy's Kitchen offers a special Birthday Bag. For more information, call (714) 781-3463.

Weddings

At Disneyland, fairy-tale weddings are a specialty. Whether you're planning a small, intimate ceremony and honeymoon or an all-out extravaganza with hundreds of invited guests, Disneyland's Fairy Tale Wedding program will help you plan the ultimate wedding and honeymoon experience.

You can hold your ceremony and reception indoors or outdoors, inside the Disneyland theme park or at one of the Disney hotels. For an especially romantic touch, the bride can arrive at Sleeping Beauty's Castle in a Cinderella coach, beneath twinkling stars, an option one out of every four brides chooses. Oh, and if you want to add Mickey and Minnie Mouse to your guest list, appearances are possible.

══FAST FACT

Past brides at Disneyland have been an imaginative bunch. One of them enlisted Snow White's Seven Dwarfs to carry the train of her dress down the aisle.

For those on limited budgets who still want to include some of the magic in their special day, the Disney wedding planners can help you plan a Fantasmic! Dessert party, Disney's Electrical Parade Rehearsal Dinner, or Mad Hatter Tea Party Brunch as part of your celebration.

When you plan your wedding through the Disney Fairy Tale Wedding program, a "fairy godplanner" will help you with every aspect from choosing Disney-themed invitations to what will be on the menu during the reception.

The most requested wedding months are May, June, October, and November, but no matter when you want to have your wedding, it's best to start planning at least a year ahead. For more information about planning a wedding at the Disneyland Resort, call (714) 956-6527.

CHAPTER 6

Ticket Prices and Admission Policies

TO HELP YOU PLAN your travel budget, this chapter outlines the 2007 ticket prices and admission policies for the theme parks and attractions highlighted in this book. The prices and special offers listed here are subject to change.

Disneyland and California Adventure

The Disney theme parks, Disneyland and Disney's California Adventure, are by far the most popular in Southern California, with options for spending one to five days.

Ticket and Pass Options at Disneyland and California Adventure

With any of these tickets, guests can re-enter the park as often as they wish during the day of use, as long as they hold on to their admission ticket and get their hand stamped on the way out.

- **Single-Day Ticket:** It can be used for either Disneyland or Disney's California Adventure but not both, and it is valid for a single day.
- **Park Hopper:** This ticket allows entry to either park any time it's valid; multiday tickets expire in thirteen days.

- **Premium Annual Passport:** This annual pass has no blackout dates, is good for 365 consecutive days, and includes free parking. It also includes dining and shopping discounts.
- **Deluxe Annual Passport:** This passport is valid for 315 preselected days a year; the blackout dates are usually the busiest days. It includes dining and shopping discounts, but an annual parking pass costs an extra $59.
- **Southern California Annual Passport:** Available only to people who live in Zip Code areas 90000 to 93599, with proof of residency, this passport allows park entry on 220 preselected days. Blackout dates include all Saturdays, some Fridays, and virtually all major holidays. It includes dining and shopping discounts, but an annual parking pass costs an extra $59.
- **Southern California Select Annual Passport:** This passport is similar to the Southern California Annual Passport, but it is only valid on 175 preselected days. An annual parking pass costs an extra $59.

These ticket prices are subject to change without notice.

TICKET AND PASS PRICES AT DISNEYLAND AND CALIFORNIA ADVENTURE		
Ticket Type	Ages 10+	Ages 3 to 9
Single Day (at the gate or call ☎(714) 781-4400)	$63	$53
1-Day Park Hopper gate or call ☎(714) 781-4400	$83	$73
1-Day Hopper (Southern California residents only)	$78	$68
2-Day Park Hopper (online or at the gate)	$122	$102
3-Day Park Hopper (at the gate)	$179	$149
3-Day Park Hopper (online)	$159	$129
4-Day Park Hopper (at the gate)	$209	$179
4-Day Park Hopper (online)	$179	$149
5-Day Park Hopper (at the gate)	$229	$199
5-Day Park Hopper (online)	$189	$159

Premium Annual Passport	$359	$359
Deluxe Annual Passport	$239	$239
Southern California Annual Passport	$154	$154

Buying your Disneyland tickets online at ✎*www.disneyland .com* not only saves you money, but you won't have to stand in line at the ticket booth when you arrive. For most of these tickets, you can buy up to nine at a time online. You can also buy advance tickets by phone at ✆(714) 781-4400, which is the only way to buy a one-day, one-park ticket in advance.

OTHER DISNEYLAND COSTS	
Item	**Price**
Parking	$11 per day
Welcome to Disneyland Tour	$24 per person
"A Walk in Walt's Footsteps" Tour	$59 per person
Discover the Magic Tour	$59 for the first two tickets, $49 for each additional

You can learn more about these special tours in Chapter 1.

Discounts on Disney Tickets

Check the combination ticket options at the end of this chapter for some of the best ways to save on Disneyland admission, but these ideas may also help:

- **Age is important.** Children under three years old get in free and senior citizens over sixty years old get a $2 discount on a one-day, one-park ticket.
- **Flexible travel schedules can help, too.** For the past couple of years, Disney has offered special discounts January through April, discounting adult admissions to the child's price level.

≡FAST FACT

Some people buy five-day Hopper tickets, use two or three days and sell the remaining days on eBay. Disneyland's policy on multiday tickets is that they are for use by the same person for all days, are not for resale and not transferable, and this option is not recommended.

- If you are an AAA, AARP, or California Teachers Association member, your organization may offer discount tickets.
- Active-duty military, Reserve, National Guard, retired military, and Department of Defense employees can get a discount that varies by time of year. Bring your ID to show at the gate.

Orange County Attractions

Disneyland isn't the only themed attraction in Anaheim, and you can read about the others in Chapter 15. Besides the Knott's Berry Farm theme park, there are also some fun, themed dinner shows.

Knott's Berry Farm and Soak City

What started out as a cute little farm stand has grown into a full-fledged theme park with fast roller coasters and lots of kid-oriented attractions. See Chapter 15 for more information about the park.

Ticket and Pass Options at Knott's Berry Farm and Soak City

Knott's tickets cover entrance to the park and all rides, shows, and attractions except Pan for Gold, Screamin' Swing, and arcade games. Soak City tickets are good for all water rides and attractions. Knott's does not give rain checks.

- **Full-Day Pass**
- **Print at Home:** Skip the line and save some money by ordering online and printing these one-day tickets on your printer.
- **Southern California Residents:** This ticket is offered only to people living in Zip Codes 90000 to 93599, who must show proof of address.
- **Late Admission:** With this ticket, you can enter after 3 P.M. at Soak City or after 4 P.M. at Knott's Berry Farm. It is offered any day the park is open past 6 P.M.
- **AAA Members**
- **Knott's Berry Farm Theme Park Annual Pass:** The pass is good for admission all year, but only at the park it was purchased for.
- **Knott's Premium Pass:** This annual pass includes theme park admission and entry to all three Southern California waterpark locations: Buena Park, Palm Springs, and San Diego.
- **Knott's California Thrill Pass:** Valid at Knott's Berry Farm and Great America in Santa Clara.
- **Knott's California MAXX Pass:** Valid at all Knott's properties, Great America, and Gilroy Gardens (formerly Bonfante Gardens).
- **Cedar Fair MAXX Passes:** Valid at theme parks owned by Cedar Fair Company all over the country.
- **VIP Tour:** The tour includes back-door access to attractions all day long and a guided tour for up to six people. Reserve forty-eight hours in advance by calling (714) 220-5298.
- **Knott's Halloween Haunt:** This special, scary event runs every evening from late September through Halloween and is not recommended for anyone under thirteen.
- **Birthday Splash Bash:** For ten to forty people, this package includes admission for guests, a special gift for the guest of honor, one kid's meal per party guest, and birthday cupcakes. Reserve at least two weeks in advance.

These ticket prices are subject to change without notice.

TICKET AND PASS PRICES AT KNOTT'S BERRY FARM			
Type	Ages 12 to 61	Ages 3 to 11	Ages 62+
Knott's Berry Farm for Southern California Residents	$35.95	$18.95	$18.95
Soak City for Southern California Residents	$21.95	$14.95	$14.95
Knott's Berry Farm Full-Day Pass	$43.95	$18.95	$18.95
Soak City Full-Day Pass	$43.95	$18.95	$18.95
Print at Home, Knott's Berry Farm	$41.00	$18.95	$18.95
Late Admission, either park	$25.00	$18.95	$18.95
KBF Theme Park Annual Season Pass	$114.95	$59.95	$59.95
Water Park Season Pass	$74.95	$44.95	$44.95
Knott's Premium Pass	$139.95	$84.95	$84.95
Knott's California Thrill Pass	$129.95	$74.95	$74.95
Knott's California MAXX Pass	$154.95	$99.95	$99.95
Birthday Splash Bash, Soak City	$26.95	$19.95	$19.95
Halloween Haunt (advance purchase)	$44.00		
Halloween Haunt (day of event)	$49.00		

Order Print at Home tickets from the Knott's Web site *www .knotts.com.*

OTHER KNOTT'S COSTS	
Item	Price
Parking	$9 per day
Bus and RV parking	$15 per day
VIP Tour	$100 per hour, four hours minimum. $1,500 during Halloween Haunt

Discounts and Specials at Knott's Berry Farm

Albertson's grocery stores in Southern California often have discount coupons, as do other locations. If you find any discount coupons, however, they'll be good only on the adult admission.

Medieval Times

Admission to this dinner and show is $49.95 for adults and $33.95 for kids under twelve years old. Add $10 per person for the Royalty Package, which includes VIP seating, or get it for only $8 if you buy online. Make online reservations at *www.medievaltimes.com* or call (888) WE-JOUST.

Pirate's Dinner Adventure

This swashbuckling dinner show costs $49.95 for adults and $33.95 for kids aged three to eleven. Little ones under age three get in free. Make online reservations at least seventy-two hours in advance at *www.piratesdinneradventure.com* or call ✆(866) 439-2469.

Los Angeles County Attractions

The big theme parks in Los Angeles are Universal Studios Hollywood, Six Flags Magic Mountain, and its water park Hurricane Harbor.

Universal Studios Hollywood

A film-themed park, Universal offers a studio tour and a variety of shows and rides based on its movies. See Chapter 19 for more information about this park.

Ticket and Pass Options at Universal Studios Hollywood

Passes include all-day admission and re-entry with a hand stamp. Unlike other parks, Universal Studios Hollywood defines a "child" (for purposes of regular ticket pricing) by height not age.

The song may say it never rains in Southern California, but don't believe it. If you visit on a day when the park receives more than one-eighth inch of rainfall by 2 P.M., you'll get a rain check good for a return visit any time in the next thirty days.

- **One-Day Pass:** This pass offers admission to the theme park for one day (all rides and attractions).

- **Southern California Residents:** This ticket is available online for people who live in Zip Codes 90000 to 93599. ID will be checked at the park.
- **Front of the Line Pass:** As the name implies, with this pass you can go straight to the front of the line at any ride or attraction. The number of these passes issued each day is limited, and they may not be available on very busy days. Order online in advance to be sure they don't sell out.
- **VIP Tour:** This tour package includes general admission, a special guided tour of the Studio Backlot, and a Front of the Line Pass.
- **Regular Annual Pass:** The pass includes twelve months of admission, 15 percent off admission for up to six guests, and discounts for merchandise and food. After the first visit, admission is subject to blackout dates.
- **Deluxe Annual Pass:** This pass offers all the features of the Regular Annual Pass but with no blackout dates.
- **Premium Annual Pass:** With this pass, a guest receives all the features of the Deluxe Annual Pass, plus free parking (after the first visit) and Front of the Line access to the Studio Tour.

These ticket prices are subject to change without notice.

TICKET AND PASS PRICES AT UNIVERSAL STUDIOS HOLLYWOOD		
Type of Pass	Adults	Children (requirement)
1-Day Pass	$59	$49 (under 48 inches tall)
Southern California Residents	$44 for all ages	
Front of the Line Pass	$99 for all ages	
Regular Annual Pass	$69 for all ages	
Deluxe Annual Pass	$89 for all ages	
Premium Annual Pass	$109 for all ages	

Buy your tickets online at *http://themeparks.universalstudios.com* and get discount coupons for food and other purchases.

OTHER COSTS AT UNIVERSAL STUDIOS HOLLYWOOD	
Item	**Cost**
VIP Experience	$149 for anyone age six and up
Parking	$10 for cars, $11 for RVs, Preferred parking $20
Fed Ex ticket delivery: $15 in the United States, $20 to addresses outside the United States	

Learn more about the Universal Studios VIP Experience in Chapter 19.

Discounts and Specials at Universal Studios Hollywood

Discounts to this park abound everywhere from their Web site to the local tourist publications, but if you buy a full-price ticket, you can get a free shuttle ride from Anaheim to Universal Studios. Children under two years old get in free.

Members of the U.S. military, including retirees, Department of Defense personnel, members of the National Guard/Reserves, dependents, and other base personnel can get special admission prices but must buy tickets in advance. Visit your local base MWR ITT/ITR ticket office or call the commander, Navy Region, Southwest at (619) 767-6000. Get started a couple of weeks ahead of time to allow for delivery.

Six Flags Magic Mountain and Hurricane Harbor

See Chapter 18 for more information. Six Flags does not offer rain checks. The water park is open seasonally, from mid-May through September only. Check their Web site at ✐*www.sixflags .com/parks/magicmountain.*

Ticket and Pass Options at Six Flags Magic Mountain

Six Flags Magic Mountain and Hurricane Harbor offer plenty of different tickets and passes. Choose the one that best meets your needs.

- **General Admission:** This ticket is good for admission for one day to the named park.
- **Two-Park Combo:** This ticket is good for one-day admission to both parks.
- **Flash Pass:** This front-of-the-line pass allows four priority boarding opportunities; for example, by four people on one ride, by one person for four rides, or by any other combination. Quantities are limited each day.
- **Play Pass:** This annual pass can be used at all nineteen Six Flags parks, with no blackout dates. It includes free concerts as well as bonus tickets and discounts for friends and family.
- **Xtreme Play Pass:** This annual pass includes Flash Pass front–of-the-line privileges on four rides per visit (subject to standard restrictions) and free parking.
- **Hurricane Harbor Premium Pass:** This pass includes unlimited admission all season long, free raft rental on every visit, and free parking, plus food and merchandise discounts.

These ticket prices are subject to change without notice.

TICKET AND PASS PRICES AT SIX FLAGS MAGIC MOUNTAIN		
Type of Pass	Adult	Children (under 48 inches tall)
Magic Mountain General Admission	$59.99	$29.99
Hurricane Harbor General Admission	$29.99	$20.99
Two-Park Combo	$69.99	
Play Pass	$59.00	$59.00
Xtreme Play Pass	$125.00	$125.00
Hurricane Harbor Season Pass	$39.99	$39.99
Hurricane Harbor Premium Pass	$100.00	$100.00

Order your Six Flags park tickets through their Web sites at *www.sixflags.com/parks/magicmountain* and *www.sixflags.com/parks/hurricaneharborla*. Print them at home or call Guest Relations at (661) 255-4142 for more information.

OTHER COSTS AT SIX FLAGS	
Item	Cost
Flash Pass	$15 Monday through Friday, $20 Saturday, Sunday, and Holidays
Automobile parking	$15 per day
Oversized vehicle parking	$20 per day
Valet parking	$30 per day

Learn more about why Flash Pass is important in Chapter 18.

Discounts and Specials at Six Flags Magic Mountain

- Children under two years old get in free.
- U. S. Military personnel can get a discount, but only if they buy in advance through their MWR or ITT recreation office.
- In the off-season, Magic Mountain often offers discounted prices, available only through their Web site.

San Diego Attractions

San Diego is full of family theme parks and attractions. These are the most popular (and expensive):

SeaWorld San Diego

SeaWorld is the home of killer whale Shamu and a host of other marine creatures. See Chapter 20 for more information about this park.

Ticket and Pass Options at SeaWorld San Diego

Most people need only one day to do everything at SeaWorld, but you can choose from a variety of tickets, and they sometimes offer a second day for free.

- **Single Day:** This ticket is valid for one day's admission.
- **Skyride and Tower:** This combination ticket gives one ride on each attraction.
- **Silver Passport:** This passport includes unlimited visits and free parking.
- **Platinum Passport:** This passport offers unlimited visits, preferred free parking, reserved seating, and guest seating tickets, along with free admission to all Anheuser-Busch Adventure Parks.

These ticket prices are subject to change without notice.

TICKET AND PASS PRICES AT SEAWORLD SAN DIEGO			
Type of Pass	Ages 10+	Ages 3 to 9	Ages 50+
Single Day	$57	$47	$57
Skyride and Tower	no extra fee		
Silver Passport	$84	$84	$84
Platinum Passport	$164	$144	$144

Buy your tickets online in advance at ✑*www.seaworld.com.*

| OTHER COSTS AT SEAWORLD SAN DIEGO ||
Item	Cost
Parking	$10 per day
RV and camper parking	$15 per day
Motorcycle parking	$6 per day
Preferred parking	$15 per day
Breakfast with Shamu	$19.95 ages 10 and up, $16.95 ages 3 to 9
Showtime Picnic	$12 for adults, $7 for kids
Behind the Scenes Tour	$11 for adults, $9 for children
Saving-a-Species Tour	$17 for adults, $14 for children
Animal Spotlight Tour	$40 for adults, $36 for children
Dolphin Interaction Program	$150 per person
Trainer for a Day Program	$150 to $495 per person, depending on level of participation
Wild Arctic Interaction	$150 per person

See Chapter 20 for a full description of these special meals and activities.

Discounts and Specials at SeaWorld San Diego

- Children under two years old get in free.
- Every Tuesday, anyone over fifty years old who buys a full-price ticket gets a free breakfast and admission to weekly symposiums on a variety of topics.
- During the off-season, SeaWorld runs special promotions, such as a second day free with the purchase of a one-day ticket. AAA members may also be eligible for a discount.

LEGOLAND California

One of four theme parks worldwide dedicated to the ever-popular toys blocks, LEGOLAND is in Carlsbad, California, about thirty miles north of San Diego. See Chapter 20 for more information about this park.

Ticket and Pass Options at LEGOLAND

Most people will only need one day to see LEGOLAND, but just in case you're besotted, there's a two-day option.

- **One-Day:** This ticket is good for one day, all attractions.
- **Two-Day:** This ticket is good for two days, but the second day must be within seven days after the first. It does not include parking.
- **Membership:** This option includes unlimited admission with no blackout days, special discounts, newsletter, and LEGO magazine subscription.
- **Membership Plus:** In addition to all the benefits of membership, this option offers free parking, a free guest pass, food, and merchandise discounts.
- **Ambassador:** This is a lifetime pass with all the benefits of Membership Plus, admission to all LEGOLAND parks worldwide, an exclusive annual session with a LEGO Builder, and four free guests passes annually.

These ticket prices are subject to change without notice.

TICKET AND PASS PRICES AT LEGOLAND			
Type of Pass	**Ages 13 to 59**	**Ages 3 to 12**	**Ages 60+**
One-Day	$57	$44	$44
Two-Day	$60	$56	$56
Membership	$106	$86	$86
Member-ship Plus		$132	$108
Ambassador	$1,000	$1,000	$1,000

Order tickets online at *www.legoland.com* and print them at home. You can order memberships online, but the passes will be mailed to you. To order an Ambassador membership, call (760) 438-LEGO.

OTHER COSTS AT LEGOLAND	
Type	**Cost**
Parking	$10
Camper and RV parking	$11
Motorcycle parking	$5
Preferred parking	$20

Don't forget to include these extra costs in your budget.

Discounts and Specials at LEGOLAND

- Children under two years old get in free.
- AAA members may be eligible for discounts or get a second day free.
- Airline employees with valid ID get a 20 percent discount on up to six tickets per visit.
- Active military personnel get a 10 percent discount on one-day admission at the ticket booth with valid ID or get a better discount at the ITT or MWR office on base.

San Diego Zoo

One of the world's most famous zoos, the San Diego Zoo is home to a wide variety of unusual animals and, of course, those cute pandas. See Chapter 20 for more information.

Ticket and Pass Options at the San Diego Zoo

The San Diego Zoo offers a couple of basic ticket types and a two-park ticket that includes the Wild Animal Park, but take a moment to figure out whether a membership might be the way to go, even if you're only visiting once. The membership options are summarized later in this chapter.

- **Admission Only:** This ticket gets you into the zoo, but it does not include any of the extras such as the tram or bus tours.
- **Best Value Admission:** This ticket includes unlimited use of the guided bus tour, express bus, and Skyfari tram.
- **Two-Park Ticket:** This ticket gives a discount on a Best Value Admission and a Wild Animal Park Nairobi Ticket when purchased together. Both must be used within five days after purchase.

These prices are subject to change without notice.

TICKET AND PASS PRICES AT THE SAN DIEGO ZOO		
Ticket Type	Ages 12+	Ages 3 to 11
Admission Only	$22.00	$14.50
Best Value Admission	$32.00	$19.75
Two-Park Ticket	$54.45	$33.55

You can buy tickets online at *www.sandiegozoo.org* or at the Zoo entrance.

OTHER COSTS AT THE SAN DIEGO ZOO	
Type	Cost
Parking	Free
Guided Bus Tour, Non-Member	$10.00
	$5.50
Skyfari Aerial Tram	$3.00 each way
Balboa Park Miniature Railroad	$1.75
ENTCO Wild Earth Safari Ride	$6.00 per player

You can learn more about these special tours and activities in Chapter 20.

Discounts and Specials at the San Diego Zoo

- Children under age two get in free any time. Every October, kids get in free if they bring along a paying adult.
- Seniors over sixty years old get a 10 percent discount off adult admission, which is not available online.
- Active-duty military personnel with a valid ID get free admission. Their spouses and dependents get 10 percent off the Best Value Admission only.

The San Diego Wild Animal Park

Run by the San Diego Zoo, this park is north of San Diego and offers a more safari-styled experience. See Chapter 20 for more information.

Ticket and Pass Options at the San Diego Wild Animal Park

The Wild Animal Park offers a two-park ticket that includes the San Diego Zoo, but take a moment to figure out whether a membership might be the way to go, even if you're only visiting once. The membership options are summarized later in this chapter.

- **General Admission:** This includes entrance into the Wild Animal Park and a ride on the Wgasa Bush Line Railway.
- **Two-Park Ticket:** This ticket gives a discount on a Best Value Admission and a Wild Animal Park Nairobi Ticket when purchased together. Both must be used within five days after purchase.

These ticket prices are subject to change without notice.

TICKET AND PASS PRICES AT THE SAN DIEGO WILD ANIMAL PARK		
Ticket Type	Ages 3 to 11	Ages 12+
General Admission	$17.50	$28.50
Two-Park Ticket	$33.55	$54.45

You can buy tickets online at *www.sandiegozoo.org* or at the Wild Animal Park entrance.

OTHER COSTS AT THE SAN DIEGO WILD ANIMAL PARK	
Item	Cost
Parking	$6 per day
RV Parking	$10 per day
Adventure Photo Caravan	$90
Cheetah Run Safari	$69
Cats and Carnivores Tour	$25 per person
A Taste of CRES Tour	$49 per person
Vet Center Tour	$49 per person
Target on Training Tour	$32 per person

Tour and other special activity prices do not include admission or parking. See Chapter 20 for a full description of these special activities.

Discounts and Specials at the San Diego Wild Animal Park

- Children under age two get in free any time.
- Seniors over sixty years old get a 10 percent discount off adult admission, which is not available online.
- Active-duty military personnel with a valid ID get free admission. Their spouses and dependents get 10 percent off the Best Value Admission only.

San Diego Zoo and Wild Animal Park Memberships

The San Diego Zoo and the Wild Animal Park are run by the same organization. As a result, annual memberships cover both parks, and because it's a nonprofit organization, membership dues are tax deductible. In addition to the benefits in the following list, members get discounts on bus tours and on parking at the Wild Animal Park. Membership levels include:

- **Membership:** Local membership is offered only to people who live in Zip Codes 90000 to 92999. Single memberships include one person in a household while dual memberships cover two. Members get unlimited admission to both the San Diego Zoo and Wild Animal Park for a year, two free guest passes, a free Skyfari Tram ride, four discount guest coupons, and four two-for-one bus tour coupons.
- **Senior memberships** are available only for locals, who get free Skyfari Tram rides, but do not get guest passes or discount coupons.
- **Koala Memberships:** These kids' memberships include unlimited admission to the zoo and Wild Animal Park, a free Skyfari tram ride and bus tour pass, and six issues of a special magazine.
- **Diamond Membership:** Good for one adult and accompanying guest or two adults in the same household, it includes free parking at the Wild Animal Park.

These prices are subject to change without notice.

MEMBERSHIP COSTS AT THE SAN DIEGO ZOO	
Membership Type	**Cost**
Local Adult Single Membership	$68
Local Adult Dual Membership	$86
Non-Local Adult Single Membership	$79
Non-Local Adult Dual Membership	$99

Senior Single Membership	$35
Senior Dual Membership	$50
Koala Child Membership	$21
Koala Junior Membership	$25 (ages 12 to 17)
Diamond Membership	$126

It's worth spending a couple of minutes with a calculator to see if a membership can save you money, and don't forget about the tax deduction.

Join online at *www.sandiegozoo.org/membership* and you'll get two extra months for free.

Combination Passes

Discounted combination tickets for Southern California attractions abound. If you're going to more than one place, check these options to see if any of them will save you money.

Southern California CityPass

This pass offers up to 30 percent savings if you're going to all the attractions it covers: a three-day Disneyland Hopper ticket, one-day admissions to SeaWorld and Universal Studios Hollywood, and one day at either the San Diego Zoo or Wild Animal Park. You'll have fourteen days to use it after you start.

The cost is $235 for adults and $189 for children. You can buy this pass online at *www.citypass.com* or at the ticket booth of any included attraction.

San Diego Zoo and Wild Animal Park Two-for-One

If you're going to both attractions, buying your tickets together will save you about 10 percent.

The cost is $54.45 for adults and $33.35 for children. You can buy this pass online at *www.sandiegozoo.org* or at the ticket booth at either location.

San Diego Three-for-One Pass

This pass is good for the San Diego Zoo, Wild Animal Park, and SeaWorld. You'll save about 10 percent over buying tickets for all three separately at full price.

The cost is $99.95 for adults and $76.95 for children. You can buy this pass online at *www.sandiegozoo.org* or at *www.seaworld.com* or at the ticket booth at any of the three locations.

San Diego Passport

This combo pass includes a host of admissions and discounts. Whether it will make sense for you depends on how many of the attractions you can visit during the time it's valid.

The cost is $79 for adults and $45 for children. You can buy this pass online at *www.sandiegozoo.org*.

Southern California Value Pass

Good for Universal Studios and SeaWorld, this pass saves you about 5 percent over buying tickets separately.

The cost is $94.94 for adults and $74.95 for children. You can buy this pass online at *www.goingtocalifornia.com*.

When evaluating any of these combination ticket packages, look into whether you can get better discounts or more extras another way. For example, you could buy a ticket that includes Universal Studios as part of a combination pack but miss out on their free shuttle from Anaheim. The discounts offered online at many attractions' Web sites, especially off-season, may also turn out to be a better deal.

CHAPTER 7

An Overview of the Disneyland Resort

WHEN IT OPENED, DISNEYLAND was a single theme park with a mere eighteen major attractions and the Disneyland Hotel next door. Today, the Disneyland Resort encompasses two large and ever-growing theme parks, three large resort hotels, a separate shopping and dining area, and plenty of other activities.

Getting to the Disneyland Resort

Both Disneyland and California Adventure are located in the same place. In fact, California Adventure sits facing the Disneyland entrance on the spot where the Disneyland parking lot used to be.

If you're staying at a Disney hotel or one of the hotels within walking distance listed in Chapter 4, it's easy. Just hoof it on over to the entrance.

If your hotel is a little farther away from the park entrance, it may offer a shuttle, but be sure you know how often it runs. You don't want to be tired and ready to head back hours before the shuttle arrives to pick you up.

If your hotel is on the Anaheim Resort Transit route, it's an easy way to get around. Not only will it take you to Disneyland, but it also goes to the Block at Orange, Anaheim Convention Center, Angel Stadium, Crystal Cathedral, and the Amtrak station. A trolley pass will cost you $3 for one day, $6 for two days, and $8 for three days. Kids under ten ride free with a pass-holding adult. Order the pass online at ✐*www.rideart.org* or buy it when you get there.

══FAST FACT

Disneyland's address may not be a coincidence. Some people think thirteen is an unlucky number, but M (for *Mickey,* or for *Mouse*) is the thirteenth letter in the alphabet and some say the double thirteen in the Disneyland address (1313 S. Harbor Boulevard) stands for M. M., Mickey Mouse's initials.

If you're driving to Anaheim from somewhere else in Southern California, take I-5 and get off at the Harbor Boulevard exit or the Disneyland exit. The main Mickey & Friends garage is on Disneyland Drive between Katella Avenue and Ball Road, and the passenger drop-off area is on Harbor. If you're using a GPS system, enter 1313 S. Harbor Boulevard, Anaheim, California.

Once you arrive at the Disneyland Resort, you'll pass through a bag inspection station and then into the central entry plaza, where you can head for the gates for either Disneyland or California Adventure.

Disneyland

Disneyland still has dozens of the classic rides and attractions created by Walt and his team of Imagineers more than fifty years ago, but this theme park also continues to be on the cutting edge, with exciting new rides, shows, and attractions designed for the entire family.

Today's Disneyland offers more than sixty rides, shows, and attractions. The park is divided into areas known as lands, and each land has a theme: adventure, the frontier, the future, fantasy, cartoons, and so on. If you're traveling with kids, you'll spend a lot of time in Fantasyland and Mickey's Toontown.

Most rides within Disneyland aren't "thrill" rides. With a few exceptions, you won't be dropped, swung, spun, tossed, or forced into a state of nausea or dizziness. What you will experience are classic moments in Disney history presented in innovative ways, often using special effects, Audio-Animatronics (robots), and beautifully designed sets or architecture.

≡ FAST FACT

It's no wonder Disneyland always looks so tidy. The cleaning crew uses 500 toy brooms, 400 dustpans, and 5,000 mop heads a year to keep the place clean, and they collect more than thirty tons of trash on a busy day.

Most of the Disneyland rides tell (or retell) a story featuring popular Disney characters. These rides tap all of your senses to create a fantasy-like experience. You can learn about each one of them in detail in Chapter 9.

California Adventure

The second theme park in the Disneyland Resort is much less focused on Disney characters and finds inspiration instead in its surroundings. As the name suggests, Disney's California Adventure salutes the state's culture, history, and lifestyle.

Many California Adventure experiences are unique to this theme park, such as Soarin' Over California, but the park offers a touch of Disney magic mixed in, and it's so well done that it often reminds Californians why they love their home state so much. In Chapters 11 and 12, you'll discover exactly what makes Disney's California Adventure such a special place to visit.

Downtown Disney

Whether you're looking for something to do after a fun-filled day at the Disney theme parks, hankering to spend an entire afternoon shopping, or looking to relax for a few hours and see a movie, Downtown Disney is the place to be. Located between the theme parks and the Disneyland Hotel, this collection of upscale stores, boutiques, and one-of-a-kind shops is also home to several themed restaurants, clubs, bars, and a twelve-screen movie theater.

During the day and evening, Downtown Disney is a great place for the entire family. At night, everyone enjoys the street performers and the energetic buzz, but most of the bars and clubs are open to adults only, allowing the older crowd to experience Disney's nightlife until around 2 A.M. (during peak seasons).

Not only does Downtown Disney boast stunning landscaping and architecture, but it also offers Disney's famous hospitality. You can find out about all its features in Chapter 14.

Parking

If you arrive at the Disneyland Resort by car, you'll find plenty of places to park. Each Disney hotel has its own separate guest parking lot, as do the theme parks and Downtown Disney. Once you're on resort property, however, it's best to leave your car parked and use Disney transportation to get around.

If you park in one of the theme park's large parking lots, expect crowds early in the morning, starting one hour before the park opens. Allow thirty minutes to get into the parking lot and into a space. You can take a ten-minute walk from the parking area to the front gate, or use the free tram.

Parking in the theme park lots costs $11 per day for automobiles. Keep your parking receipt, and you can enter and exit the lot during the day as often as you wish. No overnight parking is permitted. Don't worry about the park running out of available spots. The Mickey & Friends parking structure holds more than 10,250 cars, and an additional nearby lot holds 4,300 more.

📎 TRAVEL TIP

The Disney parking lots are huge, and all the floors of the Mickey and Friends lot look alike, except for the character they're named after. When you park your car, write down exactly where you leave it or take a picture of the area with your cell phone or digital camera. If you're driving a rental car, it's easy to forget what it looks like by the end of the day, so it may be a good idea to write down its make and model, color, and license plate number as well.

If you're traveling with anyone who might find getting onto and off the tram difficult, use the passenger drop-off areas in front of the theme parks' main entrance on Harbor Boulevard before parking your car. You'll also find designated passenger drop-off areas in front of the Disney hotels and near Downtown Disney.

Open and seemingly free parking spots at nearby restaurants and hotels may be tempting, but they are reserved for hotel/motel guests or restaurant customers. They're patrolled twenty-four hours per day, and if you aren't a guest or customer, you will most likely be towed away.

Getting Around the Disneyland Resort

You'll find a convenient tram waiting to take you from the parking lots to the park entrances and back. Once you're inside Disneyland, you can use the Disneyland Monorail to get to Downtown Disney. Otherwise, everything is within walking distance, including all three of the Disney hotels and Downtown Disney.

If you or one of your companions gets more worn-out than you expected and you need a stroller, wheelchair, or electric convenience vehicle, you can rent one in either of the parks.

 **TRAVEL TIP**

When leaving either Disney theme park, be sure to have your hand stamped at the exit and keep your Disney Passport (admission ticket) handy. You'll need both the passport and a hand stamp to re-enter the park. You're welcome to enter and exit the Disney theme parks as often as you wish on the day your passport is valid.

Avoiding the Lines

If you don't know about the long lines and waits at Disneyland and California Adventure, you're in for a surprise. On a busy day, it can take up to two hours to get onto the parks' most popular rides.

Everyone knows waiting isn't fun, and it certainly isn't what you went to the parks to do, but never fear. There are a number of ways to reduce your wait. The best of the bunch is RideMax, an inexpensive software tool that creates a custom itinerary for you, taking you to each ride when the wait is the shortest. Created by computer programmer Mark Winters to help keep his own family from waiting in line, this program can cut your wait from hours to minutes. All you do is pay $14.95 for a ninety-day subscription at *www.ridemax .com*, tell the program what you want to do and it does the rest, giving you a schedule that will keep you out of line and on the rides.

═══**FAST FACT**

Travel writers and everyday users report being able to ride every single ride in Disneyland in one day, even at the busiest times of year using RideMax, with time to spare. You can read these accounts at ✑*www.ridemax.com/tripreports.php*. They offer a money-back guarantee, so there's no risk and a lot to gain. Unfortunately, RideMax works on Windows operating systems only.

Disney's partial solution to reducing long waits is called fast-pass. At the entrance to the most popular rides in both parks, you'll find a fastpass machine. Insert your entry ticket and you'll get a pass printed with a time when you can return to the ride. When you come back, you get into a special fastpass line and onto the ride with only a short wait.

To make this system effective, it limits the number of passes issued each day, and if you arrive late, they may be all gone. There are also some restrictions. If you're holding a fastpass, you can't get another until after the return time stamped on the one you have.

JUST FOR PARENTS

If you both want to take a ride that your child is too small for, don't stand in line twice. Get in the line together and when you reach the loading area, tell the cast member that you want to switch off. The first parent can ride while the second waits near the entrance, and as soon as the first parent comes back and collects the child, the second one can get on.

A little-known fact about the lines may also help save time. Some of the popular rides, such as Soarin' Over California and Splash Mountain, offer special "single rider" lines. If you're willing to sit alone rather than next to your buddies, get in this line. Because the cast members use singles to fill in otherwise-unused seats, the wait will be much shorter. A few other tips may also help if all else fails:

- Go during less-busy times of the year or on a weekday if you can.
- Visit the most popular rides late in the day after some folks wear out and go home.
- Opinions vary about taking the most popular rides first thing in the morning. Those who support it say you can get there

before the lines build up, but others point out that too many people do the "Indy Dash" as soon as the gates open and the lines get long almost immediately. This strategy also fails if a lot of people get into the park during the early entry days offered by the Disney hotels, and it's less effective when the park opens at 9 A.M. because visitors are allowed all the way to the end of Main Street and they surge into the ride areas immediately.

- Many people stake out a spot to watch the fireworks, Fantasmic! or California Adventure's Electrical Parade up to two hours ahead of time, and many more crowd around at the last minute. If you don't mind missing those events, it's a good time to visit popular attractions such as Indiana Jones Adventure, Splash Mountain, Space Mountain, Star Tours, or Soarin' Over California.

- Lines for many attractions also are shorter when everyone breaks for lunch and dinner.

The theme parks don't have a monopoly on lines. To avoid lines at the restaurants, eat lunch before 11 A.M. or after 1 P.M.

You'll find people lined up at the ticket booths early in the morning, too. A simple way to avoid standing in this line is to order your tickets online at *www.disneyland.com*. You can print out your passes at home and then head straight for the gates when you arrive.

Meeting Your Disney Pals

You'll often find Mickey, Minnie, and other Disney characters roaming the park, greeting guests, signing autographs, and posing for pictures. While you can always find Mickey and Minnie at home in Mickey's Toontown and see them in the daily parade, they're not the only ones around. Many Disney characters make appearances throughout the day in both Disneyland and California Adventure.

To find out where the various Disney characters will be during your visit, check the Disneyland Today brochure you get at the entrance or ask the cast member at the Wait Time Board on Main Street, U.S.A. or next to the Guest Relations booth at California Adventure.

Tips for Meeting the Characters

You can meet the characters in many places in both theme parks. Some of them, such as the Little Mermaid or Winnie the Pooh, show up in special settings designed just for them, while others appear in other spots around the park. The popular character breakfasts offer an opportunity to see and meet the characters, too.

When children meet the Disney characters, they love collecting their autographs. Many of the Disney Resort gift shops sell Disney-themed character autograph books for the kids to ask their cartoon heroes to sign, and these books are one of the park's all-time bestselling souvenirs.

 JUST FOR PARENTS

To make it easy for the real people inside the character costumes to sign your child's autograph when wearing gloves twice as big as their hands, bring along a larger-size, felt-tipped pen that they can hold onto easily. If you wonder why they hold the book in front of their face to sign, it's because they can only see straight ahead through their costume's eyeholes.

Looking for Mickey?

If you want to meet Mickey Mouse during your Disneyland visit, head directly to Mickey's House in Toontown. Kids (and their parents) are Mickey Mouse's personal guests as they explore his house and stop in to say hello to him.

It's a perfect opportunity to snap a photo of Mickey with your kids, but because you're guaranteed to meet Mickey here, this attraction tends to have a long line during peak times of the day. Be patient. For kids, meeting Mickey is a highlight of their trip to Disneyland, and the picture you take of them (or yourself) with Mickey will be worth the wait.

Mickey often comes out of the Hollywood Pictures Backlot gate in California Adventure just as the park opens, wearing his California tourist outfit, stopping briefly for photos and autographs.

Both Mickey and Minnie appear in parades and live shows, and they show up around the park all day long, meeting guests.

Where the Characters Hang Out in Disneyland

Because Disneyland is so large, you'll find more characters there, and you could spend so much time greeting them all that you wouldn't get anything else done. Discuss this with your kids before you go and try to set some priorities. These are some of the places you may find the characters:

- Ariel and other Little Mermaid characters have a special grotto, located near the Triton Garden, off the path toward "it's a small world" just next to Tomorrowland.
- Pooh, Tigger, and Piglet greet guests near The Many Adventures of Winnie the Pooh ride in Critter Country.
- Goofy, Pluto, and pals appear in Toontown, along with Mickey and Minnie.
- The stars of *Toy Story 2* greet their fans in a place cowboy Woody likes: Frontierland.
- Disney princesses Snow White, Cinderella, Belle (from *Beauty and the Beast*), and others can sometimes be found in or around Once Upon a Time . . . The Disney Princess Shoppe in Fantasyland.

Another fun way to meet and interact with the characters is to take the Discover the Magic Tour, a family-oriented activity where you all work with the characters to find hidden treasure and foil the villains. It's recommended for kids between five and nine years old, and anyone under eighteen years old has to bring an adult along with them. There's an extra fee for this tour, which includes lunch and a souvenir. Call (714) 781-4400 up to thirty days in advance to reserve your spot.

Where the Characters Hang Out in California Adventure

California Adventure is where you'll find more of the newer Disney characters, from films made in the past few years.

- Flik and Atta hang out near the entrance to "a bug's land."
- You'll find a variety of characters on the main street in the Hollywood Pictures Backlot, including Stitch and the dragon Mushu from *Mulan*.
- Chip 'n Dale often show up on the boardwalk going toward Paradise Pier, just after you pass Ariel's Grotto. They make especially cute pictures with the kids.

At Christmas time, a popular character—but not one that Disney invented—can be found near the California Adventure entrance. Santa takes a break from the North Pole here, all dressed up in surfer shirt and shorts.

Character Dining

Lines to meet the characters in the parks can get quite long, especially for the most popular ones. If you don't want to wait in line so your kids can meet Mickey, Ariel, or Winnie the Pooh, consider taking them to one of the character breakfasts.

You can take your kids to a character breakfast at any of the three Disney-owned hotels, even if you aren't staying there. Goofy is the star at the Disneyland Hotel, Lilo and Stitch host the Aloha breakfast at Paradise Pier, and Chip 'n Dale appear at the Grand Californian's Critter Breakfast. Inside the park and for about half the price of the hotel breakfasts, Minnie and Friends come for Breakfasts in the Park at the Plaza Inn, while Ariel and her fellow Disney princesses show up at Ariel's Grotto restaurant in California Adventure.

 JUST FOR PARENTS

As you can imagine, these events are very popular. To avoid disappointing your child who is looking forward to meeting Chip 'n Dale while eating their Mickey Mouse-shaped pancakes, call ☏(714) 781-3483 for reservations up to sixty days and at least two weeks ahead of time.

Character Photographs

At most any spot where the characters meet their fans, you'll find a Disney photographer on hand. You may be tempted to save money by taking your own photos, but if they're digital, be sure you review them before you leave the park, just in case a finger got in the way of the lens or the exposure went awry.

 TRAVEL TIP

To capture a better picture of your kids with the characters, try to move around where there's a nice, plain background and you can see your child's face. Try to capture your little one while he or she is interacting with the character, shaking hands, or talking instead of staring at the camera. Be sure your batteries are fresh and you have plenty of digital media or film.

The pros can often capture a photo that's better than you can do yourself. Stop by Disneyland's Main Street Photo Supply Co. or California Adventure's Greetings from California shop to see what they shot, and if theirs are better than yours, you can buy a copy to take home.

CHAPTER 8

The Disneyland Theme Park

WHEN DISNEYLAND OPENED IN 1955, visitors entered through Main Street, U.S.A., just as they do today. The original four lands were Frontierland, Tomorrowland, Adventureland, and Fantasyland. Today there are eight different lands for the Disneyland visitor to explore, from the Wild West to the worlds of the future. This chapter will discuss the "lay of the lands" and also where to shop and eat while in the park.

An Overview of Disneyland

✉ 1313 S. Harbor Blvd., Anaheim

✆ (714) 781-4565

Disneyland is the only Disney theme park created under Walt Disney's direct supervision. Since the gates first opened, more than 500 million people have enjoyed the Disneyland experience.

≡FAST FACT

Disney considered Disneyland to be a three-dimensional, interactive show, which is why people visiting Disneyland are called guests and the people who work at Disneyland are called cast members.

During their visits, they've taken more than 3.4 million rides in spinning teacups, bobsledded more than 12.5 million miles on the Matterhorn Bobsleds, and purchased almost 80 million pairs of Mickey Mouse ears as souvenirs. They've also consumed more than 82 million hamburgers, enough to make a stack that would tower over 3,000 miles high, and drunk more than 35 million gallons of soft drinks, equal to 376 million twelve-ounce portions, enough for every adult in the United States, Canada, and Mexico.

Disneyland's hours of operation vary by the time of year and day of week, with its longest days starting at 8 A.M. and lasting until midnight. For the schedule during your visit, call Guest Relations or visit the Disneyland Web site at *www.disneyland.com*.

 TRAVEL TIP

Other useful-but-unofficial sites include Mouse Planet, ✑*www .mouseplanet.com*, which features weekly updates about the parks and some interesting feature stories from Disneyland behind the scenes, and About.com's California for Visitors, ✑*http://gocalifornia .about.com/od/cadisneyland*, where you can find many photographs of the Disneyland Resort and get an e-mail planner newsletter. If you're a fan of Disneyland history and the rides of yesteryear, Yesterland, ✑*www.yesterland.com*, is a must.

Some days, the main gate opens about one hour earlier than the rest of the park and guests can enter Main Street, U.S.A. for shopping and breakfast.

Tips for Visiting Disneyland

Chapter 2 will give you some tips for theme park attire. These ideas will also help you have the happiest visit possible.

- Plan your day in advance. If you are going to use RideMax to shorten your waiting time, this is essential. Otherwise, choose which attractions you absolutely must experience.

- As soon as you arrive, pick up a copy of the Entertainment Times Guide and the Souvenir Map. These helpful booklets, which are given out at the main entrance and at City Hall, contain the times for all parades and shows, describe the times and places to meet the Disney characters, and offer a detailed map of the park with all of the major attractions, restaurants, and amenities (restrooms, public phones, ATMs, etc.) marked.

- Once you get inside the park, choose a place for your group to meet in case you get separated. The Snow White Grotto next to Sleeping Beauty Castle is a good spot. It's quiet and not normally crowded, so you won't have trouble finding each other. Walk there together so everyone knows where it is.

- You'll find the Wait Time board at the end of Main Street near the Frontierland entrance. Consult it to help you figure out the best time of the day for each ride or attraction.

- If your camera batteries need charging during the day, you can take them to the Main Street Photo Supply Co. They have a few generic chargers on hand, but it's best to bring your own along to avoid any trouble.

- The Southern California sun can get hot in the middle of summer, and you won't find a lot of shade at Disneyland. If you need a spot to cool off and rest, visit the Enchanted Tiki Room or the Opera House, or take a ride on the Pirates of the Caribbean or "it's a small world." In Tomorrowland, you'll find cooling misters just below the rocket at Redd Rocket's Pizza Port.

- Throughout the day, drink plenty of liquids. You can purchase soda, juice, or bottled water throughout Disneyland, or you can take advantage of the free water fountains. Avoid dehydration by drinking liquids even if you're not thirsty.

- Disneyland usually overstates wait times by about ten minutes. If an attraction posts a twenty-minute wait, chances are you'll only wait about ten minutes.
- You can see the fireworks anywhere in the park that you can see the castle. One of the best spots to watch is just behind the rope in front of the castle drawbridge, where you'll feel as though the show is just for you, but you'll have to get there early to stake out your spot. A less-crowded place to watch is along the corridor between the castle and Toontown.

Any time you need help in Disneyland or aren't sure what to do, consult a cast member. They're trained to help with all kinds of problems and know how to answer your questions.

The Lands

Disneyland is divided into eight areas, known as lands. Each land has a theme, reflected in its rides, attractions, and shows. The park is laid out in a hub-and-spoke design, with entrances to most of the lands originating from the Hub, where you'll find the Walt and Mickey "Friends" statue.

Once you pass through the entrance gate, you're officially inside Disneyland, and will be standing in the area Walt Disney called the Lobby. Straight ahead are the Disneyland Train Station and a giant floral Mickey Mouse. This is a great photo spot, and a favorite spot for character greetings.

Main Street, U.S.A.

If you look down in the Lobby area, you'll notice that the pavement is red, to symbolize a red carpet. Walk to the left or right to pass under the train tracks and enter Disneyland's Main Street, U.S.A.

As you pass under the train tracks, look up. You'll see a sign that reads, "Here you leave today and enter the world of yesterday, tomorrow, and fantasy." Just ahead is Main Street, U.S.A. with Sleeping Beauty Castle at the far end.

JUST FOR PARENTS

Chewing gum is not sold anywhere on Disney property. If you or your kids can't get along without it for a day, you can bring your own, but the Disneyland cleanup crew asks that you dispose of it properly, and not spit it out onto the ground or stick it under your seat.

Near the entrance, you'll find City Hall (where Guest Services is located), the main Disneyland Railroad Station, and the Opera House surrounding a small park, which offers nice benches to sit on. This is an excellent place to watch the daily character parade, especially when it starts from the Main Street end of the park.

The building that looks like the Disneyland fire station isn't. Instead, it's Walt Disney's personal apartment, where he sometimes spent the night when he was too tired to go home. By tradition, the light in the window has burned ever since Disney died, to symbolize that he's still around in spirit.

Main Street, U.S.A. was inspired by Walt Disney's childhood home in Marceline, Missouri. Disney Imagineers used a technique called "forced perspective," making ground floors seven-eighths of normal size and upper floors smaller, to make it seem larger than it actually is.

While Main Street, U.S.A. is primarily a shopping and dining area, a few attractions here will be of particular interest to Disney fans and historians. They're described in Chapter 9.

≡ FAST FACT

At the center of the park is the Hub at which stands a life-size statue showing Walt Disney holding hands with Mickey Mouse. The Hub is the center of Disneyland, from which you can easily travel to any of the lands. The Hub is also one of Disneyland's most photographed areas.

The iconic Sleeping Beauty Castle, Disneyland's most recognizable landmark, stands at the end of Main Street, U.S.A. Inspired by medieval European castles, this colorful 77-foot-tall castle was created specifically for Disneyland. If you've been to other Disney theme parks, you may notice that Disneyland's castle is smaller than the others. Walt Disney wanted to be sure it didn't intimidate guests and insisted on its scaled-down size.

The castle's water-filled moat is home to many fish and is visited often by ducks and swans. In fact, the same white swans in the moat have been Disneyland guests for more than fifteen years.

Next to the castle, to the right if you're facing it from the Hub, you'll find one of Disneyland's most overlooked spots, Snow White's Grotto. Small and quiet, it's a good place to meet your group if you get split up.

Don't leave Disneyland without walking through the enchanted castle. Having your picture taken while standing in front of it will also make the perfect addition to your family photo album.

≡FAST FACT

The most popular place for marriage proposals at Disneyland is Sleeping Beauty Castle. This is also a popular spot for weddings.

Does the castle look a bit backward to you? Originally, it was supposed to face the opposite direction, but Walt Disney turned things around just before construction began to make the castle look more inviting to guests.

Adventureland

Your true adventure in Disneyland can begin in any of the lands. This one, however, takes you to exotic locales and re-creates Africa, Asia, and the South Pacific. In Adventureland, you can take a Jungle Cruise, go on an adventure with Indiana Jones, climb Tarzan's Treehouse, hear tales of Aladdin and Jasmine's Agrabah, or listen to the birdies sing in the Enchanted Tiki Room.

Critter Country

As you'll soon discover, this is Disneyland's smallest land. It offers cute, kid-oriented attractions and a special opportunity to meet Winnie the Pooh and travel through the Hundred Acre Wood, but it's also the land of Splash Mountain, one of Disneyland's most popular thrill rides.

Fantasyland

Sleeping Beauty Castle also serves as the entrance to Fantasyland, a magical place designed for the young and young-at-heart and one of the four original lands. Each Fantasyland ride and attraction features one of Disney's most famous and beloved cartoons or films. In Fantasyland, you can travel through the rabbit hole with Alice in Wonderland, visit Snow White's house, take a wild ride with Mr. Toad, fly to Neverland with Peter Pan, see an elephant fly, or spin yourself silly in a teacup.

Frontierland

Frontierland is dedicated to the pioneers of the Old West. Within its boundaries you can ride a runaway mine train, take a raft to Tom Sawyer's Island, sail on a riverboat, or see a saloon-style stage show.

Mickey's Toontown

Hollywood may be where human celebrities hang out, but the stomping ground for Disney's animated stars is Mickey's Toontown. This is Disneyland's newest land, where guests can meet and greet Mickey, Minnie, and other classic Disney characters. In fact, the entire area has the look and feel of a three-dimensional cartoon.

In Toontown, you can meet Mickey and Minnie, go for a spin with Roger Rabbit, climb into Chip 'n Dale's tree house, and ride Disneyland's gentlest roller coaster. Keep your camera ready: Even the buildings, mailboxes, fire hydrants, and manhole covers look like cartoons and the oversized "toy" cars on the main street make a great photo opportunity.

≡FAST FACT

According to legend, Mickey Mouse founded Toontown in the 1930s to get away from Hollywood's hustle and bustle, keeping it a secret from all humans except Walt Disney. Mickey convinced Walt to build Disneyland next door, and finally, in 1993, the famous mouse opened his private town to the public.

New Orleans Square

New Orleans Square offers only two attractions, but they're both Disneyland classics: the Haunted Mansion and Pirates of the Caribbean. This area is designed to look as the Crescent City did a century and a half ago, with sheltered courtyards and winding streets.

Tomorrowland

Step into the future for an exciting and positive look at what's to come. Here, you can check out cutting-edge technology and experience some space-age attractions, including Space Mountain, Disneyland's famous indoor, dark roller coaster. In Tomorrowland, you can embark on a shuttle to Endor, watch inventor Wayne Szalinski shrink a few things he wasn't supposed to, zoom around on a rocket, or take a monorail ride.

Disneyland Dining

Disneyland has plenty of places to eat, but perhaps its most famous dining spot is the Blue Bayou Restaurant. You'll also find a variety of sit-down and take-away food spots, as well as specialty refreshment carts selling items such as Mickey Mouse–shaped ice-cream bars.

To avoid crowds, have lunch before 11:00 A.M. or after 2:00 P.M. During this midday period, the lines for the popular attractions are the shortest, while the lines at Disneyland's eateries are the longest. Peak dinner hours are between 5:00 P.M. and 8:00 P.M. Once again, it's best to experience the popular attractions during these hours.

You can read about Disney's famous character meals in Chapter 7, the Disney hotel restaurants are described in Chapter 4, Chapter 14 describes dining options in Downtown Disney, and Chapter 15 offers some suggestions for other places to eat around Anaheim.

≡FAST FACT

Each year, Disneyland serves more than 4 million hamburgers, 3.4 million orders of French fries, 3.2 million boxes of popcorn, 3.2 million servings of ice cream, 1.2 million gallons of soft drinks, and 1.6 million hot dogs, but there are plenty of other dining choices available.

You can make dinner reservations for some of the Disneyland restaurants, and it's a good idea to do it as far in advance as you can. Call (714) 781-3463 up to sixty days and at least two weeks in advance.

Prices for each of the dining spots listed, as with all other prices quoted in this book, are likely to change.

Blue Bayou
Location: New Orleans Square
Meals: Lunch, dinner
Price range: $20 to $30 per person
Located at Lafitte's Landing and visible as you embark on the Pirates of the Caribbean adventure, the Blue Bayou looks lovely, with its moonlit setting under Spanish moss–draped trees. Many Disneyland visitors enjoy a meal at the Blue Bayou, and it is exceptionally

popular. If you wait until you get to Disneyland to try to get in, you will most likely find it already booked up days in advance.

 TRAVEL TIP

Even if you're over the age of twenty-one, Disneyland does not serve or allow alcoholic beverages anywhere in the theme park. However, you can enjoy beer and wine in limited areas within California Adventure.

The Blue Bayou is a full-service, sit-down restaurant whose menu includes Cajun gumbo and jambalaya, Alaskan king crab legs, filet mignon, fish, and chicken. The signature Monte Cristo sandwich is served only at lunch.

Despite all its fame and reputation, the Blue Bayou's food is mediocre at best. If you favor ambiance and the dining experience over food quality, you may enjoy it, but if you like good food, you may want to go to the Golden Vine restaurant in California Adventure instead.

Café Orleans
Location: New Orleans Square
Meals: Lunch, dinner
Price range: $10 to $30 per person

A casual restaurant that offers table service, Café Orleans offers indoor seating or tables on an outdoor terrace overlooking Rivers of America. The menu features flavors of New Orleans, including French onion soup, Monte Cristo sandwiches, and gumbo. They also serve soups and salads, sandwiches, and crepe specialties.

Carnation Café
Location: Main Street, U.S.A.
Meals: Breakfast, lunch, dinner

Price range: $10 to $20 per person

The Carnation Café serves a variety of typical American foods, such as chicken potpies, pasta, and roast beef, as well as their popular "butcher block" sandwich plates, in a casual atmosphere. Breakfasts feature croissant sandwiches and Mickey Mouse waffles, and they provide table service for breakfast and lunch.

French Market Restaurant
Location: New Orleans Square
Meals: Lunch, dinner, snacks
Price range: $10 to $20 per person

This casual dining spot is a good place to sit under the trees and enjoy the view while you eat. Dixieland jazz bands also provide mealtime entertainment. Menu highlights include Southern cooking favorites such as jambalaya, beef stew, fried chicken, soups, and salads.

Plaza Inn
Location: Main Street, U.S.A.
Meals: Lunch, dinner
Price range: $10 to $20 per person

Character breakfasts are served at the Plaza Inn every morning. The rest of the day, meals are served buffet-style with dishes such as roasted chicken, pasta, and pot roast. The dining room is nicely decorated in Victorian style with lots of ornate details.

Rancho del Zocalo
Location: Frontierland
Meals: Breakfast, lunch, dinner
Price range: $10 to $20 per person

Disneyland's only Mexican restaurant serves citrus fire-grilled chicken, burritos, tacos, and other Mexican favorites.

Redd Rocket's Pizza Port
Location: Tomorrowland
Meals: Lunch, dinner

Price range: $10 per person or less

The setting is cute, with a giant rocket ship marking the spot just next to Space Mountain, and the price is one of the most reasonable in the park. Redd Rocket's serves giant pizza slices (or whole pies), pasta, and Caesar salad.

River Belle Terrace

Location: Frontierland

Meals: Breakfast, lunch, dinner, snacks

Price range: $10 to $20 per person

Once the cherished Sunday morning breakfast spot of Walt Disney, this stately restaurant remains a sentimental favorite for breakfast, lunch, and dinner.

You can get a full breakfast at the River Belle, with scrambled eggs, country-style potatoes, bacon, sausage, and cinnamon rolls, or order some Mickey Mouse–shaped pancakes. The lunch menu includes barbecued chicken and ribs, grilled chicken salad, barbecued salmon sandwiches, vegetable stew, and clam chowder. The River Belle also offers a children's menu that includes mini corn dogs, barbecued chicken legs, or a Mickey Mouse–shaped peanut butter and jelly sandwich.

═FAST FACT

The Gibson Girl ice cream parlor on Main Street, U.S.A. sells enough ice cream every year to build a life-size replica of Fantasyland's thirteen-story-tall Matterhorn.

In late 2006, the Walt Disney Company announced new food guidelines to promote better kids' diets, with healthier choices becoming the standard offering rather than an option at all Disney-operated restaurants and snack carts. They also plan to eliminate all added trans fats and improve the nutritional value and taste of most of their food by the end of 2007.

Shopping at Disneyland

You'll find plenty of places to spend your money at Disneyland. In fact, it may be harder to keep from spending than to find something to buy.

Every major attraction has a shop that guests pass through on the way out and in between are small shops and carts selling everything imaginable.

 JUST FOR PARENTS

Disneyland's most popular souvenir of all time is a pair of Mouseke-teer ears; more than 78 million have been sold since 1955, enough to outfit every person in California, Texas, and New York. Other popular mementos include autograph books, Mickey Mouse plush toys, and balloons.

Main Street, U.S.A. Shopping

Whether you're looking to make some purchases or you just want to see some beautiful Disney-related artwork and products, spend some time browsing in the shops along Main Street, U.S.A. Much of the merchandise sold in these shops can't be purchased from the Disney Stores, the Disney Catalog, or anywhere else.

- **20th Century Music Company:** Disney CDs and videos
- **Candy Palace and Candy Kitchen:** Old-fashioned candies, caramel apples, fudge, and other sweets made on the premises
- **China Closet:** Porcelain and ceramics, Disney collectible china, and snow globes

- **Crystal Arts:** Custom blown glass and specialty crystal
- **Disneyana:** Disney animation cels, bronze statues, books, and memorabilia
- **Disney Clothiers, Ltd.:** Vintage, retro, and finer clothing with a Disney twist
- **Disney Showcase:** Disney apparel, decorative items, and pins
- **Emporium:** Disney apparel, plush toys, character hats, sweatshirts, and other souvenirs
- **Hatmosphere:** Silly hats of all kinds and custom-embroidered Mickey Mouse ears
- **The Mad Hatter:** Mickey Mouse ears (which can be monogrammed), jester caps, Goofy hats
- **Main Street Magic Shop:** Magic tricks, how-to books, practical jokes, and gag gifts
- **Market House:** Candy, gourmet food items, kitchenware
- **New Century Jewelry:** Marcasite character jewelry and gold character charms
- **New Century Timepieces:** Famous-brand timepieces, Mickey Mouse watches, custom-designed watches painted in the shop
- **Newsstand:** Film, small souvenirs, and postcards
- **Silhouette Studio:** Custom-made profile cutouts made on the spot

The Main Street Photo Co. sells Disney frames, film, disposable cameras, batteries, and digital media. This is also the place to view and purchase photographs taken by the park's roving photographers.

 ## JUST FOR PARENTS

In addition to souvenirs of all kinds, several Main Street shops sell necessities, such as sunglasses, aspirin, diapers, rain ponchos, and other items. These items aren't always on display, so if you're looking for something in particular, be sure to ask a cast member.

For unusual and inexpensive souvenirs, look for the pressed penny machines located all over the park. You drop in a penny, along with two quarters, and your penny is pressed and rolled into an elongated shape with an image imprinted. Pennies made before 1982 work best, and pressing the design on the "heads" side will give the clearest imprint. The two quarters are the price you pay for the imprinting. Park Pennies (*www.parkpennies.com*) tells you where to find the dozens of machines and what design each one presses, so you can make a project of collecting Mickeys, Tinkerbelles, or Plutos. Some of the Disneyland shops also sell albums to put your collection in, and during the holidays, you'll find special designs.

If you want to shop on Main Street, the shops are open for an hour after the attractions close. However, they're usually packed then. A better time to go is first thing in the morning on days when Main Street opens before the rest of the park, or midday when everyone else is eating lunch.

New Orleans Square Shopping

Follow winding Royal Street past the Blue Bayou Restaurant into this special shopping area. Shops here include:

- **Cristal d'Orleans:** Fine glass items of all kinds
- **Jewel of Orleans:** Art deco–style estate jewelry, rare gems, and one-of-a-kind pieces
- **L'Ornement Magique:** Disney Christmas ornaments, decorative pieces by artist Christopher Radko
- **La Mascarade d'Orleans:** Disney trading pins, lanyards, and starter sets
- **Le Bat en Rouge:** Haunted Mansion and Pirates of the Caribbean merchandise
- **Royal Street Sweets:** Mardi Gras masks, beads and boas, sweets

Also in the New Orleans Square area is the Disney Gallery. Located above the Pirates of the Caribbean ride, this space was originally designed to be Walt Disney's private apartment, but he died before its completion. Today, it's an art gallery showcasing original concept drawings; paintings; design blueprints for many of Disneyland's past, present, and future attractions; and animation cels from Disney's animated movies. Limited editions or prints of many of the works on display are for sale. The Disney Gallery also invites special guests, such as Disney Imagineers or animators, to make appearances, conduct demonstrations, and answer guests' questions.

Guest Services

You'll find Disneyland Guest Services in City Hall, just to the left of the main entrance, past the tunnel under the railroad track. No matter what you need, this is the place to go. They can cash a check, lend you an Assistive Listening Device or closed captioning activator, answer your questions, or wish you a happy birthday, and they'll try to help, no matter what you need.

The Lost and Found department is located outside the California Adventure entrance, to the left behind the wall. The Baby Care Center and First Aid Station are on the northeast end of Main Street, U.S.A. in the small side street between the Plaza Inn and the Main Street Photo Company.

Disney security is highly trained in dealing with lost-child situations. If a young child (under the age of ten) in your party gets lost in Disneyland, before you panic, seek help from security or report the missing child to any Disneyland cast member and follow their instructions. The missing kid is likely to end up in the same location as the Baby Care Center. Guests over ten years old who get separated from their group can leave a written message at City Hall.

CHAPTER 9

Disneyland Rides

TODAY, DISNEYLAND OFFERS MORE than twice the number of rides and attractions than when it opened more than fifty years ago. Disneyland boasts forty-four rides and attractions and sixteen shows spread over eight themed lands. Twelve million people visit it every year. This chapter describes what's where, what happens, and who might enjoy it. You may want to get out the Attraction Selection Worksheet in Appendix C as you read this section so you can mark the things you want to do.

Main Street, U.S.A.

Disneyland's main thoroughfare expresses the essence of small-town life around the turn of the twentieth century. It's filled with shops, places to eat, and various guest services, but it has a few attractions that will be of particular interest to true Disney fans and Disney historians.

Attractions on Main Street, U.S.A. include:

The Disneyland Opera House

Ages 2–4:	N.S.
Ages 5–10:	★
Ages 11–15:	★
Ages 16–adult:	★★

For a review of the rating system, see below.

The Disneyland Opera House (which was a lumber mill during Disneyland construction and later a television studio for the original Mickey Mouse Club) contains a small museum and theater.

While waiting for the show, guests enjoy the Disney memorabilia exhibits in the lobby. During the Disneyland fiftieth anniversary celebration, Disneyland replaced Great Moments with Mr. Lincoln, the Opera House's normal attraction with a special film called *Disneyland: The First 50 Magical Years*, hosted by actor Steve Martin and Donald Duck.

When this book was written, the anniversary celebration was officially over but *Disneyland: The First 50 Magical Years* was still showing.

★	Rides and attractions that earned just one star aren't worth waiting for and could be skipped, especially if your time within the theme park is limited.
★★	Rides and attractions that earned two stars are good, but they don't fall into the "must-see" category.
★★★	The rides and attractions that earned three stars are definitely worth seeing and should not be missed.
N.S.	This denotes rides and attractions that are "not suitable" for a specific age group.

The Disneyland Railroad

Ages 2–4:	★★
Ages 5–10:	★★
Ages 11–15:	★★
Ages 16–adult:	★★

Walt Disney loved trains and railroads, and a train appeared in his earliest sketches of the attraction that eventually became Disneyland. Five different trains run continuously on the circular track, with stops near the main entrance, New Orleans Square, at the back of Tomorrowland behind Autopia and Innoventions, and in Fantasyland near the entrance to Mickey's Toontown. Each station is designed to complement the theme of the area it's located in.

The Disneyland Railroad provides a transportation alternative to using your feet, but more important, the trip between Tomorrowland and Main Street, U.S.A. is also the only way you'll get to see a couple of hidden Disneyland attractions, Primeval World, which features huge Animatronic (robotic) dinosaurs that kids will love, and Grand Canyon. Taking an entire loop around the park on the train takes about twenty minutes, but you can get off and board at any stop.

The train offers a great overview of the entire theme park. If you want to go on the Disneyland Railroad without waiting too long, your best bet is to climb aboard at the Main Street, U.S.A. station.

The Main Street Cinema

Ages 2–4:	N.S.
Ages 5–10:	★
Ages 11–15:	★
Ages 16–adult:	★★

When you're standing on Main Street, U.S.A. and facing Sleeping Beauty Castle, you'll find a movie theater on the right side of the street. There's no charge to enter, and what you'll see inside is a must for fans of early Mickey Mouse cartoons. Shown on six screens are some of Mickey's original animated films, including *Steamboat Willie*, *Plane Crazy*, *Mickey's Polo Team*, *The Moose Hunt*, *Traffic Trouble*, and *Dog Napper*.

═══FAST FACT

Walt Disney first created Mickey Mouse for the 1939 New York World's Fair, and both Mickey and his girlfriend, Minnie, made their debut in the film *Steamboat Willie*.

All of these films are in black and white, with Walt Disney providing Mickey's voice. The films run constantly, so you can enter and exit the theater whenever you wish. It's seldom crowded, and watching a short movie in a nice air-conditioned theater is a nice respite from the crowds outside. Adults have to remain standing, but there's a place for kids to sit down.

True Disney fans and historians shouldn't miss these films, but kids might find them somewhat boring.

Main Street Vehicles

It's easy to get a lift from one end of Main Street, U.S.A. to the other. Four different antique vehicles make the trip on a regular basis, adding to the old-fashioned, small-town atmosphere while providing guest transportation. They run from a stop near the Main Street Train Station to Sleeping Beauty Castle. There's seldom a wait, but you can only ride one-way. You can choose your vehicle from among the following:

- A horse-drawn streetcar, modeled after the vehicles found in many cities well into the early twentieth century, runs on a track down the middle of the street and around the Hub.
- A bright red fire engine that kids just can't resist runs on Main Street. It is a beauty, built for Disneyland but based on turn-of-the-century designs. It's been around since Disneyland's opening day.
- A horseless carriage fulfills your dream of having your own chauffeur. You'll have to share your jaunt with up to nine other people, though.

- A double-decker bus, or omnibus, was added in 1956 along with the horseless carriage. Head for the upper level for a different view.

The Penny Arcade

Forget about the hottest video games with their 3-D graphics and surround sound. The Penny Arcade on Main Street, U.S.A. will take you back to the days before Pac-Man, Space Invaders, and Mortal Kombat. Here, you'll see arcade machines from the early 1900s. They still work, but you'll have to pay to try your skill at them. For a more modern selection of games, trek on over to Starcade in Tomorrowland.

TRAVEL TIP

While you're walking down Main Street, look up at the second-story windows. Many of them contain subtle tributes to former Disney employees, such as the one found above Main Street Photo Supply, dedicated to Renié Bardeau, Disneyland's chief photographer and photo archivist for forty years.

Drum major Mickey Mouse puts the Disneyland Band through its paces on Main Street, U.S.A., serenading guests with classic marching band favorites and familiar Disney tunes. Depending on the day of the week, they perform at the main entrance, Sleeping Beauty Castle or in Town Square. The Dapper Dans barbershop quartet also performs in the same area. The daily parade makes its way down Main Street twice a day, traveling alternately between "it's a small world" and the Mad Hatter shop at the end of Main Street. The sidewalk is a good place to watch the parade, but a bad place to try to walk through while it's going on, despite cast members' best efforts to keep the walking area on sidewalks clear.

Check the Disneyland Entertainment Times Guide or the Wait Time board to find out when and where these performances happen during your visit.

Sleeping Beauty Castle

Sleeping Beauty Castle is Disneyland's best-known landmark, and its mere outline is enough to identify it as belonging to Disneyland. It also serves as the entrance to Fantasyland and the backdrop for countless photographs. Look above it, and you'll see the wires that guide Tinkerbelle's flight to light the fireworks.

What you may not know is that visitors cannot go inside the castle. You'll find a small shop just past the drawbridge, but otherwise the castle is just ornamental.

≡FAST FACT

The drawbridge at the castle's front entrance can raise and lower. However, it's only been raised twice, at Disneyland's opening in 1955 and again during the Fantasyland renovation in 1983.

Instead of going straight across the drawbridge into Fantasyland, veer to the right along the moat and you'll come to the little-known Snow White Grotto, a quiet little corner that's a good place for your group to rendezvous if they split up.

Adventureland

All of Disneyland is an adventure, but in this land, the escapade takes you all over the world, to Aladdin and Jasmine's Agrabah, to Polynesia, on a cruise down the world's rivers, on an archaeological expedition, and into a tree house.

Aladdin and Jasmine's StoryTale Adventures

Ages 2–4:	★★★
Ages 5–10:	★★★
Ages 11–15:	★★
Ages 16–adult:	★

The stars of the popular animated film take the stage in Aladdin's Oasis several times daily, to spin tales of love and adventure in the land of Agrabah.

If your children want to participate in the interactive part of the show, make sure they sit in the floor seating area in front of the stage. After the show is over, Aladdin, Jasmine, and Kazoo stick around for a photo and autograph session.

Enchanted Tiki Room

Ages 2–4:	★
Ages 5–10:	★★
Ages 11–15:	★★
Ages 16–adult:	★★

The Enchanted Tiki Room was the first Disneyland attraction to feature Animatronics, a technology that allows Disney Imagineers to make models of people and animals appear to move and speak. Sit down, relax, and see if you can resist singing along.

The Enchanted Tiki Room has been a popular attraction at Disneyland since 1963, and while it certainly doesn't offer state-of-the-art entertainment, it does offer a pleasant break from a hectic day. The show is presented on an ongoing basis throughout the day. You'll seldom wait more than a half hour, and once you're inside, you'll find the room is air-conditioned.

⎯⎯FAST FACT

If you go to the Walt Disney World Resort in Orlando and visit the Magic Kingdom's Enchanted Tiki Room, you'll find the show totally revamped, but the Disneyland version sticks to Walt's original vision.

Guests waiting to enter the Enchanted Tiki Room enter in a small park area, complete with benches where you can rest your tired feet. The Tiki Juice Bar just outside sells tropical pineapple treats, and some Disneyland fans think their Tiki Room visit isn't complete unless they've had a Dole whip or a pineapple spear snack while waiting.

A few minutes before the show begins, the Polynesian gods' statues around the waiting area come to life and explain their role in Polynesian culture. Inside, four parrots named Fritz, Jose, Pierre, and Michael host a seventeen-minute, fun-filled musical performance featuring dozens of Animatronic birds and 225 Animatronic performers in all.

Some of the scenes—a thunderstorm and some briefly angry gods—may be a little too intense for small children, but the biggest risk is that the song will get stuck in your head: "In the tiki-tiki-tiki-tiki room. . . ."

Indiana Jones Adventure

Ages 2–4:	N.S.
Ages 5–10:	★★★
Ages 11–15:	★★★
Ages 16–adult:	★★★

One of the most popular Disneyland attractions, Indiana Jones Adventure is based on the live-action movies featuring the swashbuckling archaeologist Indiana "Indy" Jones.

Because the main part of the attraction is actually located outside the park boundaries, the entry queue is quite long. However, it's one of the best decorated in the park, littered with the gear of a jungle expedition and passing through an ancient temple. The line stops near the boarding area, where Sallah, Indy's partner from the films (played by John Rhys-Davies) narrates a short safety film.

After splitting into two lines, guests board twelve-passenger off-road vehicles that look a little like a dirty, topless Hummer. Take off your hat and make sure your glasses, purse, camera bag, and any other loose belongings are secure.

As you pass through a door, you trip a booby trap by looking into the Eyes of Mara, and then you're off. Would-be treasure hunters embark on a fast-paced and extremely turbulent trip through the simulated jungles of India and the Temple of the Forbidden Eye, passing several Animatronic Indiana Jones figures along the way before returning to safety. Among the things you'll experience are a bridge collapsing over a fiery pit (with your vehicle on it); a lunging, ten-foot-tall cobra; a creepy bunch of bugs; and a house-size boulder rolling straight at you. The experience lasts three minutes.

≡ FAST FACT

If the troop transport vehicle you see outside Indiana Jones Adventure looks familiar, it should. It dragged Indy in a high-speed chase scene in *Raiders of the Lost Ark*. Other props from the popular film franchise can be seen as you move through the line. Once inside, there are 160,000 possible combinations of twists, turns, plunges, and other maneuvers, so you never experience the same journey twice.

Because Indiana Jones is one of the most popular Disneyland attractions, you can expect to wait in long lines (up to two hours) if you don't use RideMax or fastpass. If you're trying to do it on the fly, the lines are usually shorter early in the morning, late at night, or during a parade. Wait times are somewhat overstated, and if you see a posted wait of fifteen minutes, it really means there's no wait at all. It will take you five minutes or more just to walk through the long entry area and get to the loading zone, and you'll usually get right on.

Although not a roller coaster in the traditional sense of the word, Indiana Jones Adventure is extremely erratic, with lots of jerks and sudden moves. Anyone with back or neck trouble or any other condition that might be aggravated by all the quick movements, young children less than 46 inches tall, and anyone who doesn't like being jolted and jostled should not try it.

Jungle Cruise

Ages 2–4:	N.S.
Ages 5–10:	★★
Ages 11–15:	★★
Ages 16–adult:	★★

The Jungle Cruise is one of Disneyland's original rides, although it has been modified over the years. The line snakes through the offices of an African river cruise company before guests board a boat that takes thirty-two people on a quiet cruise down a manmade river. River scenes include Animatronic hippos, elephants, hungry piranhas, and a ransacked jungle camp.

FAST FACT

The Jungle Cruise is a truly international journey, replicating sections of rivers in Burma and Cambodia, the Nile, the Congo River, and the rapids of Kilimanjaro. When you see the gorillas, look closely and you may spot a crate labeled "WED Safari." WED stands for Walter Elias Disney and refers to WED Enterprises, now called Walt Disney Imagineering.

Disney cast member/boat drivers should get hazardous duty pay to tell you some of the worst jokes you'll hear all day long. Cringe, laugh, and groan out loud and some of them will take the bait and get better.

The Jungle Cruise is cute, entertaining, and suitable for people of all ages. The trip lasts seven minutes.

Tarzan's Treehouse

Ages 2–4:	N.S.
Ages 5–10:	★★★
Ages 11–15:	★★
Ages 16–adult:	★★

This artificial tree (which Disney's Imagineers dubbed *Disneydendron semperflorens grandis* meaning "large everblooming Disney tree") was the Swiss Family tree house, modeled after Disney's 1960 movie *The Swiss Family Robinson*. Nowadays it offers a Tarzan theme, based on Disney's animated film.

≡ FAST FACT

Tarzan's Treehouse is 70 feet tall, weighs 150 tons, and has 450 branches bearing 6,000 leaves.

While the tree might look real, it's all artificial and good for climbing and exploration. Think of the tree house as a giant jungle gym for your kids (although it's suitable for adults, too). There's seldom a long line, it takes about ten minutes to walk through, and it's something that kids really enjoy. Because of the stairs involved, Tarzan's Treehouse is not accessible by wheelchair or electric convenience vehicle (ECV).

Critter Country

Disneyland's smallest area, Critter Country is home to some tame rides and attractions and is a good place to take the little ones, but it's also where you'll find the popular Splash Mountain.

Meet Winnie the Pooh

Near the entrance of the Many Adventures of Winnie the Pooh, you and your kids can meet Pooh, Eeyore, and Tigger at their favorite Thotful Spot, a specially designed place that makes a great photo backdrop as Pooh signs kids' autographs.

A Disney photographer will be on hand, but you can take your own photos, too.

Davy Crockett's Explorer Canoes

Ages 2–4:	N.S.
Ages 5–10:	★★
Ages 11–15:	★★
Ages 16–adult:	★★

In the heart of Disneyland is the Rivers of America, a circular river surrounding Tom Sawyer Island. Several Disneyland rides take you on the river, but this one does it in a 35-foot-long fiberglass canoe.

Originally called Indian War Canoes, they've been around since 1956.

 **TRAVEL TIP**

There are other ways to travel on the Rivers of America, including the *Mark Twain* paddle wheeler and the *Columbia* sailing ship, but oddly, Disney assigns them to Frontierland and the canoes (which are just around the bend) to Critter Country.

Sixteen guests and two cast members board each boat. Guests are expected to paddle the canoe and should be able to do so. However, no one makes a fuss if you don't. Although the river is only about waist deep, small children will be required to wear a life vest.

The canoes only run when the weather is good, may be closed during slack days in the off-season, and stop running around dusk. The trip takes about five minutes, but it may feel longer if your arms get tired.

The Many Adventures of Winnie the Pooh

Ages 2–4:	★★★
Ages 5–10:	★★
Ages 11–15:	★
Ages 16–adult:	★

Based on the Winnie the Pooh stories by A. A. Milne, *The Blustery Day* and *The Floody Place*, this dark ride (like Peter Pan or Mr. Toad) makes a trip through the Hundred Acre Wood, past Pooh's house, and ends in Pooh's birthday party. Guests travel in beehive-shaped vehicles that can hold seven adults or nine children.

Lines are usually short, it's suitable for everyone, and the trip lasts a little less than three minutes. You'll get a much better view if you sit in the front row, and you can ask the cast member at the boarding area to put you in the next car if you're assigned to a backseat.

Splash Mountain

Ages 2–4:	N.S.
Ages 5–10:	★★★
Ages 11–15:	★★★
Ages 16–adult:	★★★

Based on Disney's 1946 movie *Song of the South*, Splash Mountain gives you a chance to relive the adventures of Brer Rabbit, Brer Fox, and Brer Bear, along with a colorful cast of more than a hundred other Animatronic creatures, but most people board Splash Mountain for the thrill at the end.

Riders board logs that accommodate six passengers each, straddling a center bench and sitting one behind another. The nine-minute trip starts as a slow-paced, calm, relaxing boat trip. Your heart and imagination will be captivated by the classic Disney music and exciting visuals, and after you leave Splash Mountain, you could be singing the "Zip-A-Dee-Doo-Dah" song for the rest of the day. Everyone knows what's coming at the end, though, and the adventure concludes with a 52-foot drop (at a 47-degree angle) that creates a big splash. The drop is scary but surprisingly smooth, and you'll probably get wet, especially if you're sitting in front.

≡FAST FACT

Disneyland is the original recycler, taking portions of older attractions and incorporating them into newer ones. Splash Mountain includes more than 100 Animatronic figures rescued when the America Sings attraction closed in 1988.

If you're wondering what your face looks like when you let out a scream as you plummet downward during the final drop, you can purchase a color photo of yourself as you leave. With or without the picture, Splash Mountain is not something you'll soon forget.

Waits for Splash Mountain can top an hour. It's a fastpass attraction and offers Child Swap and a Single Rider line. Lines are shorter in the evening, but there's a reason. Think twice before getting on it then, because you'll have to walk around soggy and cold after getting soaked.

TRAVEL TIP

The child swap policy gives both adults (Mom and Dad, for example) the opportunity to enjoy the various thrill ride attractions that aren't suitable for kids, without the double wait. To take advantage of this policy, one parent waits in line with a small child while the other parent rides the attraction. When the first adult exits the attraction and returns to the loading area, he or she takes custody of the child while the second parent rides—without having to wait in line.

Guests must be over 40 inches tall and over three years old. Splash Mountain is not recommended for anyone who can't handle steep drops. The log vehicle does not have seat belts, and even if your children are old enough to ride, you may want to evaluate their ability to follow instructions, keep their arms inside, and stay seated before you let them get on board.

Teddi Barra's Swinging Arcade
The arcade combines old-fashioned machines with some of the newest video game hits. You'll need to purchase tokens to play these games because they're not included in the Disneyland admission price.

Fantasyland

Located behind Sleeping Beauty Castle, Fantasyland is home to many of Disneyland's classics and filled with activities smaller children will enjoy. Because of its location close to the castle, where the fireworks explode, most of Fantasyland closes during the fireworks display.

Alice in Wonderland

Ages 2–4:	★★★
Ages 5–10:	★★★
Ages 11–15:	★
Ages 16–adult:	★

Generations have grown up hearing the story of *Alice in Wonderland*, but only at Disneyland can you leap down the rabbit hole and meet Tweedledee, Tweedledum, the Cheshire Cat, the Queen of Hearts, and other characters from the classic story.

Guests sit in caterpillar-shaped vehicles as they travel through this colorful, enchanting "dark" ride. Like all of the Fantasyland attractions, Alice in Wonderland is designed for kids but suitable for guests of all ages. The journey lasts three minutes and ends with a very sweet surprise—an exploding "unbirthday" cake.

Alice in Wonderland is one of the few Disneyland rides to close when it rains.

Casey Jr. Circus Train

Ages 2–4:	★★★
Ages 5–10:	★★★
Ages 11–15:	★
Ages 16–adult:	★

The Disney animated classic *Dumbo* inspired this train ride, which was actually designed before Dumbo the Flying Elephant, but the attraction was not quite finished on opening day, opening shortly afterward in July 1955. The train is the circus train that carried the big-eared elephant from city to city, pulled by an engine named Casey Jr. Guests travel in train cars (including the popular monkey car) to make a three-and-a-half-minute journey around Storybook Land, providing a different view of the area than the one you get from the Storybook Land Canal Boats. Young children will enjoy themselves, and older guests may find it nostalgic. This ride also closes when it rains.

Dumbo the Flying Elephant

Ages 2–4:	★★★
Ages 5–10:	★★★
Ages 11–15:	★
Ages 16–adult:	★

Of all the rides at Disneyland, Dumbo the Flying Elephant is one of the true classics. It's been experienced by guests since Disneyland's earliest days.

≡ FAST FACT

When U.S. president Harry Truman—a Democrat—visited Disney-land, he refused to go on Dumbo the Flying Elephant because elephants are a symbol of the opposing political party.

Young children (who should definitely be accompanied by parents) can hop on Dumbo's back and take a two-minute journey into the air as they fly in circles at a speed that'll thrill most young people, without scaring them. It's popular because a child and parent can ride together, with the child controlling the vehicle's height. It lasts a minute and a half.

Disney Princess Fantasy Faire

Ages 2–4:	★★★
Ages 5–10:	★★★
Ages 11–15:	★
Ages 16–adult:	★

Located near the entrance of Mickey's Toontown and the Disneyland Train Station, Fantasyland Theatre has staged many shows over the years, but currently it's the home of the Disneyland Princess Fantasy Faire.

All day long (11 A.M. to 6 P.M. weekdays, 10 A.M. to 6 P.M. Friday through Sunday), it's Disney princess overload at the Faire, with multiple activities going on at once. They include a meet-and-greet area where kids can meet the princesses and a crafts area where young guests can make their own paper crowns. Several times a day, Snow White, Cinderella, Aurora, or Belle appears to tell her story. The Royal Coronation Ceremony teaches youngsters what it takes to be a knight or a bona fide princess, and there's a Royal Dance.

Ages 2–4:	★★★
Ages 5–10:	★★★
Ages 11–15:	★★★
Ages 16–adult:	★★★

"it's a small world"

Walt Disney's team of Imagineers created this attraction to be the Pepsi Cola Company's display at the 1964 New York World's Fair, and it moved to the park in

1965. The theme is world peace, understanding, and friendship, and it's been dubbed "the happiest cruise that ever sailed." Riders' opinions seem equally divided: They either love it or swear they'll never set foot near it again.

 TRAVEL TIP

> Most families visit the park early. As the day progresses, however, kids get hungry and tired. By evening, most families with kids tend to leave the park, making late afternoons, evenings, or nights the best times for adults to experience Fantasyland and some of the other areas most popular with families and small children.

Outside the ride, you'll find a fine collection of topiary animals, and you can enjoy looking at the exterior decorations and watching the complicated cuckoo clock that goes off every fifteen minutes. The twelve-minute boat ride floats through a series of colorful and magical sets filled with more than 300 Audio-Animatronics dolls, representing countries from around the world, all of them singing the famous theme song in their own language.

The attraction closes in November to get dressed up as a winter wonderland for the holidays. It closes again in early January to put everything back together again.

King Arthur Carrousel

Ages 2–4:	★★★
Ages 5–10:	★★★
Ages 11–15:	★★★
Ages 16–adult:	★

This musical carousel is an antique, built in 1876 in Germany, upgraded in Toronto, Canada, in 1921 and bought by Walt Disney in 1955. The original carousel featured a variety of animals, but Disney wanted his carousel to have all horses, so the carousel's train cars were recycled to the Casey Jr. Circus Train, and additional horses were purchased and reconfigured into a jumping pose.

The carousel's seventy-two horses were originally painted in different colors with only one white one, but the single white horse proved so popular that all the horses were painted white when the carousel was renovated in 1976. It's suitable for all ages, but small children should use the seat belts and adults should stick very close to the littlest ones.

Mad Tea Party

Ages 2–4:	N.S.
Ages 5–10:	★★★
Ages 11–15:	★★★
Ages 16–adult:	★★

Here's a classic ride for anyone who wants to take a spin in a giant teacup. Inspired by a scene in Disney's *Alice in Wonderland* animated movie, the teacups were Disneyland's first "thrill ride" back in 1955, and they've been spinning ever since.

Guests climb into a giant teacup-shaped vehicle that spins in circles around other teacups. At the same time, riders (three or four per cup) can make their own teacup spin quickly or slowly around its own axis, adding to the dizzying thrill.

Extremely young children should not ride the Mad Tea Party. Even though it only lasts a minute and a half, all the spinning is quite hard on anyone who suffers from motion sickness, so if you do, either stay away or use your favorite remedy.

Matterhorn Bobsleds

Ages 2–4:	N.S.
Ages 5–10:	★★
Ages 11–15:	★★★
Ages 16–adult:	★★★

The Matterhorn Bobsleds can be seen from miles around Disneyland. It was the tallest structure in the park until the Tower of Terror appeared at California Adventure. In reality, the fake mountain is only 147 feet tall, but the Disney Imagineers use forced perspective to make it look a lot taller.

Inside the snowcapped mountain is a roller coaster that was state-of-the-art when it first opened. It's since been upgraded, so it continues to make you feel as if you're riding in an actual bobsled down, through, and around a giant mountain.

Guests ride in bobsleds made up of two cars, each holding up to eight people. The cars climb to the top of the eight-story-tall ride and drop back down while circling the mountain. The ride lasts two minutes. Along the way, you'll pass the abominable snowman, whose glowing red eyes sometimes frighten smaller children. It may be best to warn them before you go.

≡FAST FACT

Disneyland's Matterhorn Bobsleds ride was the world's first tubular-steel roller coaster. The attraction took its inspiration from a film called *The Third Man on the Mountain*, made in 1959.

You can expect one of the longest waits in the park on a busy day, but if you enjoy roller coasters, it's worth it. This high-speed ride is teen- and adult-oriented, not suitable for very small children, and you must be 35 inches tall to ride. Guests who suffer from a weak back, heart condition, or any other condition that might be aggravated by careening around at high speed should not ride. If you're prone to motion sickness, use your favorite remedy.

Meet a Disney Princess

Near Sleeping Beauty Castle, you may find the Disney princesses available to meet visitors and sign autographs. They show up daily but are not around during the parade. Ariel, the Little Mermaid, can be found nearby in her grotto, which is in Triton's Garden next to Tomorrowland.

Mr. Toad's Wild Ride

Ages 2–4:	★★★
Ages 5–10:	★★★
Ages 11–15:	★★
Ages 16–adult:	★

As one of the classic rides at Disneyland, Mr. Toad's Wild Ride is based on the 1949 Disney movie *The Wind in the Willows*. Guests ride in high-speed, car-like vehicles driven by Mr. Toad, who is not the best of drivers.

≡FAST FACT

Look for J. Thaddeus Toad's coat of arms in Mr. Toad's Wild Ride and you'll find the motto *Toadi Acceleratio Semper Absurdia*, which means "speeding with toads is always absurd."

In addition to the kid-oriented thrill element, there's a lot to see along the two-minute journey, so keep your eyes open. This indoor dark ride is suitable for guests of all ages.

Peter Pan's Flight

Ages 2–4:	★★★
Ages 5–10:	★★★
Ages 11–15:	★★
Ages 16–adult:	★

Also one of the original Disneyland rides, Peter Pan's Flight is an indoor dark ride. It's much like Mr. Toad's Wild Ride, except the vehicles, which look like pirate ships, are suspended from the ceiling to give more of a feeling of flying. As you wait in line, listen carefully and you may hear Peter Pan and Wendy laughing.

Based on the classic animated film, the ride takes guests flying over a scale model of the city of London, soaring through the air in Never Land and seeing many familiar sights from the popular film. The ride lasts two minutes.

Peter Pan is suitable for guests of all ages. Although guests ride in a moving vehicle that simulates flight, the movement isn't too fast-paced or scary.

Pinocchio's Daring Journey

Ages 2–4:	★★★
Ages 5–10:	★★★
Ages 11–15:	★★
Ages 16–adult:	★

Disney's *Pinocchio* animated film, which premiered in 1940, inspired this ride. Guests travel in slow-moving vehicles as the Pinocchio story unfolds before their eyes. Jiminy Cricket is the guide, and Animatronics, holograms, fiber optics, and other effects add a touch of Disney-style magic that kids in particular will enjoy. The ride lasts two minutes.

Pinocchio's Daring Journey is suitable for everyone.

Snow White's Scary Adventures

Ages 2–4:	★★
Ages 5–10:	★★★
Ages 11–15:	★★
Ages 16–adult:	★

Based on Disney's classic animated film *Snow White and the Seven Dwarfs*, this is one of the park's classics. The dark ride has been in Disneyland since it first opened, although it was named merely Snow White's Adventures until 1983.

Traveling in cars that accommodate four adults each, riders see Bashful, Happy, Dopey, and their buddies, visit their house, and hear music from the movie soundtrack.

Snow White's adventure is far more enchanting than scary, since it's designed primarily for Disneyland's young guests. Like many Fantasyland rides, it lasts about two minutes.

Storybook Land Canal Boats

Ages 2–4:	★★
Ages 5–10:	★★
Ages 11–15:	★
Ages 16–adult:	★

Your gentle ride begins as Monstro, the giant whale from the Pinocchio story, swallows the boat. The balance of the five-minute cruise along a manufactured canal takes riders past expertly crafted miniatures that re-create scenes from many Disney movies and other classic stories, including the town of Agrabah from the *Aladdin* film. Adults will truly appreciate the incredible detail of the miniatures, while kids will enjoy the boat ride.

Sword in the Stone Ceremony

Ages 2–4:	★★
Ages 5–10:	★★
Ages 11–15:	★★
Ages 16–adult:	★

Held in the courtyard between the carousel and the castle, this daily event features wizard Merlin and a volunteer from the audience who, after much difficulty and urged on by Merlin's humorous chatter, manages to extract the sword from the stone.

Frontierland

One of Disneyland's original areas, Frontierland has the kind of themes its names lead you to expect, of cowboys and the Old West.

Big Thunder Mountain Railroad

Ages 2–4:	N.S.
Ages 5–10:	★★★
Ages 11–15:	★★★
Ages 16–adult:	★★★

Frontierland's most action-packed ride is a runaway railroad (actually a roller coaster) that takes sharp turns at pretty fast speeds, but offers no really big drops, making it pretty tame as far as thrill rides go. When Disneyland was built, Big Thunder Mountain was the park's most expensive and massive construction effort, but in terms of cost, recent attractions have exceeded its price tag many times over.

═FAST FACT

Disney Imagineers shopped at swap meets and scoured ghost towns and abandoned mines to find some of the items used to set the scene at Big Thunder Mountain Railroad, including a 1,200-pound cogwheel and a 100-foot-tall mill stamp made in 1880.

Lots of attention was paid to putting detail and realism into the ride, which helps compensate for the lack of big drops and dips. The track is almost half a mile long and the train goes up to 28 miles per hour.

Big Thunder Mountain is a popular attraction that offers fastpass and Child Swap during busy times. Add it to the list of thrill rides that'll appeal to guests over 40 inches tall who don't suffer from any physical limitations that prevent them from experiencing high-speed, turbulent rides.

Big Thunder Ranch

Big Thunder Ranch is basically a petting zoo. Critters on display include a horse, a cow, pygmy goats, and a few baby sheep. After the kids get their fill of petting, you'll find a large wash area just before you get to the exit, and you'll also find hand sanitizer stations throughout the area. Big Thunder Ranch usually opens around noon (on low-attendance days, it may not open at all) and closes well before dusk so the animals can bed down for the night.

══FAST FACT

In November 2005 and 2006, Big Thunder Ranch gained some famous residents. In what's becoming a new Thanksgiving tradition, after the President of the United States ritually "pardons" a turkey from the dinner table, the relieved animal and its backup take off to Disneyland, where they live out their lives at Big Thunder Ranch.

Frontierland Shootin' Exposition

Ages 2–4:	N.S.
Ages 5–10:	★
Ages 11–15:	★
Ages 16–adult:	★★

How's your aim? You can find out at an arcade-style shooting range that features replicas of rifles from the 1800s. These rifles use infrared beams instead of bullets as you aim and shoot at targets. Just like all of the arcades in Disneyland, the cost of shooting is extra—fifty cents for twenty shots. The most fun is guessing what will happen when you hit a target.

Golden Horseshoe Stage

Ages 2–4:	N.S.
Ages 5–10:	★
Ages 11–15:	★★
Ages 16–adult:	★★

Billy Hill and the Hillbillies perform in an old-fashioned saloon setting. Four brothers—all named Billy—perform bluegrass music and slapstick comedy. The show is free, but food and drinks cost extra.

Laughing Stock Co.

Ages 2–4:	N.S.
Ages 5–10:	N.S.
Ages 11–15:	★★
Ages 16–adult:	★★

This comedy show, made up of humorous skits with an Old West theme, runs several times daily.

Mark Twain Riverboat

Ages 2–4:	N.S.
Ages 5–10:	★★
Ages 11–15:	★★
Ages 16–adult:	★★

Located in the heart of Disneyland is Tom Sawyer Island, and surrounding the island is a body of water called the Rivers of America. The *Mark Twain* sails on the "river." Not only was this one of Disneyland's original attractions, it was one that Walt Disney paid for partially out of his own pocket. It looks like an antique paddle-wheel steamboat, but in fact it was the first new, functioning steamboat built in the United States in almost fifty years, constructed in a San Pedro, California, shipyard south of Los Angeles.

The *Mark Twain* offers a fourteen-minute cruise and provides a look at parts of Frontierland, New Orleans Square, Critter Country, and Tom Sawyer Island. Climb to the upper decks for the best views.

The boat operates constantly during the day, and a night cruise is nice, but when the Fantasmic! show is running, the cruises end in the early evening so the boat can get ready for its role in the show.

Sailing Ship *Columbia*

Ages 2–4:	★★
Ages 5–10:	★★
Ages 11–15:	★★
Ages 16–adult:	★★

Disneyland's other large ship traveling the Rivers of America is a replica of the first American ship to circumnavigate the globe. When not sailing (which it frequently isn't), *Columbia* remains moored at Fowler's Harbor, located near the Haunted Mansion. If you have the opportunity to cruise on the *Columbia*, be sure to visit the maritime museum that's located belowdeck.

Tom Sawyer Island

Ages 2–4:	N.S.
Ages 5–10:	★★
Ages 11–15:	★★
Ages 16–adult:	★★

Tom Sawyer Island is a great area for the kids to play. It's filled with dozens of places to explore and climb, just as Tom Sawyer would have done. Be sure to drop by the new Pirate's Lair, which opened in May, 2007. The island is open only during daylight hours and can only be reached by taking a motorized raft ride. The island closes early any night when Fantasmic! takes place.

Mickey's Toontown

All of Toontown looks like a giant cartoon, from the flat painted hills in the background to the cars on the street, the light posts, and the wobbly Jolly Trolley.

JUST FOR PARENTS

Mickey's Toontown often closes earlier than the rest of Disneyland because of preparations for the fireworks show. Be sure you get there early enough so the kids can see everything.

Families with small children will enjoy spending time in Toontown.

Chip 'n Dale Treehouse

Ages 2–4:	★★★
Ages 5–10:	★★★
Ages 11–15:	★★
Ages 16–adult:	N.S.

Chip 'n Dale's "branch" office is a walkthrough attraction where kids can run upstairs and check out the cheerful chipmunks' digs, and work off their excess energy. If they don't linger, it will take them about ten minutes to go through the whole place.

The treehouse is suitable for all ages, but because it requires climbing stairs, guests must be ambulatory to enjoy it.

Donald's Boat

Ages 2–4:	★★★
Ages 5–10:	★★★
Ages 11–15:	★★
Ages 16–adult:	N.S.

Everyone knows Donald Duck, but did you know he has a passion for sailing? Donald keeps his colorful, cartoon-like boat, the *Miss Daisy*, docked (on land) in Toontown. Young guests can explore the boat, climb rope ladders, turn the steering wheel, and pretend they're sailing the high seas with Donald.

Gadget's Go Coaster

Ages 2–4:	★★★
Ages 5–10:	★★★
Ages 11–15:	★★★
Ages 16–adult:	N.S.

Named for Gadget, the mouse in the *Chip 'n Dale Rescue Rangers* series, this brightly colored roller coaster was created just for Disneyland's young guests. It's a gentle ride suitable for children over 35 inches tall, but it's still a roller coaster with turns and dips and comes with all the standard cautions for people who might have problems with the movement.

≡FAST FACT

At the entrance of each ride with a height limit, you'll find a measurement device. If there's any question, the cast members will use it to decide if your child is tall enough to ride. They know all the tricks; don't try to fool them.

Goofy's Playhouse

Ages 2–4:	★★★
Ages 5–10:	★★
Ages 11–15:	N.S.
Ages 16–adult:	N.S.

In Goofy's Playhouse, kids can kick off their shoes and bounce around...literally. This is one place where they can climb all over the furniture without getting in trouble and peek through rope-covered windows to see their parents and other onlookers.

Jolly Trolley

For a quick tour of Toontown, hop aboard the Jolly Trolley, a fun (and somewhat bouncy) ride that will take you from one end of this cartoon-like town to the other. It's a short trip but exciting for kids.

Mickey's House

Ages 2–4:	★★★
Ages 5–10:	★★★
Ages 11–15:	★★
Ages 16–adult:	★

If you want to meet Mickey Mouse during your Disneyland visit, head to Mickey's Toontown. Kids (and their parents) can be Mickey Mouse's personal guests as they explore his house. After looking around and walking through Mickey's costume closet, visitors get a chance to meet Mickey in person.

You're guaranteed to meet Mickey, so lines are often long during peak times of the day.

Minnie's House

Ages 2–4:	★★★
Ages 5–10:	★★★
Ages 11–15:	★★
Ages 16–adult:	★

Being the ultimate hostess, Minnie Mouse loves to meet and greet her guests as they tour her house. The imaginative house is as cute outside as it is inside, and it looks like a cartoon come to life. Minnie's House is entertaining for everyone, and kids seem to especially like the kitchen, where they can turn on the dishwasher and watch it spin.

Roger Rabbit's Car Toon Spin

Ages 2–4:	★★★
Ages 5–10:	★★★
Ages 11–15:	★★★
Ages 16–adult:	★★

Based on the animated film *Who Framed Roger Rabbit?* this is Toontown's most popular ride and the one most likely to appeal to adults.

Although not a roller coaster, this ride makes a lot of quick turns as guests travel in taxi-like vehicles past scenes from the film. It's fast-moving but not at all scary, and riders can control how much their vehicle spins. The whole trip takes three and a half minutes.

The wait can be quite long, but you can fend off boredom by looking around the nicely decorated waiting area, examining Jessica Rabbit's dressing room and eavesdropping on some plotting weasels. Waits can be more than forty minutes, but using a fastpass can shorten that.

New Orleans Square

New Orleans Square offers two classic Disneyland attractions that have been loved for generations: the Haunted Mansion and Pirates of the Caribbean. Both are suitable for people of all ages, but might be a bit scary for very young kids.

New Orleans Square is also home to Club 33, the exclusive, private club located in Walt Disney's former VIP dining room. Look for the door marked number 33 just to the right of the Blue Bayou restaurant.

💼 TRAVEL TIP

The Disneyland Railroad stops at New Orleans Square and can take you to any of the other stations located throughout Disneyland, such as the main entrance, Mickey's Toontown, or Tomorrowland.

The Bilge Rats and the Bootstrappers

This bunch of pirates and miscreant musicians supposedly just escaped from the Pirates of the Caribbean story. They play to pay off their debt to the owner of the Faithful Bride Tavern, one of the places you'll pass on the ride. You'll find them in the area between the water and the shopping street.

Haunted Mansion

Ages 2–4:	N.S.
Ages 5–10:	★★★
Ages 11–15:	★★★
Ages 16–adult:	★★★

Before Haunted Mansion opened, Walt Disney held media interviews during which he invited all homeless ghosts to come live at Disneyland. Construction began in 1963, but it wasn't completed and opened to Disneyland guests until 1969.

Since then, millions of guests have dropped in on the 999 ghosts who live in the mansion. Perhaps one of the most elaborate haunted houses anywhere, this one uses all sorts of special effects to entertain and scare visitors.

After entering a lobby area, guests move into a room (actually an elevator), the lights go out, lightning flashes, and the room seems to grow taller. At the end, a body is seen hanging from the ceiling. After walking down a hallway lined with amusing paintings and decorations, guests board moving loveseats, called "Doom Buggys," to travel past several richly decorated scenes and dozens of smaller sights and details, including a ghostly dinner party.

At the end, each car picks up a hitchhiking ghost who appears to be in the car with the riders. The trip takes seven minutes.

≡FAST FACT

At Disneyland, they have a hard time keeping the Haunted Mansion dirty, and the maintenance crew regularly has to bring in new cobwebs and dust to replace what the air-conditioning system sucks out.

Haunted Mansion closes every September to get decked out for Haunted Mansion Holiday, an even more richly themed affair based on Tim Burton's animated film *The Nightmare Before Christmas*, a look at what might happen if Halloween tried to create Christmas. It stays decorated from October through the end of the year and then closes again for all the decorations to be taken down.

Haunted Mansion is suitable for everyone, but parts of it may be too scary for the kids, and the very dark and noisy growing room often sends little ones into tears. Lines can get long, especially during the holidays but fastpass is available then to help shorten the wait.

Pirates of the Caribbean

Ages 2–4:	★
Ages 5–10:	★★★
Ages 11–15:	★★★
Ages 16–adult:	★★★

Walt Disney always loved pirates, which is the reason he insisted that Disneyland guests have the opportunity to take a boat ride through the pirates' world.

After being one of Disneyland's most popular attractions for many years, the ride inspired a Disney film, *Pirates of the Caribbean: The Curse of the Black Pearl*, which became so popular that it spawned two sequels, *Pirates of the Caribbean: Dead Man's Chest* and *At World's End*. In turn, the popular films prompted Disney to start a major renovation of the ride shortly before the second film debuted.

The updated Pirates of the Caribbean follows the same basic story of a pirate attack on a Caribbean village, with riders embarking at Lafitte's Landing and following the event from the initial attack through the burning, pillaging, and plunder. The Animatronic pirates and animals underwent significant improvement in 2006, making their movement more natural, and the rest of the attraction was spruced up, cleaned up, and brightened.

The song "Yo-Ho, Yo-Ho, A Pirate's Life for Me" plays throughout the cruise, so by the end of the cruise, you'll probably be singing along.

Pirates of the Caribbean is air-conditioned. It lasts longer than most rides and attractions, so it's an ideal place to cool off and relax in the middle of a hot day. The Blue Bayou restaurant is located inside the same building. Riders can watch the diners (and vice versa) as they float through the first part of the trip.

The thirteen-minute boat ride is one of Disneyland's most popular attractions, suitable for anyone, but a bit noisy for some of the smaller folks. Just after your cruise begins, the boat takes two very short (three-second) drops, otherwise your cruise will be smooth, slow, and extremely enjoyable. However, if you are sensitive to sudden movements, the rafts sometimes bump into each other while waiting to unload.

Tomorrowland

One of Disneyland's original lands, Tomorrowland has changed significantly over the years, along with our ideas of what the future will bring.

Astro Orbitor

Ages 2–4:	★
Ages 5–10:	★★★
Ages 11–15:	★★
Ages 16–adult:	★★

This ride is a spectacular sight, an intricate design based on an orrery, a planetary model popular from the fifteenth through nineteenth centuries, and it's especially striking when lit up at night. Aside from the pretty design, it's a simple ride quite similar to Dumbo the Flying Elephant. The ride rotates the rocket jets and the riders control the altitude. It lasts ninety seconds.

Astro Orbitor is a popular ride among kids, and the lines move slowly, which means the wait can be long. Although the experience is fun, if there's a long wait, you might want to think twice about whether it's worth it.

Ages 2–4:	N.S.
Ages 5–10:	★★★
Ages 11–15:	★★★
Ages 16–adult:	★

Autopia

For kids, driving a car on their own is always in the future. At Autopia, originally called the Freeway of the Future, they can get an early start. Guests take off in model sports cars (sort of like go-carts) along a predefined track, but the cars don't move until the checkered flag waves. The cars are about 10 feet long, weigh 1,100 pounds, and have real motors. They travel at a fast-paced 7 miles per hour but can't leave their track. Kids get to control the speed and steering as they go around curves, over bridges, and even try off-roading. They are sure to find Autopia a lifelike and fun driving experience. And adults can get an idea of what it will be like when their kids are driving!

≡FAST FACT

Suzy, the cute little coupe that's one of the three Autopia vehicles, is based on Walt Disney's 1952 short animated film, *Suzy the Little Blue Coupe*. An off-road vehicle and a little sports car are the other two designs.

Anyone who already has a driver's license will probably want to skip Autopia, especially since waits can be so long that it's a fastpass attraction.

Kids over 52 inches tall can ride Autopia alone. Smaller children can ride with an adult, but they must be at least one year old. Autopia is suitable for most people, but sometimes the cars get bumped sharply from behind.

Buzz Lightyear Astro Blasters

Ages 2–4:	N.S.
Ages 5–10:	★★★
Ages 11–15:	★★★
Ages 16–adult:	★★

Part ride and part game, Astro Blasters is an interactive ride. Two people ride per vehicle, shooting at targets and accumulating points. One of the riders can also control the car's rotation. In a modern twist, online players can affect what happens to riders in the park. The whole thing lasts about five minutes.

Astro Blasters is popular and lines can get long. fastpass is available. Riders of all ages are allowed, but it can intimidate small children. The ride is noisy, and there are lots of flashing lights.

Disneyland Monorail

When the Disneyland Monorail opened in 1957, it was the first of its kind. It travels through Disneyland and Disney's California Adventure, crossing the replica Golden Gate Bridge that spans California Adventure's entrance and stops in Tomorrowland and in Downtown Disney.

Round trips are not allowed, and you'll have to get off and re-board if you want to go right back where you came from.

Finding Nemo Submarine Voyage

Inspired by the Disney/Pixar film *Finding Nemo*, this new ride was scheduled to open in summer 2007 when this book was written. It is located in the space once occupied by the Submarine Voyage and recycles eight of the submarines from that ride, and guests will embark on a mission to observe an undersea volcano. Characters from the animated film will appear swimming just outside the windows, and riders will get involved in the hunt to find Nemo.

Don't worry about sinking. The "submarines" do not submerge. Instead, they're really boats with the passenger seating located below the water level.

"Honey, I Shrunk the Audience"

Ages 2–4:	N.S.
Ages 5–10:	★★★
Ages 11–15:	★★★
Ages 16–adult:	★★

Based on the humorous film *Honey, I Shrunk the Kids*, this 3-D show features inventor Wayne Szalinski (played by actor Rick Moranis) who is to accept the Inventor of the Year award. Guests get a preview of things to come while waiting in line and then enter the auditorium. Things go awry (of course), and the hapless innovator ends up shrinking the audience. Eventually most everything returns to normal, but not without some startling moments along the way, including a "fourth dimension" effect of scurrying mice.

This attraction is suitable for everyone, but smaller children may not be able to keep their 3-D glasses on, and some of the effects may be a little scary for them.

Innoventions

Ages 2–4:	N.S.
Ages 5–10:	★★
Ages 11–15:	★★
Ages 16–adult:	★★

Innoventions is a showcase for current and future technology, more of a mini-museum or display than a ride. In the past, featured technology has included the Segway human transporter (and a chance to take a short ride on one), but the current feature attraction is Honda's walking robot ASIMO.

Innoventions is intended to showcase cutting-edge technology. Unfortunately, cutting edge quickly becomes trailing edge, and at any time, some of the displays may seem a bit outdated.

Space Mountain

Ages 2–4:	N.S.
Ages 5–10:	★★
Ages 11–15:	★★★
Ages 16–adult:	★★★

Perhaps one of Disneyland's most famous and popular attractions, this roller coaster takes you for a fast-paced ride through space. A renovation completed in 2005 left the track unchanged but with new effects added.

After waiting in a space station–themed queue and boarding area, twelve passengers board each "rocket" and soon find themselves traveling in the dark—at speeds up to 30 miles per hour—whizzing around sharp turns. Hollywood-style special effects surround you with stars and galaxies that make you feel as if you're on a rocket flying through space.

What sets Space Mountain apart from most roller coasters is that it travels fast but offers no steep drops. Even if you tend to get scared riding a traditional roller coaster, since you're in virtual darkness and don't experience any massive drops, the whole experience is rather enjoyable.

≡ FAST FACT

The term *E-ticket ride*, which now means an exciting experience, comes from the way Disneyland tickets were once sold, in lettered categories A through E, with an *E* ticket giving entrance to the most expensive and exciting rides.

Space Mountain should not be experienced by children less than 40 inches tall, pregnant women, anyone with a heart condition, weak back, or any type of physical problems that might be aggravated by the high speeds and g-forces. Because it's in the dark, motion sickness is not such a big problem as with other roller coasters, but if you're prone to it, you may still need your favorite remedies. Make sure you secure all loose items, including your glasses before you get on.

There's always a wait for Space Mountain, which can be as much as ninety minutes or more on busy days. You will definitely want to take advantage of fastpass.

Starcade

Starcade features some of the hottest new arcade games, plus some of your old favorites. Like all of the Disneyland arcades, it accepts tokens (which are not included in the cost of admission to the park).

Star Tours

Ages 2–4:	N.S.
Ages 5–10:	★★
Ages 11–15:	★★★
Ages 16–adult:	★★★

Based on George Lucas's *Star Wars* movies and featuring characters like R2-D2 and C-3PO, Star Tours is a simulator ride.

An elaborate preshow includes Animatronic characters from the *Star Wars* movies and video monitors that feature Star Tours travel information. The storyline is that you are an intergalactic tourist on a shuttle ride to Endor.

When you reach the ride, you and thirty-nine other guests will board a StarSpeeder, but it turns out that your pilot is inexperienced, and you end up on a whirlwind tour of the galaxy by mistake.

Using flight-simulator technology, the StarSpeeder is on hydraulic lifts and its movements are synchronized with the movie you watch on the ship's main view screen. The overall effect is that you'll feel as if you're traveling at ultra-fast speed through space, when in reality, your StarSpeeder is only a few feet off the ground.

◼ TRAVEL TIP

The best time to ride the Star Tours attraction is late in the evening. If the line doesn't extend out the front door, the wait will be less than twenty minutes.

Star Tours is a fast-paced, turbulent ride with a *Star Wars* twist. It's suitable for people of all ages, except children under 40 inches tall and people who suffer from back problems, heart conditions, motion sickness, and so on. Once you board the StarSpeeder, stow all of your loose articles and fasten your seat belt. The ride is bumpy but not scary. It lasts about five minutes.

Be prepared for long lines while you're waiting to board the StarSpeeder (up to forty minutes), but the waiting is somewhat offset by the decorated waiting area, which looks like a star base.

Tomorrowland Terrace Stage

As you chow down on snacks from the nearby Tomorrowland Terrace Refreshment Stand (where hamburgers, hot dogs, French fries, drinks, and other goodies are available), you can often enjoy live musical performances or hang out with Disney characters. This is also a great place to sit down (at tables covered with large umbrellas to block the sun) and rest for a few minutes.

CHAPTER 10

Disneyland's Parades, Shows, Special Events, and Fireworks

THIS CHAPTER DESCRIBES THE parades, shows, and live entertainment offered throughout Disneyland. Disney brings their signature style to everything in the Disneyland Resort, and these diversions are no exception. Expect a fun time, no matter which ones you choose to see. In fact, if you aren't interested in the rides and attractions, you could spend most of a day just seeing all the shows and parades.

Disneyland Parades

Most Disney vacationers take time out of their busy theme park schedules to watch a parade. While a parade may seem less enticing than the rides and fireworks displays, you should try to make it to at least one of the parades offered to truly capture the essence of Disneyland.

Walt Disney's Parade of Dreams
Location: Main Street, U.S.A.

Once or twice a day (depending on the season), a lavish parade winds its way down Main Street, compete with colorful floats, upbeat music, dancing performers in colorful costumes, and, of course, all of the popular Disney characters. You're guaranteed to see Mickey,

Minnie, Donald Duck, and many other Disney favorites as part of this parade, so have your camera handy.

═FAST FACT

To keep Disneyland looking its best, more than 5,000 gallons of paint are used each year. In addition, the park uses more than 100,000 light bulbs, including 11,000 rim lights to outline the buildings along Main Street.

Although the theme of the parade changes every year or two, the daytime character parade has been a staple since the early days. The parade represents the fun and excitement this park offers—especially to young people. The current version, Walt Disney's Parade of Dreams, salutes Disneyland's fiftieth anniversary. The parade features more than 100 performers, 20-foot-tall floats, confetti blasts, oversized puppets, and a cast of characters you've grown to love. Tinkerbelle appears atop the train on the lead float, an Animatronic Geppetto pulls the strings on some human marionettes, Alice in Wonderland characters dance in the street, and Mickey and Minnie bring up the rear, waving from the balcony of a replica Sleeping Beauty Castle.

TRAVEL TIP

Many digital cameras can also take short movies, a perfect way to capture the fun of a Disneyland parade. Resist the temptation to turn the camera sideways while filming; it's not easy to rotate the videos afterward. You'll need a fully charged battery or two and plenty of room on your digital media.

The parade takes about thirty-five to forty minutes to cover the entire route and about twenty minutes to pass a single spot. The first parade usually starts in midafternoon and the second one runs around dark. For parade times during your visit, see the Entertainment Times Guide or stop by the Wait Time board on Main Street, U.S.A.

The parade route begins at the end of Main Street, next to the Mad Hatter shop in the Town Square area, proceeds along the entire length of the street and around the Hub, turns to the right toward the Matterhorn Bobsleds, and concludes at the parade gate near "it's a small world." If there's a second parade, the route is reversed.

When the park is busy, stake out your viewing spot about one hour early. If you'll be visiting Disneyland over several days and have seen the parade once, use parade time during the remaining days to do something else, taking advantage of shorter lines at the most popular rides and attractions.

TRAVEL TIP

Good parade-viewing locations include the platform of the main Disneyland Railroad station, and in and around Town Square (in front of the train station, near the flagpole). However, some of the best places to watch are from the terraced area along the Small World corridor, where surprisingly, you can often get a good spot even ten minutes before the parade starts.

Disneyland Band

The Disneyland Marching Band has been appearing at Disneyland since the park first opened in 1955. In that time, the band has marched over 3,500 miles up and down Main Street, U.S.A. It's not a parade on such a grand scale as the daily character parade, but it's fun to watch as drum major Mickey Mouse marches the players around the Hub while the brass band plays a selection of marching band favorites and Disney tunes.

Disneyland Shows

A number of shows happen daily in Disneyland. The Disneyland Entertainment Times can give you their times.

- Aladdin and Jasmine's StoryTale Adventures (Adventureland)
- Billy Hill and the Hillbillies (Frontierland)
- Disney Princess Fantasy Faire (Fantasyland)
- Enchanted Tiki Room (Adventureland)
- "Honey, I Shrunk the Audience" (Tomorrowland)
- Laughing Stock Co. (Frontierland)
- Sword in the Stone Ceremony (Fantasyland)
- The Bilge Rats and the Bootstrappers (New Orleans Square)
- Tomorrowland Terrace Stage

For more detailed information about these shows, see Chapter 9. Many of the sit-down restaurants (such as the Corner Café on Main Street, U.S.A.) also offer live music throughout the day and evening.

≡FAST FACT

The public areas of the park always look spotless because the streets are swept and steam-cleaned every night after the park closes. During a typical day, 30 tons of trash are removed from the park; however, each year, the park recycles 3.1 million pounds of cardboard, 500,000 pounds of office paper, and more than 9,400 pounds of aluminum cans.

Besides all the other goings-on, character greetings happen all day long, and "Streetmosphere" performers and Disney characters may show up anywhere, adding to the festivity.

Fantasmic!

Location: New Orleans Square

A twenty-five-minute show performed along the Rivers of America, Fantasmic! is a fireworks, laser, fog, fiber optics, lighting effects, shooting water, motion picture effects show like nothing you've seen before. This Disneyland original, still unique among theme park entertainment, began in 1992. The show was an instant hit and still draws huge crowds every time it plays.

Fantasmic! begins in darkness as Mickey, the Sorcerer's Apprentice, appears on Tom Sawyer Island and starts to dream. He brings the river to life in a blaze of lights, water, and pyrotechnics. Three large curtains of spraying water rise from the river, each thirty feet tall by fifty feet wide; much of the show is projected on them.

As fog rises from the river, a host of Disney characters appear, including Captain Hook (in his pirate ship, which is actually the sailing ship *Columbia* decked out in pirate décor). More characters follow, including the Disney princesses.

When Snow White shows up, the Wicked Witch Maleficent is never far away, appearing on stage in a burst of flame, her magic mirror conjuring a cadre of Disney villains, as she transforms herself into a dragon. Mickey battles the enormous monster and wins as the creature disappears in a shower of fairy dust. To close the show, Tinkerbelle appears and the *Mark Twain* steamboat sails by with Steamboat Willie at the helm.

Fantasmic! is a somewhat seasonal show. During summer and other peak times, it's presented twice a night, but the rest of the year, it may only be done on weekends.

Fantasmic! is very popular, and all the best viewing spots often fill up hours before the first show. When there are two shows, it may be easier to get a good spot to see the second one, slipping in as viewers from the first show leave.

TRAVEL TIP

Disney offers two paid programs that guarantee you a seat for Fantasmic! For $59, you can reserve one of eighteen seats for the dessert buffet held at the Disney Gallery. Another 100 seats are reserved near the Haunted Mansion ($59 each for guests aged ten and over, and $49 for those under ten), where guests receive a selection of desserts brought to their chairs. To make reservations, call ✆(714) 781-4400 promptly at 8 A.M. Pacific Time thirty days before you want to attend. They sell out fast.

The Fantasmic! "stage" is the entire Rivers of America area in front of Tom Sawyer Island, so you can see the show from almost anywhere in New Orleans Square. The best seats are in front, but you can usually get a spot to watch (albeit with a limited view) even fifteen minutes before it begins.

JUST FOR PARENTS

This musical show is impressive and suitable for the entire family; however, at times it's very dark, the giant dragon and snake are intense, and the fireworks and pyrotechnics are noisy. This adds up to an experience that may overwhelm small children (and some adults, for that matter).

If you are in a wheelchair or an electric convenience vehicle, ask a cast member to show you to the special Fantasmic! seating area. Hearing-impaired visitors can request a complimentary sign-language interpretation by calling (714) 300-7710 at least a week ahead of time.

Fireworks Spectacular

Location: Above Sleeping Beauty Castle

At Disneyland, every day is a celebration, capped with an extravagant fireworks presentation high above Sleeping Beauty Castle. This pyrotechnic show features more than 200 blasts synchronized to classic Disney music.

 TRAVEL TIP

You can take some stunning souvenir photos of your family in front of the castle with the fireworks exploding overhead during the show. If you can find a way to prop your camera on something to steady it, use the longest exposure time you can so you can capture the fireworks going up and exploding.

Actress Julie Andrews (who played Mary Poppins) introduces the show, saying there was once a place where you could wish on a star. Music follows, you hear Pinocchio wishing to be a boy, Ariel wishing to be on dry land, and Aladdin wishing Genie his freedom, and then Tinkerbelle flies through the air toward Sleeping Beauty Castle to touch off the fantasy in the sky. An audio clip of Walt Disney's 1955 dedication speech plays, and the rest of the show is a tribute to favorite Disneyland rides and experiences: Main Street, the Tiki Room, Indiana Jones, Haunted Mansion, Pirates of the Caribbean, and each of the lands. The show ends with more wishes and a fireworks finale. It lasts seventeen minutes.

This fireworks show is typically presented late in the evening but is coordinated with Fantasmic! so guests can experience both shows in a single evening.

JUST FOR PARENTS

> This fireworks spectacular is a must-see show, but the loud bangs and bright flashes may frighten young children. Because the fireworks explode high in the sky, you can see them from anywhere you can see the castle, so watching from a little farther away (Main Street Station or Rivers of America) may be a better idea.

The Central Plaza (Hub) is the only place where you can see everything that goes on during the fireworks, but not all spots are created equal. Check to see if trees or other objects might block your view. To get a front-row seat, you should arrive at least an hour before the fireworks start. Other excellent viewing areas include the platform at the Disneyland Station, which affords a good overall view and a quick exit. If you've just watched Fantasmic! your best bet may be to stay put, moving to the left side if you aren't there already. The views are good, the departing crowds will make it difficult to move anyway, and all the best spots around the castle will already be taken. If all this seems too much to remember, just focus on this: If you have an unobstructed view of the castle, you'll see the entire fireworks show.

For safety reasons, some park areas close during the fireworks. This includes all of Toontown. The fireworks are launched from there and it closes early so staff can get ready. Most of Fantasyland and the walkway in front of and through Sleeping Beauty Castle will also be closed. If you don't like fireworks or have already seen the show, this is another time when you'll find short lines at some of the park's busiest rides.

TRAVEL TIP

If you want to see the show but don't want to get stuck in the crowds leaving afterward, take the tram to the Mickey & Friends Parking Lot, go to the top floor and watch from there. If you're parked there, you can head straight for your car, or take the tram back to the main resort area.

Disneyland at Halloween

In 2006, Disney started getting gussied up for Halloween, with special fall- and Halloween-themed decorations. Pumpkin Mickeys sprout up everywhere, including a 16-foot-tall Mickey Mouse jack-o-lantern on Main Street that's a perfect backdrop for a photo. The Haunted Mansion takes on its "Nightmare Before Christmas" décor for the event, with a special holiday effect replacing the hitchhiking ghosts that normally appear near the end. The characters don their Halloween costumes, and you can buy special jack-o-lantern Mickey ears as a souvenir.

The Halloween festivities start in early October, and the park gets extraordinarily crowded on the first day the decorations are up. If you want to see it on opening weekend, go on Sunday.

Disneyland at Christmas

The Disneyland holidays don't stop at the end of October. Starting in early November and lasting through the end of the year, "The Happiest Place on Earth" becomes "The Merriest Place on Earth." Special holiday activities include the Christmas Fantasy Parade, a special fireworks show, and a new round of seasonal decorations.

The "Nightmare Before Christmas" decorations stay up at Haunted Mansion Holiday (but the hitchhiker changes), all the dolls in "it's a small world" don their holiday finery, new lights and decorations go up, and the music changes to a holiday theme. Main Street, U.S.A.

is decorated with thousands of lights and poinsettias, along with a 60-foot-tall Christmas tree decorated with more than 6,000 twinkling lights. Toontown glitters with shiny balls and garlands.

 TRAVEL TIP

For an even more magical holiday visit, take the Holiday Time at Disneyland guided tour. You'll get express boarding at Haunted Mansion Holiday and "it's a small world" Holiday, reserved seating for the parade, and a commemorative pin. The two-and-a-half-hour tour costs $59 per person.

Goofy stands in for Santa in Toontown, Mrs. Claus settles into Disneyland's Big Thunder Ranch, turning it into a temporary "West Pole," while over at California Adventure, Santa himself shows up in a surfer shirt and shorts.

A Christmas Fantasy Parade
Location: Main Street, U.S.A.

In this special version of the daily character parade, a full band of tin soldiers entertains, Pinocchio and Geppetto help Santa make toys, and Mickey and Minnie skate on an icy pond while Goofy and Max make a gingerbread house. Suitable for the entire family, it's well worth the time to stop and watch it.

 JUST FOR PARENTS

If your children will enjoy interacting with the parade's characters, seat them in the front row anywhere along the route or on the curb along Main Street, U.S.A. They'll get a good view and the characters often wave back to nearby onlookers or stop to speak to them.

The Christmas Fantasy Parade follows the same route as the regular parade, and all of the same tips about finding a spot to watch the daily parade apply for it, too. The steps in front of the Disneyland Train Station at the end of Main Street, U.S.A. make a particularly good place to watch the Fantasy Parade if you want an overall view. If you want to take pictures of the Christmas Parade, choose the earlier time while it's still light. After dark, the moving floats and figures are very hard to photograph.

"Believe...In Holiday Magic" Fireworks Spectacular

For the Christmas season, the daily fireworks spectacular takes on a soundtrack of favorite holiday songs, but the big surprise is the snowfall at the end. The sight is especially pretty when viewed from the Disneyland Train Station.

Gay Day

Although not officially sponsored or sanctioned by the Walt Disney Company, Gay Day happens at Disneyland every October. According to the Web site of the organization sponsoring this unofficial event: "Years ago, Disneyland used to have a private party one night of the year for gays and lesbians...Gay Day Anaheim is a 'mix in,' meaning gay people and straight people mingle together; the park is open to the general public... we wear red shirts to identify one another and show our numbers."

Activities held during Gay Day include parties and a traditional group photo in front of the castle. For more information, visit *www .gaydaysanaheim.com*.

Not satisfied with just one Gay Day a year, some attendees have now launched a mini–Gay Day, a more mellow event held in April.

Disneyana Convention

Although they no longer hold their annual Disneyana convention, Disney memorabilia collectors host other events throughout the year at the Disneyland Resort. These may include special release parties for new pins and other products, sometimes with special artists' autograph events. Visit *www.disneygallery.com* to find out the dates.

CHAPTER 11

Disney's California Adventure

LOCATED DIRECTLY ACROSS FROM Disneyland, Disney's California Adventure is a five-year-old, fifty-five-acre, completely separate theme park that pays tribute to the state of California through its unique rides, shows, and attractions. Everything you'll see and do within this park somehow tells a story about the state's culture, diversity, and history. This chapter will explore the areas of California Adventure as well as the best places to eat and shop within the park.

The History of Disney's California Adventure

The Disney Company wanted California Adventure to be a different kind of park, to enhance visitors' experience but not compete with Disneyland. While Disneyland revolves around the Disney characters (as well as the company's television and movie franchises), California Adventure has the look and feel of a Disney theme park, but many rides, shows, and attractions are based on something else.

California Adventure is more teen- and adult-oriented than Disneyland. Many of its rides could be classified as thrill rides, and some of what's offered might even be considered educational or culturally enlightening, which appeals more to adults. Nevertheless, California Adventure offers something for the entire family.

If you visited Disneyland before California Adventure was built, you'd probably think the place was already stuffed full, with the theme park, hotels, and parking lots taking up all available land surface. Disney was faced with a challenge. How could they add a new hotel, a new theme park, and a new shopping and dining complex without spreading out? The solution was to build a multistory parking structure capable of holding up to 10,000 vehicles, the largest in North America when it was completed. This oversize parking garage has six floors, ten toll booths, six entrance and exit lanes, and a separate ramp for each floor to improve traffic flow.

With the land freed up, it was only a matter of time and money— five and a half years of construction and an outlay of $1.4 billion—to complete the Disneyland Resort. California Adventure opened to the public on February 8, 2001.

An Overview of California Adventure

✉1313 S. Harbor Blvd., Anaheim

✆(714) 781-4565

Much of what California Adventure offers is totally new, but they did borrow a few attractions from other Disney parks. The *It's Tough to Be a Bug!* 3-D movie can also be seen at Disney's Animal Kingdom in Orlando, and Jim Henson's Muppet*Vision 3-D and Twilight Zone Tower of Terror were copied from Disney/MGM Studios in Orlando. California Adventure is also the home of what was once Disneyland's Main Street Electrical Parade (now called Disney's Electrical Parade), a Disneyland staple since 1972.

California Adventure will provide a family with about a day's worth of entertainment. It's a separate theme park from Disneyland and requires its own admission ticket. If it's the only thing you want to see, you can buy a single-day pass good for California Adventure only, or you can buy a pass that lets you travel between both parks using a single ticket (passport), a practice called "park-hopping." You can read about ticket options and pricing in Chapter 6.

💼 TRAVEL TIP

If you plan on park-hopping, be sure to keep your admission ticket handy and get your hand stamped as you leave each park. If you leave California Adventure and try to return later that day without a stamp, you will be stopped by security even if you're holding a valid ticket.

California Adventure's hours of operation vary by the time of year and day of the week, but it normally opens later than Disneyland and closes earlier. For the schedule during your visit, call Guest Relations or visit the Disneyland Web site at *www.disneyland.com*.

Whatever time the park officially opens, the main gate may open an hour earlier. On those days, you can shop in the area near the gate and enter Sunshine Plaza, but won't be able to go into the other areas until the official opening time. Some days, Mickey Mouse comes out of the Hollywood Pictures Backlot gate just as the park opens, wearing his California tourist attire.

═ FAST FACT

If you're staying at any of the three Disney hotels, one of the perks is that you can get into Disneyland and California Adventure one hour before regular ticket holders on selected days of the week. However keep in mind that the three Disney hotels combined have almost 2,000 hotel rooms and all the people staying in them will be doing exactly the same thing you are.

Tips for Visiting California Adventure

In general, you will find California Adventure less crowded than Disneyland, in part because its pathways are wider and its sight lines more open. However, the most popular rides and attractions still develop long lines and on a busy day, they may even run out of fastpasses.

Chapter 2 will give you some tips for theme park attire. These ideas will also help you have the happiest visit possible.

- Plan your day. If you are going to use RideMax to shorten your waiting time, this is essential. Otherwise, choose which attractions you absolutely must experience.
- As soon as you arrive, pick up a copy of the Entertainment Times Guide and the Souvenir Map. These helpful booklets, which are given out at the main entrance and at the Guest Services window near the entrance, contain the times for all parades and shows, describe the times and places to meet the Disney characters, and offer a detailed map of the park with all of the major attractions, restaurants, and amenities (restrooms, public phones, ATMs, etc.).
- Once you get inside the park, choose a place for your group to meet in case you get separated. The big sun sculpture in Sunshine Plaza is a good spot. It's easy to find and there are places to sit down. Walk there together so everyone knows where it is.
- You'll find the Wait Time board near the Guest Relations booth. Consult it to help you figure out the best time of the day for each ride or attraction.
- The Southern California sun can get hot in the middle of summer, and you won't find a lot of shade at California Adventure. If you need a spot to cool off and rest, visit any of the indoor shows. The lobby of the Animation building is also air-conditioned and has some benches you can sit on while watching Disney animated film clips play on the walls around you.

- Throughout the day, drink plenty of liquids. You can purchase soda, juice, or bottled water throughout California Adventure, or you can take advantage of the free water fountains that are also located throughout the park. Avoid becoming dehydrated by drinking liquids even if you're not thirsty.
- California Adventure typically overstates wait times by about ten minutes. If an attraction posts a twenty-minute wait, chances are you'll only wait about ten minutes.
- One of the last spots to fill up for watching the Electrical Parade is also one of the best. The area just in front of the Golden Zephyr looks like a bad spot to stop because it's brightly lit and the parade is best seen in the dark, but when the parade starts, the lights go off. As a bonus, you'll be near the exit if you want to leave right afterward.

Any time you need help in California Adventure or aren't sure what to do, consult a cast member. They're trained to help with all kinds of problems and know how to answer your questions.

The Areas

The California theme begins before you enter the park's gates, with 11.5-foot-high letters spelling *california* like an old-fashioned picture postcard and beautiful, mosaic tile murals flanking the entrance gate portraying California scenes. A model of San Francisco's Golden Gate Bridge spans the entry area, and beyond the gates, a 50-foot-tall titanium-and-bronze sun gleams above a flowing water fountain.

California Adventure is divided into five areas, similar to Disneyland's "lands." Each has a theme, reflected in its rides, attractions, and shows. The park is laid out around Sunshine Plaza, and if you lose your way, you can go there to get to any other part of the park.

Sunshine Plaza

Many of the park's guest services are located in Sunshine Plaza. In this area, you'll find a few shops and places to eat, and you can often meet and greet popular Disney characters, get their autographs, and take pictures with them. During the Christmas holidays, Santa also holds his Beach Blast in Sunshine Plaza.

You'll find a Wait Time board near Guest Services, just inside the entrance, where you can find out how long ride and attraction lines are and see listings of times for the live entertainment (shows and parades).

If you have a few free moments in Sunshine Plaza, you can get a peek at how Disney makes sure that this spot always lives up to its sunny name. Since sunshine can't fall directly on the metallic sun all day long, the Imagineers erected a bank of mirrors opposite the sculpture that follow the real sun and always reflect light toward the sculpture.

"a bug's land"

By far the cutest part of California Adventure, "a bug's land" looks like the characters from the film *A Bug's Life* must have built it themselves. Walk through the entry to Flik's Fun Fair and you'll find an area created just for the little ones, with only one ride that has a minimum height limit. Adults will enjoy the cute way it's built as much as the kids like the rides. You'll see hot-air balloons made out of leaves and paths lit by fireflies, and even the entry tunnel looks as though it's made from a cardboard box. Just outside the entrance, Flik and Atta often greet guests, and next door, you can see the 3-D show *It's Tough to be a Bug*.

Hollywood Pictures Backlot

This fun-filled area salutes Hollywood's past and present. You can get a behind-the-scenes look at Disney animation, laugh through a 3-D movie starring the Muppets, help Mike and Sulley rescue little Boo on a chase through Monstropolis, drop in at the Hollywood Tower Hotel, watch musical shows, and chat with Crush the turtle from the Disney/Pixar film *Finding Nemo*.

Golden State

The rides and attractions in this area of California Adventure salute California's diversity and heritage. Golden State is divided into six mini-areas simulating the legendary Edwards Air Force Base, the Sierra Nevada Mountains, the state's "salad bowl" agricultural areas, Wine Country, seaside fishing ports, and the San Francisco Bay Area.

RAINY DAY FUN

By necessity, California Adventure's most exciting rides such as California Screamin' and Mulholland Madness are outside and will close when it rains, so a rainy day is a good time to get inside and see the things you might otherwise miss. Take the tortilla factory and sourdough bread–making tours, or see the Golden Dreams show. It's always clear and sunny at Soarin' Over California, so why not do it twice?

In Golden State, you can soar over California, take a whitewater raft trip, learn how things are made, have a gourmet meal served with a flight of award-wining wines, or eat breakfast with Ariel, the Little Mermaid.

Paradise Pier

The largest area of California Adventure looks like a seaside amusement park and has a "fun in the sun" theme. If you enjoy traditional amusement park thrill rides, that's exactly what's in store for you. Some of the rides are suitable for people of all ages (including young kids), but some are much better suited for thrill-seeking teens and adults. Of course, if you want a totally mellow experience, you can always skip the rides and check out the carnival games and shopping area.

In Paradise Pier, you can ride a screaming fast roller coaster or a Ferris wheel with a surprise, go mad on Mulholland Drive, swing inside a giant orange or in a silver space ship, and drop through a colorful kelp forest. This area is especially pretty at night, when all the lights reflect in the water.

Dining at California Adventure

You can read about Disney's famous character meals in Chapter 7, the Disney hotel restaurants are described in Chapter 4, Chapter 14 describes dining options in Downtown Disney, and Chapter 15 offers some suggestions for other places to eat around Anaheim.

Throughout California Adventure, there are many dining areas, most of which offer fast food. You can find sit-down dining in three places and can make a priority seating reservation at any of them by calling (714) 781-3463 up to sixty days and at least two weeks in advance.

Prices for each of the dining spots listed here (like all other prices quoted in this book) are likely to change.

The Vineyard Room at the Golden Vine Winery

Location: Golden State
Meals: Dinner only
Price Range: $30 or more per person

The beautiful dining-room mural and balcony views of Paradise Pier make the Vineyard Room a special enough place, but the menu is equally unique, featuring food and wine designed to complement each other.

≡FAST FACT

Alcohol is served at several dining locations in Disney's California Adventure. However, Disney security will not tolerate disorderly conduct from people under the influence of alcohol.

While its menu includes some items suitable for children, the Vineyard Room is better suited for adult diners.

Wine Country Trattoria at the Golden Vine Winery

Location: Golden State
Meals: Lunch, dinner
Price Range: $10 to $20 per person

More relaxed and casual than the Vineyard Room, the trattoria still reflects California Wine Country's emphasis on fine cuisine. They serve lasagna, pasta, grilled sandwiches, and salads in an atmosphere reminiscent of a Napa Valley winery.

Ariel's Grotto

Location: Paradise Pier
Meals: Lunch, dinner
Price Range: $10 to $20 per person

If you or your kids want to dine with the Disney princesses, this is the place to go. Ariel and her royal friends Snow White, Belle, Sleeping Beauty, and Cinderella all show up here to meet and greet diners.

Many people visiting California Adventure prefer a less expensive and less formal lunch or dinner experience. Hollywood & Dine (in the Hollywood Pictures Backlot area) and the Taste Pilot's Grill (in the Condor Flats area) are both great places to stop with the family for lunch or dinner. So are the fast-food spots at Pacific Wharf, which include the Pacific Wharf Café, a favorite stop for clam chowder or soup in a sourdough bread bowl, and Cocina Cucamonga Mexican Grill.

≡FAST FACT

Many of California Adventure's shops and attractions make a joke from the names of California places. Some are more obvious, like Maliboomer (Malibu), Bur-r-r- Bank Ice Cream, or Baker's Field Cookies. Others are merely cute: Award Wieners, Taste Pilot's Grill, or Pizza Oom Mow Mow. There's also Man Hat 'n Beach (Manhattan Beach), Rushin' River Outfitters (Russian River), and Cocina Cucamonga, named for Rancho Cucamonga in San Bernardino County.

For snacks, you can buy cotton candy, shaved ice, hot dogs, and other items from vendors all over the park.

TRAVEL TIP

Just a short walk away from California Adventure is Downtown Disney, which offers an even greater selection of theme-oriented, sit-down restaurants suitable for the entire family.

California Adventure Shopping

Just like Disneyland, California Adventure offers a wide range of shops where guests can purchase all kinds of souvenirs. Whether you're looking for plush toys, Disney clothes, toys, or other items, there are plenty of shopping opportunities within this park.

Sunshine Plaza Shopping

Near the entrance gate, you'll find two fun shops to browse through.

- **Engine Ears Toys:** A well-stocked toy store shaped like a train

- **Greetings from California:** California Adventure-, California-, and Disney-themed merchandise

Golden State Shopping
- **Fly 'n' Buy:** Ladies' and men's apparel, flight jackets, and Soarin' Over California merchandise
- **P. T. Flea Market:** Limited edition pins, lanyards, and trading accessories
- **Rushin' River Outfitters:** A general store selling Disney T-shirts, fleece clothing, and toys

Hollywood Pictures Backlot Shopping
- **Gone Hollywood:** Hollywood-themed souvenirs, toys, and costumes
- **Off the Page:** Disney animation cels, collectors' prints and figurines, animation books, and souvenirs
- **Studio Store:** Muppets and Monsters Inc. apparel, toys, and souvenirs
- **Tower Hotel Gifts:** Collectible pins and souvenirs from the Tower of Terror

Paradise Pier Shopping
- **Dinosaur Jack's Sunglass Shack:** A three-story-tall pink dinosaur with yellow spots and shades for the whole family
- **Man Hat 'n' Beach:** Hats and visors, swimwear, towels, and other beach-themed items
- **Pacific Ocean Photos:** Have a souvenir photo taken in front of a variety of backdrops
- **Point Mugu Tattoo:** A temporary tattoo parlor with T-shirts and beach-themed merchandise
- **Slideshow Shirts:** T-shirts, tank tops, and beach fashions
- **Souvenir 66:** Travel and tourism-themed gifts, postcards, and personalized items
- **Treasures in Paradise:** Adult Disney clothing, fleece items, T-shirts, and candy

Throughout California Adventure (and Disneyland), you'll find Disney Collector Pin Trading Centers kiosks. Here you can purchase collectible pins (many of which are limited editions) and trade them with cast members or other guests. Many collectors wear their pins on baseball hats, on specially made lanyards, or on their clothing.

Like Disneyland, California Adventure has a number of pressed penny machines. They make a relatively inexpensive collectible for kids age eight and up, and occasionally become quite valuable. You can read more about them in Chapter 8.

Guest Services

You'll find California Adventure Guest Services just to the left of the main entrance. No matter what you need, this is the place to go. They can cash a check, supply an audiotape tour or Braille guidebook, lend you an Assistive Listening Device or closed captioning activator, answer your questions, or wish you a happy birthday. They'll try to help, no matter what you need.

The Lost and Found department is located outside the California Adventure entrance, to the left behind the wall. The Baby Care Center and First Aid Station are in Golden State, near the Mission Tortilla Factory. To get there from the entrance, follow the walkway that goes to the right of Sunshine Plaza past "a bug's land."

Disney security is highly trained in dealing with lost child situations. If a child (under age ten) in your party gets lost, seek help from Disney security or report the missing child to any Disneyland Cast Member and follow their instructions. The missing kid is likely to end up at Guest Services. Guests over ten years old can leave a written message at Guest Services near the entrance.

Parades, Shows, and Special Events

California Adventure, like Disneyland, offers a wide range of shows, parades, and special entertainment, including one of the most popular Disney parades of all time.

Disney's Electrical Parade

Location: From Paradise Pier near the Maliboomer to Sunshine Plaza

When the sun sets, California Adventure becomes the stage for a classic Disney parade that was a Disneyland staple for decades. Guests of all ages will enjoy this charming presentation featuring classic Disney characters and dozens of parade floats covered in colorful, sparkling lights.

≡FAST FACT

The Main Street Electrical parade ran for more than twenty seasons at Disneyland, between 1972 and 1996. It was so well loved that Disney brought it back, with a new name at California Adventure in 2001. Its theme song is "Baroque Hoedown," written in 1967 by Gershon Kingsley and Jean-Jaques Perrey.

The twenty-minute parade features floats and live performers, all covered in twinkling lights. You'll see Cinderella and Dumbo, twinkling butterflies, Captain Hook's pirate ship, and the Seven Dwarfs' mine train, among others. The parade ends with Pete's Dragon, followed by "To Honor America," a patriotic salute in lights. The bouncy, synthesized soundtrack is triggered by radio control so it's synchronized with the passing spectacle. Disney's Electrical Parade creates a truly magical entertainment experience that most people never forget.

Disney parades come and go, but this one continues to be a favorite. It's definitely worth seeing, even if it means leaving the park in the afternoon, taking a nap, and returning after dark for the parade.

For the best viewing location, stake out your spot along the parade route at least thirty minutes before the scheduled parade time. On nights when the parade is presented twice, the later show is always less crowded.

Disney's Electrical Parade is seasonal and does not happen every day. Check with Guest Services, the Disneyland Web site, or the Entertainment Times brochure to find out if it's scheduled during your visit.

 TRAVEL TIP

Many people try to photograph the Electrical parade, but get disappointing results. If your camera takes movies (and even many pocket-type digital cameras do), it's a fun way to record both movement and sound. Just be sure you have plenty of batteries and digital media on hand. Otherwise, try to snap your picture while the parade is stopped, and steady your camera on a nearby object like the top of a trashcan or the side of a pole.

Block Party Bash

Location: From the Hollywood Pictures Backlot gate past Sunshine Plaza to Paradise Pier, with Party Zones near Golden Dreams and at Sunshine Plaza

This bash is really a parade featuring characters from the Disney/Pixar animated films. It lasts about fifty minutes from beginning to end, with an eleven-minute performance stop in the middle. You'll see Woody and Buzz Lightyear from *Toy Story*, Mike and Sulley from *Monsters, Inc.*, and Flik and Atta from *a bug's life*, along with a host of other characters such as the Green Army Men, Mr. and Mrs. Incredible, and more.

FAST FACT

The Block Party Bash stops one time. If you want to see the best performances, stand in one of the party zones. The show is intended to be interactive, so if your kids want to join the fun, playing and dancing with the characters, stand in the front of the crowd. If you or your kids have a favorite show or character you'd like to see, ask a cast member where to stand to see them perform.

The performance part of the parade is especially energetic, accompanied by music from every decade from the 1950s through the 1970s. It includes sixty dancers, three trampolines, electric scooters, people on stilts, and flying acrobats.

High School Musical Pep Rally

Location: Sunshine Plaza and near Golden Dreams

Based on the Disney Channel television program, this outdoor performance features tunes from the show, cheerleaders, and more on a moving stage that stops at Sunshine Plaza and near the Golden Dreams theater, inviting onlookers to shoot some hoops and dance along.

Hyperion Theater

Location: Hollywood Pictures Backlot

You'll find this 2,000-seat theater at the end of the main street in Hollywood Pictures Backlot. It currently features a forty-minute show called *Disney's Aladdin—A Musical Spectacular*, a stage show based on the popular animated film featuring singers, dancing genies, and soaring carpets. The theater has three levels, and getting to the top two requires climbing stairs, although an elevator is available.

The show runs several times a day, and if you want a front-row seat, get in line about twenty-five minutes early.

Turtle Talk with Crush

Location: Hollywood Pictures Backlot

The wisecracking, 152-year-old sea turtle Crush from the film *Finding Nemo* introduces a new level of technology for bringing animated characters to life. He has unscripted, real-time conversations with the audience. For instance, he might stop in the middle of the show, look out at the audience and say "Hey you—dude in the righteous Hawaiian shirt—what's that on your head?" Introduced for the Disneyland fiftieth anniversary celebration, this attraction is similar to one at Florida's Epcot Center, which has been a huge hit.

"Playhouse Disney—Live on Stage!"

Location: Hollywood Pictures Backlot

The name of this show reveals its format. During the twenty-minute musical, members of the audience are invited to go on stage to join performers including Jim Henson's Bear from *The Bear in the Big Blue House*. The show runs several times a day and is located just inside the Hollywood Pictures Backlot gate.

≡ FAST FACT

Walt Disney wanted his theme park always to be growing and changing, and California Adventure continues the tradition. Don't be surprised if the live entertainment you find during your visit is different than what's described here.

A number of other, smaller shows happen daily in California Adventure. They include the following:

- **Golden Dreams (Golden State):** Narrated by actress Whoopi Goldberg, a film of the story of California history
- *It's Tough to Be a Bug!* ("a bug's land"): A 3-D show featuring Flik and the other bugs
- **Muppet*Vision 3-D (Hollywood Pictures Backlot):** A fun show with singing pigs, penguin musicians, and hecklers in the balcony
- **The Magic of Brother Totem Ceremony (Golden State):** Featuring characters and stories from the film *Brother Bear*
- **Animation Academy (Hollywood Pictures Backlot):** Learn how to draw a Disney cartoon character

Besides all the other events, character greetings happen all day long, and performers and Disney/Pixar characters may show up anywhere, adding to the festivity.

California Adventure Holidays

California Adventure joins Disneyland in celebrating the holidays, although they typically don't go as all-out as their sister park does.

California Adventure at Halloween

During the Halloween celebration in 2006, the California Adventure letters were transformed into giant pieces of candy corn, making a very popular photo backdrop. Inside the park, Golden Dreams temporarily becomes Golden Screams, a place for Disney villains to show their scary stuff, and at the Tower of Terror, hotel staff and guests step out of the fifth dimension to tell stories of the creepy goings-on in the Hollywood Tower Hotel.

≡FAST FACT

A few events happen at the Disneyland Resort every year that involve both Disneyland and California Adventure. See Chapter 5 for more about them, and Chapter 10 to learn about Gay Day and Disney collectors' events.

California Adventure at Christmas

While California Adventure doesn't get as dressed up for the holidays as Disneyland does, it doesn't lose track of the calendar, either. One of the most enjoyable Christmas events is Santa's Beach Blast, when the Jolly Old Elf trades his red suit for surfer shorts and Hawaiian shirt and settles into Sunshine Plaza for a little "R and R." In this area, you'll also find fun activities such as a Sand Castle Wreath toss or a limbo contest.

CHAPTER 12

California Adventure Rides

CALIFORNIA ADVENTURE BOASTS THIRTY-THREE rides, attractions, and shows spread over five named areas. One of the ways California Adventure differs from Disneyland is in its rides. In Disney's California-themed park, you'll find more rides designed to appeal to older children and adults, including the world's fifth-longest roller coaster. The little ones aren't neglected, though. They have their own amusement area, where people of any height can go on almost every ride. This chapter describes what's where, what happens, and who might enjoy it.

Sunshine Plaza

Sunshine Plaza, California Adventure's equivalent of Main Street, U.S.A., acts as the gateway to the park. While it doesn't have any specific rides or attractions, you will often see characters there and Santa sets up Beach Blast in the plaza during the Christmas holidays. It's also a stop for most parades including the Disney Electric Parade and other entertainment like the Block Party Bash.

In Sunshine Plaza you'll see a 50-inch golden sun "shining down" over a perpetual wave fountain, making this a great photo spot. You can also shop at the Engine Ears Toys and Greetings from California shops and grab a bite to eat at Bur-r-r Bank Ice Cream and Baker's

Field Bakery while listening to classic California tunes like, "I Love LA," "California Dreamin'," and "Route 66."

≡FAST FACT

The sun sculpture is able to shine continuously due to some creative engineering. If you look around the plaza, you'll see the flower-shaped heliostats that reflect the sun's light onto the titanium-covered sun sculpture. The heliostats are programmed to track the sun and to move every few seconds so that the solar highlights on the sun sculpture move as well, thereby making the sculpture shine continuously.

The Sunshine Plaza also features a replica of the Golden Gate Bridge, which guests pass under to enter the park and the monorail passes over as it brings guests into the park.

"a bug's land"

Designed mostly for younger, smaller guests, "a bug's land" depicts the world from a bug's point of view, as inspired by animated film *A Bug's Life*.

You'll often find Flik and Atta greeting guests near the entrance to Flik's Fun Fair, which features a number of very cute rides suitable for almost anyone:

Flik's Flyers

Ages 2–4:	★★★
Ages 5–10:	★★
Ages 11–15:	★
Ages 16–adult:	★

For a reminder of the rating system, see page 120.

The ride is simple, making slow circles, but the design is almost too cute for words, with riders traveling in hot-air balloons made from leaves and empty food cartons.

Francis's Ladybug Boogie

Ages 2–4:	★★★
Ages 5–10:	★★
Ages 11–15:	★
Ages 16–adult:	★

Francis's ladybug-shaped vehicles move much like the teacups in Disneyland, with riders controlling how fast they spin. Three to four riders can sit in each "bug." The ride lasts ninety seconds.

 TRAVEL TIP

If your party includes only adults and older children, you may be tempted to pass right by Flik's Fun Fair, but don't do it. Even if you don't want to ride anything there, it's worth a brief visit to see the cutest rides and decorations in all of California Adventure.

Heimlich's Chew Chew Train

Ages 2–4:	★★★
Ages 5–10:	★★
Ages 11–15:	★
Ages 16–adult:	★

You may remember Heimlich the caterpillar from the animated film. He's a hungry guy, and while you ride in a caterpillar-shaped train, you'll hear him muttering about his favorite foods. The ride lasts two minutes.

It's Tough to Be a Bug!

Ages 2–4:	N.S.
Ages 5–10:	★★★
Ages 11–15:	★★★
Ages 16–adult:	★★★

If you thought being a human was difficult, you're about to discover that life is harder as a bug. Featuring characters from the Disney/Pixar animated film, the 3-D show plays in a custom-built theater that harbors some unexpected effects. It will appeal to everyone who liked the movie. It's lighthearted, visually rich, and the extra-special effects are extremely realistic.

JUST FOR PARENTS

It's Tough to Be a Bug! includes some noisy scenes, a few moments of darkness, and some realistic effects that may scare younger children. If you're not sure how your youngsters will react, go all the way to the far side and back of the auditorium when you enter so you can make a quick escape.

Princess Dot Puddle Park

Ages 2–4:	★★★
Ages 5–10:	★★
Ages 11–15:	★
Ages 16–adult:	★

The kids will have a ball running around and getting wet (or trying not to).

Tuck and Roll's Drive' Em Buggies

Ages 2–4:	★
(if over 36 inches tall)	
Ages 5–10:	★★
Ages 11–15:	★★
Ages 16–adult:	★

Unlike the bumper cars at the local county fair, these buggies are very slow and gentle, but the kids don't seem to care. The ride lasts two minutes, and riders must be at least 36 inches tall. This ride may not be suitable for people with conditions that might be affected by all the bumping.

Golden State

The largest area of the park is dedicated to California's natural and artificial beauty and to the people who follow their dreams to the Golden State.

The Boudin Bakery Tour

Ages 2–4:	N.S.
Ages 5–10:	★
Ages 11–15:	★
Ages 16–adult:	★★

A San Francisco fixture, Boudin's Bakery makes a unique style of sourdough bread. On the bakery tour, you'll learn how their signature product is made and get a look at a few of the cute shapes that the bakers like to form from the dough. The lines are typically short, and adults in particular will find it interesting. If all the watching makes you hungry, you can get the bread in the adjacent Pacific Wharf Café, which serves Boudin's traditional soup in a sourdough bread bowl or scrambled eggs in a bread bowl for breakfast.

 JUST FOR PARENTS

The ride listings in this book include suggested age groups for whom the rides are most suitable. The abbreviation N. S. means not suitable. However, these are only general guidelines. Before you put your children on any ride, consider their maturity, likes and dislikes, and their ability to stay seated and follow directions. As long as they are tall enough to meet the rides' height requirements, the ultimate decision about whether your child can go on the ride is yours.

Bountiful Valley Farm

Ages 2–4:	N.S.
Ages 5–10:	★
Ages 11–15:	★
Ages 16–adult:	★

This outdoor exhibit showcases many plants, trees, and shrubs native to California, along with California crops. You'll find yourself in a park-like environment that you can walk through at your own pace.

Golden Dreams

Ages 2–4:	N.S.
Ages 5–10:	★
Ages 11–15:	★
Ages 16–adult:	★★★

A twenty-minute documentary movie, *Golden Dreams* will appeal mainly to adults. It offers a brief history of California using stunning movie footage and still photography. Narrated by Whoopi Goldberg, the film takes you on a whirlwind tour through time. *Golden Dreams* is shown throughout the day and evening in an air-conditioned, indoor theater.

During October, *Golden Dreams* becomes Golden Screams, a place where all the nastiest Disney villains congregate to create the biggest screams they can.

Golden Vine Winery

Ages 2–4:	N.S.
Ages 5–10:	N.S.
Ages 11–15:	N.S.
Ages 16–adult:	★★

Designed for adults, this attraction includes a small recreation of a Napa Valley vineyard. The focus here is on California's wine industry, and a seven-minute movie details its history and growth. You'll see how wine is made and learn about the famous Napa Valley wine country. At the end, you'll be invited to sample some of California's best-known wines during a wine tasting (for adults only).

Adults who enjoy sampling wine will find Golden Vine Winery to be informative and mildly entertaining. That is, if you're not put off by the infomercial-like quality of the overall presentation.

TRAVEL TIP

If you purchase wine at the Golden Vine shop, you must take advantage of the Package Express service and have it delivered either to the front of the park (to pick up on your way out) or directly to your room (if you're staying at a Disney hotel).

The lines for the film are always short. The movie theater holds fifty people at a time, and the film airs continuously throughout the day and evening. You'll also find two restaurants here, along with a wine shop that sells a large selection of California wines.

Grizzly River Run

Ages 2–4:	N.S.
Ages 5–10:	★★
Ages 11–15:	★★★
Ages 16–adult:	★★★

Grizzly River Run is similar to the white-water rafting rides found at many theme parks. Six riders sit in an oversize, circular "raft" that floats down a manmade river. The main difference between Grizzly River Run and similar rides is that it takes you higher to begin with, so you can have more fun on the way down.

It's almost impossible to keep from getting wet as you weave around the sometimes uneven river because the rafts turn constantly. If you're carrying cameras or any other electronics, make sure they're protected. It's best to ride in midday (but not just before going into an air-conditioned restaurant) and wear clothing that will dry out quickly, or have a change of dry clothing.

Grizzly River Run is suitable for people of all ages who are in good enough condition to stand the turns and sudden drops. It's a lot of fun and not too scary, except when you experience the river's two drops (one of which falls 21 feet). Because the river has many twists and turns, it's often hard to see what thrills are coming next, which adds to the excitement.

Riders must be at least 42 inches tall and able to stand some drops and turns. Grizzly River Run is very popular, especially on hot summer days, making it a fastpass attraction. A Single Rider line is also available.

Mission Tortilla Factory

Ages 2–4:	★
Ages 5–10:	★
Ages 11–15:	★★
Ages 16–adult:	★★

This short, walk-through attraction, located just across from the Boudin Bakery, demonstrates how flour and corn tortillas are made. At the end of the tour, you'll get a free sample. Mission Tortilla

Factory is a self-paced, indoor attraction that you can get through in three to five minutes, and the lines are typically short. Kids and teens might find the working machinery interesting, but smaller children may be bored.

Redwood Creek Challenge Trail

Ages 2–4:	★★★
Ages 5–10:	★★★
Ages 11–15:	★
Ages 16–adult:	★

A good place for the kids to work off any excess energy, Redwood Creek is an interactive (outdoor) play area that looks like a California redwood forest. Youngsters will find all kinds of places to climb net ladders, walk over suspension bridges, slide down, and explore the playground/obstacle course. Parents are encouraged to watch from a nearby area. Most people spend about twenty minutes here. Some of the activities have a 42-inch height limit.

The Magic of Brother Bear Totem Ceremony, featuring the characters Koda and Kenai from the animated film *Brother Bear*, is held here several times a day.

Soarin' Over California

Ages 2–4:	N.S.
Ages 5–10:	★★
Ages 11–15:	★★★
Ages 16–adult:	★★★

To many people, Soarin' Over California is the best experience at California Adventure, if not the entire Disneyland Resort. It combines motion-simulator and Omnimax movie technologies to make you feel as if you're soaring over California in a hang glider, taking an airborne tour of historic landmarks and national parks.

Riders walk through a mildly themed entry area lined with photographs of California's aviation pioneers before dividing into groups to enter one of the two simulator theaters. Each theater has three "gliders," each holding thirty-six people in three rows of twelve. The gliders move 45 feet into the air and into the middle of an almost-hemispherical Omnimax screen. The film is all you'll see around you, and the glider's movements synchronize with the movie to enhance the feeling of flying. To add an extra dimension of reality, you'll also smell orange blossoms, pine trees, and salty air.

TRAVEL TIP

The best seats available for Soarin' are in the first row, where you get an unobstructed view without anyone's feet dangling in front of you. If you're directed to a second or third row seat, politely tell the cast member you want to sit in the first row. It will be worth the short extra wait.

Soarin' has a 40-inch minimum height restriction, but it's a smooth, easy ride that most anyone will enjoy. However, the experience is so realistic that a few brief scenes may bother those prone to motion sickness.

Soarin' is a fastpass ride that often develops long lines, but it's well worth the wait to experience the four-minute "flight" across California and you may find yourself running back to the fastpass machine as soon as you get out so you can see it again. It also offers a Single Rider option.

As you enter or exit Soarin' Over California, you're in the park's Condor Flats section. The California Adventure design team visited legendary Edwards Air Force Base in the California desert to duplicate the look of their runway tarmac in every detail, down to the cracks and repairs.

You'll also find street entertainment in Golden State, with the Mariachi Divas performing at Pacific Wharf and the Miner 49ers hanging out on Highway 49, serenading guests with Disney songs.

Hollywood Pictures Backlot

The real Hollywood may be more of a state of mind than a physical place, but at California Adventure, the imagined place becomes real.

You can be cast as the voice of a Disney character or try your hand at being an animator.

The setting looks very much like a real studio back lot, with a fool-your-eye blue sky at the end of a street made to look longer than it is by using forced perspective.

Disney Animation

Ages 2–4:	★
Ages 5–10:	★★★
Ages 11–15:	★★★
Ages 16–adult:	★★★

Disney Animation is really four attractions in one. By experiencing them all, you'll discover how Disney animation is created and get reacquainted with classic Disney characters. The Disney Animation building houses a series of walk-through exhibits, hands-on interactive activities, live shows, and demonstrations.

Before you set out to explore the exhibits, stop to enjoy Animation Courtyard where film clips from classic Disney films are hypnotically choreographed to run on dozens of screens. You'll feel as if you've stepped into one of Disney's animated adventures. The show lasts thirty minutes, giving you a good excuse to sit down and rest. From the courtyard, you can enter the sections in any order:

- **Animation Academy:** You have to do some work at the academy, where you'll learn how to draw a Disney cartoon character (the one with the big round ears). The best seats in the 230-seat theater are in the fourth row (toward the center of the room). No matter which seat you wind up in, however, you'll see and hear everything.
- **Sorcerer's Workshop:** In the workshop, you can take a quiz to find out what Disney character you're most like, make your own little cartoon and watch it run, practice being the voice of a Disney character, and more. The most fun, however, is standing in the library from *Beauty and the Beast* and watching it transform as the last petal falls from the rose.

- **Turtle Talk with Crush:** The 152-year-old sea turtle Crush from the film *Finding Nemo* interacts directly with the audience. Using some very impressive, real-time animation effects, he asks questions about the human world and answers questions about his world.

Plan to spend at least an hour enjoying the self-paced activities. You exit Disney Animation through a gift shop that has the best Disney collectibles in California Adventure.

Jim Henson's Muppet*Vision 3-D

Ages 2–4:	★★
Ages 5–10:	★★★
Ages 11–15:	★★★
Ages 16–adult:	★★★

Fans of the classic television series *The Muppet Show* will get a touch of comic nostalgia watching Kermit, Miss Piggy, and the rest of the Muppet gang perform in a fun-filled 3-D movie.

While waiting to go inside, you'll see an amusing preshow. The theater itself was custom-designed to look like the set from *The Muppet Show* television series, and the mayhem is typical Muppet style. During the movie, the theater becomes part of the show.

Special 3-D glasses are provided, but don't put them on until you're comfortably seated in the main theater. The wait for the show is not usually very long, and while in line, you'll enjoy the Muppet characters and signs that line the entrance queue.

Monsters, Inc. Mike & Sulley to the Rescue!

Ages 2–4:	★★
Ages 5–10:	★★
Ages 11–15:	★★
Ages 16–adult:	★★

Step into Monstropolis as you experience Mike and Sulley's mad rush to save little Boo in a dark ride inspired by the animated film *Monsters, Inc.*

═FAST FACT

If you visited California Adventure when it first opened, you may think Mike & Sulley to the Rescue feels vaguely familiar. It began as the Superstar Limo, using the same vehicles, but is now re-themed from limousines running around Los Angeles to taxis running around Moustropolis.

The taxi-style vehicles hold six people. On the left side of each row, a television monitor shows news coverage of events as a human child gets loose in the monsters' city. You can sit in a left-most seat to get the best view of its screen, but the rest of the attraction is more interesting.

While this is by no means a thrill ride, it does make some abrupt direction changes. The most enjoyable part is the trip through the scare factory and the door rooms shown in the film.

The Twilight Zone Tower of Terror

Ages 2–4:	N.S.
Ages 5–10:	★★★
Ages 11–15:	★★★
Ages 16–adult:	★★★

You can see the Tower of Terror from anywhere in the Disneyland Resort. At 183 feet, it's the tallest structure in the area, and at first, you might mistake it for a new hotel, which it is. However, the Hollywood Tower Hotel is not a place you'll want to spend the night.

The classic television program *The Twilight Zone* inspires the ride's story. In this "lost" episode, you are about to enter the fabled zone as you check into a hotel with a past. After waiting in the 1930s-style lobby, groups of twenty-one people enter a library. While waiting, you'll learn about a bizarre incident that happened some years ago. Lightning struck the ill-fated hotel, and a bellhop and guests in the elevator simply vanished.

After a cast member dressed as a bellhop leads you through a realistically constructed boiler room, you'll enter the "service elevator." Moments later, you join the lost elevator occupants as their ghostly figures beckon you from the hallway.

Suddenly everything breaks loose, and the elevator shoots up—very fast—only to fall equally as fast. Cables groan and the car creaks, and doors fly open on the thirteenth floor, where the lightning blasted the wall away. You experience a few seconds of weightlessness during which your seat belt seems to be the only thing keeping you from flying upward. Four minutes after you went in, it's all over.

If you've seen Tower of Terror at Disney-MGM Studios in Florida, the California Tower is quite similar, except that the cars only move vertically and not horizontally.

As you might expect, Tower of Terror is very popular, and a fast-pass can help you get on more quickly on a busy day. Riders must be at least 40 inches tall and in good enough physical shape to tolerate the abrupt ups and downs.

Paradise Pier

Paradise Pier celebrates the glory days of California's seaside amusement parks when Californians and tourists alike sought sun and fun at the beach. It sports an authentic boardwalk and some modern interpretations of classic amusement park rides.

California Screamin'

Ages 2–4:	N.S.
Ages 5–10:	N.S.
Ages 11–15:	★★★
Ages 16–adult:	★★★

At first glance, California Screamin' looks like a classic wooden roller coaster, but when you notice riders going heels over head through a vertical loop, you realize the wooden framework is really a façade that cleverly conceals a tubular steel track.

When it was built, California Screamin's 6,072-foot track was the world's fourth longest, and designers didn't waste a single foot of it packing in turns, drops, and twists, including the signature

360-degree loop around Mickey's face. The trains are broken into six 4-person units, which catapult from zero to 55 miles per hour in just 4.7 seconds.

Due to its popularity, waits can be ninety minutes or longer. fast-pass is available and so are Single Rider line and Child Swap options. Riders must be at least 48 inches tall and in good enough condition to stand all the fast twists, turns, and drops.

For a beautiful view of California Adventure, ride California Screamin' in the evening or at night when the park is lit up. That is, if you can keep your eyes open as you fly around the track. Souvenir photos taken during your ride will be on sale at the exit.

Games of the Boardwalk

Along the boardwalk, you'll find a handful of skill- and luck-based carnival games, priced between $1 and $2 per play. Prizes include plush toys. It's a fun way to spend some time, if you don't mind spending a bit more money.

Golden Zephyr

Ages 2–4:	★★
Ages 5–10:	★★
Ages 11–15:	★★
Ages 16–adult:	★★

A simple, rotating swing ride, Golden Zephyr is gentle enough for just about anyone, unless you're extraordinarily prone to dizziness. The silver rocket ships hold fourteen people each (seven rows with two people per row), and they swing around in the air for about two minutes.

Jumpin' Jellyfish

Ages 2–4:	N.S.
Ages 5–10:	★★
Ages 11–15:	★★
Ages 16–adult:	★★

Jumpin' Jellyfish is a little bit like a gentler version of Maliboomer, lifting riders into the air and then raising and lowering them in a series of successively shorter drops, all of which takes about a minute. Two people can ride per seat. Jumpin' Jellyfish is a pretty ride that isn't scary, unless you're afraid of heights.

It's most suitable for children up to age twelve, who are at least 40 inches tall.

King Triton's Carousel

Ages 2–4:	★★
Ages 5–10:	★★
Ages 11–15:	★★
Ages 16–adult:	★★

As you can guess from its name, this beautiful carousel has a water theme. Instead of riding horses, guests sit on colorful sea creatures, such as fish, dolphins, and seahorses. Some of the creatures are stationary, while others move up and down as you go around. The ride lasts about two minutes. Parents can stand next to their child or ride with them. There's also a nice viewing area where you can take pictures of the kids as they ride.

Maliboomer

Ages 2–4:	N.S.
Ages 5–10:	N.S.
Ages 11–15:	★★★
Ages 16–adult:	★★★

What comes down must go up first—in this case, extremely fast. The theme is an old-fashioned carnival test of strength: Use a hammer to hit a lever and ring the bell, but Disney hits the hammer and you fly up to ring the bell. Maliboomer shoots you (four people per bench) 180 feet into the air in four seconds. After that, you bounce a few times before returning to the ground. The whole thing takes about forty-five seconds. The view from Maliboomer is beautiful at night, but the thrill is the same anytime.

Riders must be at least 52 inches tall and able to stand some fast ups and downs (especially the ups). This fairly popular ride offers a Single Rider option, but no fastpass.

Mulholland Madness

Ages 2–4:	N.S.
Ages 5–10:	★★★
Ages 11–15:	★★★
Ages 16–adult:	★★

Designed for those not brave enough to experience California Screamin', Mulholland Madness is a traditional roller coaster, but one designed for young people. It offers a much tamer, although fun experience as you race along the track, and its biggest thrill is the feeling that you're going to plummet off the track before your car abruptly turns. The best place to experience the sensation is the front row, but riders who are afraid of heights may be more comfortable in the back.

Riders must be at least 42 inches tall and able to stand the turns and drops. To reduce the wait, use fastpass or take the Single Rider option.

Orange Stinger

Ages 2–4:	N.S.
Ages 5–10:	★★★
Ages 11–15:	★★★
Ages 16–adult:	★★

You'll know when you've reached the Orange Stinger because it's shaped like a giant half-peeled orange. Inside the over-size piece of fruit are single-person swings that rise into the air and spin around. This family-oriented ride is suitable for anyone over 48 inches tall, unless they're prone to dizziness.

S.S. rustworthy

Ages 2–4:	★★★
Ages 5–10:	★★★
Ages 11–15:	★★
Ages 16–adult:	N.S.

The *rustworthy* looks like an old fire-boat full of things to climb and fire hoses to squirt. Kids under the age of twelve will enjoy playing here. Anyone who experiences the S.S. *rustworthy* is going to get wet, so it's best to have a change of clothes on hand.

Sun Wheel

Ages 2–4:	★★
Ages 5–10:	★★★
Ages 11–15:	★★★
Ages 16–adult:	★★★

The Ferris wheel with a giant, grinning sun on its face isn't quite as simple as it might look at first glance. Stand and watch it for a minute, and you'll realize that some of the gondolas are mounted on oval tracks that make them slide around and rock back and forth, while others remain fixed.

Four adults can ride in each gondola, and you go around twice: the first time starting and stopping to let people board and then once without stopping. The view from the Sun Wheel is great—you can see all of the park and beyond—but the wire-mesh enclosure prevents taking good pictures unless your camera has a very small lens.

Before you get on, watch the ride for a minute and decide which kind of car you want to ride in. Some people get quite unnerved by the moving cars while others love them. The fixed ones go higher and the line to get on them is shorter. After you've decided, pick the line that matches your choice.

Most Popular Rides

Some California Adventure rides have become almost instant classics. Any fan can name them, and so can you after you read this list. All are fastpass rides.

- California Screamin' (Paradise Pier)
- Grizzly River Run (Golden State)
- Mulholland Madness (Paradise Pier)
- Soarin' Over California (Golden State)
- Tower of Terror (Hollywood Pictures Backlot)

Rides for Very Little Ones

These rides are mostly in the Flik's Fun Fair section of "a bug's land," where everything is bug-built and kid-size.

- Flik's Flyers ("a bug's land")
- Francis' Ladybug Boogie ("a bug's land")
- Heimlich's Chew Chew Train ("a bug's land")
- King Triton Carousel (Paradise Pier)
- Princess Dot Puddle Park ("a bug's land")

Rides by Height of Rider

For safety's sake, some California Adventure rides have a minimum height requirement. The requirement is set to help keep riders from falling out or otherwise getting hurt.

MINIMUM HEIGHT REQUIREMENTS FOR CALIFORNIA ADVENTURE RIDES	
Minimum Height	**Rides**
36 inches (91 cm)	Tuck and Roll's Drive'Em Buggies
40 inches (102 cm)	Tower of Terror, Jumpin' Jellyfish, Soarin' Over California
42 inches (107 cm)	Mulholland Madness, Grizzly River Run, some parts of Redwood Creek Challenge Trail
48 inches (122 cm)	Orange Stinger, California Screamin'
52 inches (131 cm)	Maliboomer

At the entrance of each one, you'll find a height-measurement device. If there's any question, the cast members will use it to decide if your child is tall enough to ride. They know all the tricks; don't try to fool them.

Smooth and Quiet Rides

These rides won't rattle your nerves or your bones. They're tame and quiet, with no sudden starts and stops, jerks, or noisy surprises.

- All the rides in Flik's Fun Fair ("a bug's land")
- Golden Zephyr (Paradise Pier)
- Soarin' Over California (Golden State)
- Sun Wheel's fixed cars (Paradise Pier)

Thrill Rides

While California Adventure isn't Southern California's most extreme theme park, these rides are quite exciting.

- California Screamin' (Paradise Pier)
- Maliboomer (Paradise Pier)
- Sun Wheel's swinging cars (Paradise Pier)
- Tower of Terror (Hollywood Pictures Backlot)

Great Places to Cool Off

If the Southern California sun seems a little too hot at California Adventure, these are all good places to cool off (and rest your feet, too).

- Disney's Aladdin—A Musical Spectacular (Hollywood Pictures Backlot)
- Disney Animation (Hollywood Pictures Backlot)
- Golden Dreams (Golden State)
- It's Tough to Be a Bug ("a bug's land")
- Muppet*Vision 3-D (Hollywood Pictures Backlot)
- "Playhouse Disney—Live on Stage!" (Hollywood Pictures Backlot)

Accessible Rides

Almost everything in California Adventure is accessible, but riders have to transfer from their wheelchairs into the ride itself. At Monsters, Inc., Sun Wheel, and King Triton's Carousel, electric convenience vehicle riders transfer to a wheelchair. All shows and other attractions are fully accessible.

Most rides and attractions that have an audio component offer closed captioning, Assistive-Listening devices, and/or reflective captioning. You can find out which ones offer which assistance by looking at the codes on the California Adventure map brochure, and you can pick up Assistive-Listening devices at Guest Services.

CHAPTER 13

Special Services at the Disney Theme Parks

OVER THE YEARS, hundreds of millions of people have visited the Disneyland Resort. With an eye toward customer service and a lot of experience handling their guests' needs, the Disney theme parks offer a wide range of special services. This chapter describes many of these services and how to take advantage of the most commonly needed ones. If you need help with something not mentioned here, call Disneyland Guest Services at (714) 781-4101.

ATMs

In Disneyland and Disney's California Adventure, as well as in Downtown Disney, you'll find plenty of ATMs (automated teller machines). Ask any Disney cast member for directions to the closest machine or check the maps available at the entrance gates.

JUST FOR PARENTS

Disneyland has its own currency, Disney Dollars, available in $1, $5, and $10 denominations and exchanged on a dollar-for-dollar basis with U.S. currency. You can spend your Disney Dollars just like cash anywhere in the Disneyland Resort. Enhance your kids' feeling that they're going someplace special by exchanging your currency at Guest Services. Keep a dollar or two for a souvenir.

With proper identification, you can cash a check, made payable to "Disneyland," at Guest Services in each theme park. Disneyland hotels offer a similar check-cashing service but only for hotel guests.

FAST FACT

You'll find foreign currency exchange services at Travelex in Downtown Disney, City Hall in Disneyland, the Guest Relations Lobby at California Adventure, and the front desks of the Disney hotels.

Most shops and restaurants at the Disneyland Resort accept cash (U.S. currency), Disney Dollars, traveler's checks, personal checks, Visa, MasterCard, American Express, JCB, the Disney Credit Card, and Discover Card. However, some of the small food and merchandise kiosks located throughout the parks do not accept credit cards.

Telephones

Throughout the Disneyland Resort, in public areas of the hotels, in the theme parks, and in Downtown Disney, there are plenty of public telephones. Most of them accept coins, credit cards, or prepaid phone cards.

Most nationwide cellular telephone services work in the Anaheim area. Depending on your service contract, however, you may incur per-minute, out-of-area roaming fees, so contact your cellular service provider for details.

Both parks have typewriter phones for the hearing impaired. Ask a cast member for their location.

Lockers

Both Disney theme parks offer lockers for rent. Storing the extra items you bring into the park—such as a change of clothes, jackets for the evening, a blanket to sit on while you watch the fireworks—or things you purchase is a good way to keep these extras from weighing you down and tiring you out. Renting a locker is a lot more convenient than running back and forth to your parked car or hotel room, both of which require a long walk, drive, or tram ride.

Depending on the size of the locker, rental rates range from $6 to $12 per day. Locker space is somewhat limited, and on busy days, they tend to be filled by noon at the latest.

Lost and Found

The Lost and Found office is next to the Guest Services window outside California Adventure. It's tucked behind the wall to the left of the entrance gate.

If you lose something, report it missing as quickly as possible. If someone returns your lost item while you're still at the park, you can pick it up at the Lost and Found window. If your lost article is important to you and it isn't found before you leave, keep checking. If it turns up in a reasonable amount of time, Disneyland will ship it to you at their expense.

If you find something and no one claims it, you may eventually be allowed to claim it yourself. Ask about this policy when you turn in the lost item.

The Disneyland Lost and Found telephone number is (714) 817-2166.

≡FAST FACT

Disneyland's Lost and Found department finds almost 400 misplaced items a day. Some of the most unusual ones they've encountered include a glass eye, a coffee pot, and a canary. The glass eye was returned, the coffee pot's owner is still trying to find some caffeine, and the canary was last seen flying toward the Enchanted Tiki Room.

If you lose your child (or parent), contact the nearest cast member. They're experts at reuniting separated people.

Medical Emergencies

No matter what type of emergency you experience, medical or otherwise, head for the First Aid center or contact the nearest Disney cast member. Disneyland employees know how to deal with all kinds of emergencies, including lost children, medical-related problems, and lost or stolen items.

Disneyland and Disney's California Adventure both offer fully equipped first-aid stations. Some routine items such as pain relievers, sunblock, and bandages can also be purchased at many of the gift shops, including those along Main Street, U.S.A. (in Disneyland).

If you need refrigeration facilities for prescription medications (such as insulin or antibiotics), the first aid office of both theme parks and the Disney hotels will provide them, free of charge. Contact Guest Relations for more information.

If you need medical attention while you're in Anaheim, Western Medical Center is nearby at 1025 S. Anaheim Boulevard, and the UC Irvine Medical Center is a few miles away at 101 The City Drive South in the city of Orange.

 **TRAVEL TIP**

Before you leave on vacation, get copies of any prescriptions for medications you might need and take along contact information for your doctor and medical insurance company. If you lose something and need to refill your prescription, it will be much less of a hassle.

If you'd rather not go out looking for a doctor, HouseCall Physicians can arrange for one to come to your hotel room for a consultation, twenty-four hours a day. You can reach them at (800) 362-7911 or *www.housecallphysicians.org*. This is a licensed medical practice, not a telephone referral service, and it is not operated by or affiliated with the Walt Disney Company.

Package Express Service

If you're staying at a Disney hotel, Package Express is one of the extra services provided. Whenever you buy something at a shop in one of the parks, you can have it delivered directly to your hotel room, free of charge. This means you won't have to carry your purchases or store them in lockers.

 TRAVEL TIP

By the end of a long day, it's easy to forget about the package you left to pick up early in the morning. To keep from forgetting your goodies, do something that will help you remember, such as wrapping your receipt around your hotel or car key or tying something to that rented stroller that will jog your memory when you see it.

If you aren't staying at a Disney hotel, you can still enjoy the convenience of Package Express. Just leave your purchases at the Newsstand near Disneyland's main entrance, at Star Trader in Tomorrowland, or at the Pioneer Mercantile in Frontierland and pick them up at the same place before you leave. In California Adventure, the drop-off point is Engine Ears Toys near the entrance.

Babies and Children

Baby Centers in both Disney theme parks provide clean facilities where you can prepare formulas, warm bottles, nurse, or change diapers. For a small fee, you can also buy some baby products at these locations. You'll also find changing tables in almost all of the public restrooms in the theme parks.

The Disneyland Resort doesn't offer baby-sitting services to guests, but if you're staying at one of the Disney hotels, you can coordinate private baby-sitting services through the concierge or front desk. Disney's Grand Californian Hotel offers Pinocchio's Workshop, a child activity center that's open from 5 P.M. to midnight.

The Disneyland parking lot trams require you to fold your stroller when you get on, so be prepared.

Stroller Rental

Both theme parks offer stroller rentals for $8 per day. You'll find a stroller rental booth near the entrance of each park. Stroller rentals are not available in Downtown Disney. When renting a stroller, be sure to keep the receipt with you at all times.

If you park your rented stroller and find it gone when you return, simply go to a stroller replacement center or the main rental area to get another one, or ask any Disney cast member to help you.

JUST FOR PARENTS

Because you can't take a stroller on to attractions, on the Disneyland Railroad, or on the Monorail, you'll have to leave it unattended and parked outside each attraction you experience. To avoid worries about theft, rent a stroller at the theme park, but don't forget to take your valuables out each time you leave it somewhere.

Accessibility

The Disneyland Resort offers a wide range of services for guests with special needs. A special Braille guidebook is available, free of charge, from City Hall (in Disneyland) or Guest Relations (in Disney's California Adventure). However, you may find it a little outdated.

Closed captioning is available at many movie- or video-based attractions, you can get written storylines for most of the rides and attractions, and some of the rides and attractions use Assistive-Listening systems. Pick an assistive-listening receiver at City Hall in Disneyland or at California Adventure's Guest Relations.

Wheelchair-accessible attractions in Disneyland include Inno-ventions, King Arthur Carrousel, *Mark Twain* Riverboat, Mickey and Minnie's Houses, Tom Sawyer Island, and most of the shows, including Fantasmic! In California Adventure, wheelchairs can go on the Boudin Bakery Tour, into Disney Animation, Princess Dot Puddle Park, Redwood Creek Challenge Trail, S.S. rustworthy, and most shows. At many other rides and attractions, it's possible to transfer from a wheelchair on to the ride. Cast members at any entrance can give you more information and direct you to special wheelchair entrances.

Disneyland provides shuttles just to carry people who need special assistance from the parking lots to the gate. Ask a cast member for assistance.

All of the Disney hotels, as well as most Anaheim-area hotels, offer special accommodations for the disabled. These accommodations must be reserved in advance to ensure that the services you need will be available when you visit.

TRAVEL TIP

For more information about services available for disabled guests, call Guest Relations at ✆(714) 781-7290. Disneyland's TTY telephone number is ✆(714) 781-4569. Their free Guidebook for Guests with Disabilities offers information about accessibility to rides, shows, attractions, shops, and restaurants in the theme parks. This guide is available from Guest Relations, or you can find an electronic copy at the Disneyland Web site ✍www.disneyland.com by searching for "disabilities guidebook."

If you have special dietary needs, speak with your server or the chef at any of the sit-down restaurants in the Disneyland Resort, including Downtown Disney.

Wheelchair and Electric Convenience Vehicle Rental

Wheelchair rental costs $8 per day for a manual wheelchair, and electric convenience vehicles (ECVs) rent for $35. Each requires a $20 refundable deposit. Wheelchair rentals are not available in Downtown Disney.

Pet Care

Even if you consider your pet a member of the family and usually travel with it, you may want to reconsider before you take your pet with you to the Disneyland Resort. Most Anaheim-area hotels do not allow pets in their rooms, and only service animals are allowed in the theme parks, so you won't get to spend much time with them.

If you're bent on bringing your animal with you no matter what, Extended Stay Anaheim, Lemon Tree Hotel, Marriott Residence Inn Anaheim Maingate, Marriott Anaheim Suites, Marriott Residence Inn Anaheim, Sheraton Anaheim Hotel, Sheraton Park Hotel Staybridge Suites, and Towneplace Suites allow pets, although most charge an extra nonrefundable deposit or daily fee.

During the day, Disney offers pet owners an air-conditioned kennel called the Disneyland Pet Care Kennel. Any cast member can show you where it's located.

 TRAVEL TIP

Although Disney provides kennel facilities, the cast members who work at the kennels do not handle the pets. Guests must place their pet in an assigned cage and are encouraged to visit their pet several times during the day and night to walk and feed the animal.

For $15, a pet can be boarded during the day, but they cannot stay overnight. For more information about rates and availability, call (714) 781-4565. Disneyland Kennel Club rules and Orange County law require you to show rabies and distemper vaccination certificates from your vet to board dogs over four months old.

CHAPTER 14

Exploring Downtown Disney

WHETHER YOU'RE LOOKING FOR Disney-oriented nightlife or an escape from the Disney theme parks, Downtown Disney can provide many hours of entertainment, shopping, dining, and activities for people of all ages. Adults will enjoy the boutiques, bars, and cafés, while younger people will appreciate the toyshops, novelty stores, candy shops, and theme restaurants.

The Lowdown on Downtown Disney

✆(714) 300-7800

✉*www.disneyland.com*

Located along a central thoroughfare between the Disneyland Hotel and the Disney theme park entrances, Downtown Disney adds a fun twist to the dining and shopping experience all day long, with a wide range of family-oriented restaurants and cafés, plenty of upscale shopping, and a handful of attractions.

Whether you want to relax and have breakfast before spending a day at one of the Disney theme parks, enjoy a sit-down lunch or dinner, or need a late-night snack, Downtown Disney offers many dining options.

 TRAVEL TIP

As soon as you arrive at Downtown Disney, pick up a free Downtown Disney Show Schedule, available from any information kiosk (not the merchandise kiosks) or ticket counter. It will provide you with special event show times and let you know what's happening during the week at ESPN Zone, House of Blues, AMC Theatres, Ralph Brennan's Jazz Kitchen, and other locations.

If you don't find the perfect gifts and souvenirs in the Disneyland or California Adventure, you may find them in the many shops of Downtown Disney. Some of these shops are exclusive to Downtown Disney, while others (like Illuminations and Sephora) are chain stores.

When it comes to entertainment, many of the restaurants offer live shows, and the AMC Theatres boast a dozen state-of-the-art theaters showing the latest movies. The House of Blues contains an indoor theater where well-known recording artists perform.

Lovely landscaping that includes fountains and waterfalls surrounds the shops, restaurants, and attractions.

JUST FOR PARENTS

Downtown Disney lights up at night and offers a festive atmosphere for an evening stroll, an alfresco meal, or a quick shopping spree. Kids and adults enjoy the buzz and like listening to the street performers.

There is no separate admission charge to visit Downtown Disney, and anyone can visit it at any time.

Getting to Downtown Disney

Conveniently located a short walk from Disneyland and Disney's California Adventure, Downtown Disney has its own monorail station, complimentary bus and tram transportation, and two parking lots.

If you're staying at one of the Disney-owned hotels, the easiest way to get around is to leave your car parked and walk or to take the complimentary bus or tram to Downtown Disney instead of driving. Some independent hotels, motels, and resorts also offer complimentary shuttle bus transportation to and from Downtown Disney.

If you are driving to Downtown Disney from Interstate-5 southbound, take the Disneyland Drive/Ball Road exit. At the end of the exit ramp, turn left on Disneyland Drive; then stay in one of the two right-hand lanes. Follow the Downtown Disney signs. After passing Ball Road, turn right on to Magic Way and get into the leftmost lane. As you approach the Downtown Disney North Parking Lot, turn left into the lot.

From northbound I-5, take the Katella/Disney Way exit. At the traffic light (at the end of the exit ramp), turn left on to Katella. Pass straight through the Harbor Boulevard intersection. The following intersection will be Disneyland Drive. Turn right at this intersection (on to Disneyland Drive), and take an immediate left into the Downtown Disney South parking lot.

If you're visiting Downtown Disney along with one of the theme parks, it's cheaper to park in the theme park's parking lot (for a flat rate of $11 per day).

If you're going just to Downtown Disney, you'll find two conveniently located parking lots off Disneyland Drive. For self-parking, the first three hours are free of charge, and you can get two more hours free with validation from the AMC Theatres or any sit-down restaurant in the area. After that, there's a $6 per hour parking fee (billed in twenty-minute increments), and a $30 per day maximum. Add $14 if you want valet parking service.

Bicycles can park for free any time, and you'll find guest drop-off areas at Magic Way and Downtown Drive (near Rainforest Café) and on Harbor Boulevard, just south of the Esplanade intersection.

If you're already in the Disneyland Resort, the Disney Tram service operates continuously, connecting Downtown Disney, Disneyland, Disney's California Adventure, and the theme park parking lots. The tram operates for two hours after the Disneyland and Disney's California Adventure theme parks close. After that, it's a ten-minute walk from Downtown Disney to the Mickey & Friends lot.

≡FAST FACT

When it first opened in 1959, the Disneyland Monorail was the only regularly operating monorail in the Western Hemisphere. Vice President Richard M. Nixon was on hand for the ribbon-cutting ceremony, and guides on the "Walk in Walt's Footsteps" Tour like to tell the story of how Walt whisked Nixon into the train so fast that his Secret Service agents were left behind.

If you're in Disneyland and want to get to Downtown Disney the easy way, the Disneyland Monorail goes from Tomorrowland to the Downtown Disney station. You can get back into the park at the same monorail station, but you must have a valid Disneyland Passport to get on.

Activities and Attractions

Shopping and dining are the main offerings at Downtown Disney. Besides the live entertainment offered at many of the restaurants and the performances on the street, you can also experience the following activities and attractions:

AMC Theatres
✆(714) 769-4AMC
✉*www.amctheatres.com*
To rest your feet after a day at one of the Disney theme parks, or perhaps to fill time during a rainy day or evening, you can catch a movie at the AMC Theatres located near the Disneyland Hotel. Each

of the twelve screens offers state-of-the-art THX sound system and stadium seating.

RAINY DAY FUN

If you're caught in a downpour, you can seek refuge at the ESPN Zone, grab a show at the AMC Movie Theatre, or take the little ones over to the LEGO shop for a bit of play.

ESPN Zone

☎(714) 300-3776

✍*www.espnzone.com*

The popular, sports-oriented cable-television network ESPN offers a theme-dining experience combined with a state-of-the-art sports bar and an arcade sure to please sports fans of all ages.

Located near the main entrance of ESPN Zone is an ESPN Radio studio, where you'll often find live radio broadcasts taking place. The post-football television show *Sports Zone* also broadcasts from the ESPN Zone.

Besides watching the live sports programming that originates from this location, you can also watch almost any live televised sporting event on the dozens of high-definition television screens located throughout the complex. Don't worry if you need to use the restroom during a televised sports event—there are video monitors located in the restrooms, too.

TRAVEL TIP

Throughout Downtown Disney, you must wear a shirt and shoes at all times. California law prohibits smoking inside all stores, dining areas, and restrooms. You may not ride on skateboards, in-line skates, bicycles, and scooters in the public areas of Downtown Disney.

On the second floor, the Sports Arena features dozens of sports-oriented arcade games and interactive activities. As with any arcade, guests pay for each game or activity separately. Game cards (used instead of quarters or tokens) are available in $5 increments. Of course, there's also an ESPN gift shop, where you'll find a wide range of ESPN logo merchandize and other sports-oriented memorabilia.

Exotic Bird Show

Just outside the AMC Theatres and near the Rainforest Café, you'll find a small area where an exotic bird show takes place throughout the day. Not only is this a chance to learn about the colorful birds and see them perform tricks, but having your picture taken with one of the birds makes for an awesome photo opportunity and an inexpensive souvenir. Kids in particular enjoy this interactive show.

House of Blues Stage

✆(714) 781-4560

✍*www.hob.com* or ✍*www.ticketmaster.com*

This popular theme restaurant often features live entertainment in the main dining room, and big-name recording artists perform on the House of Blues Stage, an intimate concert setting. Don't be fooled by the name of this establishment. There's more here than just blues music, including pop, R & B, hip-hop, and rock-and-roll.

Ticket prices for the evening concerts start around $25 for well-known performers. Although tickets can be purchased in advance from Ticketmaster, you can sometimes pick up day-of-show tickets at the House of Blues box office.

Shopping in Downtown Disney

Downtown Disney is made for shopping. You'll find plenty of Disney merchandise as well as a large selection of specialty stores.

You can get a complimentary Downtown Disney map from any Disneyland information kiosk, the Compass Newsstand, or any Disney-owned hotel.

Ann Geddes Shop

☏(714) 533-2663

✐*www.anngeddes.com/stores/disney.aspx*

You'll recognize the signature style of Ann Geddes and her charming photographs of babies right away. In her flagship store, you can buy plush toys, decorative items, diaper bags, baby clothing, and a host of other items bearing her images.

Basin

☏(714) 808-9293

✐*www.basin.com*

Transform your bathroom at home into a lavish spa when you purchase any of the fancy soaps, shampoos, body, and bath products available from this upscale store, or pick up a bath bomb or massage bar to help you relax in your hotel room. The prices aren't cheap, but the products are among the best from around the world, and they make great gifts for friends or loved ones who enjoy pampering themselves.

Build-A-Bear Workshop

☏(714) 776-5980

✐*www.buildabear.com*

It's not just a store. It's a real teddy bear factory where kids (and adults) can create their own teddy bear, watch it getting stuffed, choose an outfit for it, adopt it, and take it home.

Club Libby Lu

☏(714) 772-3793

✐*www.clublibbylu.com*

"It's a girl thing" at this shop made for young princesses, offering enough sparkly, pink, pretty, and precious stuff to set any young woman's heart a-twitter.

Compass Books & Café

📞(714) 502-9999

✉*www.booksinc.net*

If you're looking for a bestseller to read by the pool or want to browse this bookshop's large selection of travel books, step into Compass Books & Café. Modeled after a 1900s-vintage New York Explorer club, Compass is an upscale bookstore that also offers an impressive children's book section. In addition to the latest book releases, the café area serves gourmet coffees and bakery products.

Department 56

📞(714) 772-6828

✉*www.department56.com*

It's Christmas every day at Department 56. You'll find an extensive selection of holiday decorations and collectibles, many miniature Christmas village displays, as well as other holiday-themed decorative items. A visit here will definitely help get you into the Christmas spirit, even if it's mid-July.

Disney Vault 28

✉*www.disneyvault28.com*

This contemporary boutique features designer items with a Disney "edge." Items available include vintage Disney wear as well as exclusive house-label items. They often host trunk shows of clothing and home décor items.

≡FAST FACT

Located near ESPN Zone and the AMC Theatres, you'll find the Compass Newsstand. They carry a wide selection of newspapers and magazines and double as an information booth. This is a great meeting place for family members who get separated when exploring Downtown Disney.

Disney's Pin Traders

✍*www.disneypins.com*

Whether you're an experienced Disney pin trader who wants to swap with fellow collectors, a novice who wants to learn how to get started in pin trading, or simply a tourist who wants to buy a single pin as a souvenir, this kiosk near the Monorail station has everything you need, from starter sets to collector cases.

Fossil

✆(714) 808-1939

✍*www.fossil.com*

You'll find a wide range of watches, sunglasses, leather goods, and more at this store, but if you're looking for a watch featuring one of the Disney characters, you should go to the watch shop on Main Street, U.S.A. instead.

Illuminations

✆(714) 991-4719

✍*www.illuminations.com*

This is the same chain store found in many upscale malls, selling scented candles of all shapes and sizes. In addition, you'll find a wide selection of candleholders and accessories that can help you create a beautiful candlelit ambiance in any setting. After a long day at the theme parks, you can pick up a soothing aromatherapy candle to help you relax in your hotel room.

Island Charters

✆(714) 635-9499

✍*www.islandcharterstore.com*

Adult clothing and accessories with a nautical and aviation theme are offered here. Whether you're looking for casual wear or beachwear, you'll find popular designer labels in this shop, and they carry a nice collection of handmade replica airplanes and boat reproductions.

LEGO Imagination Center

✑www.lego.com

Kids of all ages enjoy exploring this large, colorful store that offers everything related to LEGO building blocks. In addition to life-size LEGO statues of Darth Vader and R2-D2 from *Star Wars* and the sleepy old man on the bench outside, you'll discover that this shop sells every current LEGO set in existence. There are also play areas for young people to build small projects, and the shop sells a wide range of LEGO accessory products and logo merchandise, such as watches and T-shirts. If you're planning a visit to LEGO-LAND in San Diego, you may want to wait and buy your LEGO's by the pound there.

Marceline's Confectionery

Almost any sweet tooth can be satisfied with a visit to this upscale candy store that offers prepackaged candies and gourmet jelly beans, along with homemade treats that you can watch being made, such as caramel apples, fudge, and cookies. This is the perfect place to stop for dessert on-the-go.

═══FAST FACT

Marceline's Confectionery takes its name from Walt Disney's birthplace, Marceline, Missouri, a town of 5,000 people. Disney lived in Marceline for the first ten years of his life, before the family moved to Kansas City.

Quiksilver Boardrider's Club Store

✑www.quiksilver.com

This shop features boys' and young men's sports apparel including trunks, boardshorts, shirts, sweats, caps, accessories, shoes, and more.

Sephora

✆(714) 758-1700

✐*www.sephora.com*

Some of the world's best-known skincare products, cosmetics, fragrances, and soaps (for both men and women) are available at this large store.

JUST FOR PARENTS

If the kids are getting restless in Downtown Disney, you can entertain them by looking for Hidden Mickeys. You'll find the outline of Mickey's head cleverly concealed in the fancy *M* and *C* of Marceline's Confectionery and some cute little blue Mickeys tucked into the corners of the World of Disney's entrance sign.

Something Silver

✆(714) 254-0007, ✐*www.somethingsilver.com*

As the name suggests, this store offers silver jewelry, including bracelets, earrings, necklaces, and charms. The prices are reasonable and their selection is large.

Starabilias

✆(714) 284-1055, ✐*www.starabilias.com*

Located across from the Rainforest Café, this unusual shop gives you a chance to take home valuable pieces of pop culture and history. Whether you consider yourself a collector or you just like to gawk, Starabilias is fun for adults and teens to explore. You'll find genuine items, such as an antique Coca-Cola vending machine ($8,995), a 1930s Texaco gas pump ($10,000), or a Ty Cobb autographed baseball bat ($10,000), along with autographed memorabilia from politicians, recording artists, Hollywood's superstars, and historical figures. The inventory changes regularly, and if your budget is more modest, you'll find a selection of inexpensive toys and collectibles.

☰FAST FACT

If you're staying at a Disney-owned hotel, you can arrange to have your purchases delivered to your hotel room, so you don't need to carry them around with you.

Sunglass Icon

If you forgot your sunglasses, lost them on a roller coaster, or are shopping for a more stylish pair, you'll find a large selection of designer sunglasses for men, women, and children at Sunglass Icon.

World of Disney

This block-long store offers the world's second-largest collection of Disney clothing, jewelry, household items, toys, collectibles, artwork, sporting goods, plush toys, Disney movie merchandise, costumes, and many other items featuring Mickey, Minnie, and all of the other Disney characters.

Like a regular department store, World of Disney is divided into sections, each featuring its own type of Disney-themed merchandise. For example, there's a separate men's, women's, and children's clothing section, a toy department, and an area where household merchandise is showcased. They also carry some collector-quality items.

Besides all the Disney items on sale, this store is full of cute and imaginative decorations. Don't forget to look up and all around to see them.

▮ TRAVEL TIP

If you're looking for nice Disney collector's items, don't stop with the World of Disney. Look for some of the small carts selling collector's items in Downtown Disney, especially the one offering crystal-studded statues near the Monorail station. Be sure to stop by the collector's shops on Main Street, U.S.A. and in California Adventure's Animation Studio.

Kiosks

Throughout Downtown Disney, you'll find kiosk carts selling a wide range of products and souvenirs. One of the most popular offers hair wraps, colored threads interwoven with beads and hair to create simple or complex designs and styles. Hair wraps are a favorite among kids and teens.

Downtown Disney Dining

Downtown Disney is loaded with exciting places to eat, whether you're looking for an expensive sit-down dinner, a light lunch, or a quick late-night snack. Many of the restaurants are open for breakfast, lunch, and dinner, and most offer a special children's menu. However, restaurants with a club atmosphere (that offer full bars), such as House of Blues aren't necessarily suitable for young children in the evening.

Some of the restaurants at Downtown Disney could be considered theme-dining experiences, and consequently, you'll pay a premium to experience the atmosphere.

 TRAVEL TIP

If you're a Disneyland Annual Pass Holder, you can save 10 percent when you dine at many of the participating restaurants in Downtown Disney.

Options for a quick snack at Downtown Disney include Haagen-Dazs ice cream, Jamba Juice fruit smoothies, and Wetzel's Pretzels.

To help you find a restaurant that fits your dining budget, the following symbols describe the price range of an average meal: appetizer, entrée, and dessert (but no alcoholic drinks).

$:	Under $10 per person
$$:	Under $20 per person
$$$:	Over $20 per person

Catal Restaurant & Uva Bar, $$$ and $$ (respectively)

✆(714) 774-4442

✑www.patinagroup.com/catal

You'll find two separate places to eat here, both sharing the same kitchen. The restaurant offers indoor seating and an outdoor patio that's a great place to watch the fireworks, while the bar offers outdoor seating on the ground level, allowing you to enjoy the ambiance of Downtown Disney and get in a little people-watching. The menu features Mediterranean dishes, as well as burgers and salads. Some of the house specialties include Greek chicken and lemon kabobs, North African steamed mussels, and Moroccan tuna skewers. A variety of vegetarian entrées are also available.

Compass Books & Café, $

✆(714) 502-9999

✑www.booksinc.net

This bookstore and coffee shop combination offers a selection of freshly brewed gourmet coffees and teas, plus an assortment of snacks. A limited amount of outdoor seating is available. While this is a great place for adults to take a breather and enjoy a cup of java, you won't find too many menu selections suitable for children.

ESPN Zone Restaurant, $$/$$$

✆(714) 300-3776

✑www.espnzone.com/anaheim

The perfect dining experience for sports fans of all ages, this 35,000-square-foot complex includes a full-service restaurant and a state-of-the-art sports bar (adults only). The restaurant offers a family dining experience with main entrées including cedar plank salmon, grilled chops, and New York strip steak. As you enjoy your lunch or dinner, or watch your favorite college team play while you eat your weekend breakfast, you might catch a live broadcast from the television studio located in the main dining room.

House of Blues Restaurant, $$/$$$

✆(714) 778-BLUE

✐*www.hob.com*

Besides offering live musical entertainment at the House of Blues Stage, this establishment features a full-service restaurant. Since this is a popular, family-oriented restaurant, you'll probably want to make lunch or dinner reservations, or be prepared to wait for a table. A full menu including vegetarian dishes and a children's menu is served daily. House specialties include Memphis-style ribs, salmon with watercress-jicama salad, and pan-seared Voodoo shrimp. On Sundays, the House of Blues serves a Gospel Brunch buffet with a side order of inspiring musical performances.

La Brea Bakery Café, $/$$/$$$

✆(714) 490-0233

✐*www.labreabakery.com*

A branch of a longtime Los Angeles favorite founded by chef Nancy Silverton, the La Brea Bakery Café is really two dining establishments in one. You can get a quick snack to enjoy while on the go or sitting outside, or head for the more formal dining area for indoor and outdoor seating and a full menu that includes freshly baked breads and pastries, gourmet coffee drinks, sandwiches, and full entrées. Roasted chicken with crushed potatoes and bitter greens is a specialty.

Naples Ristorante e Pizzeria, $$/$$$

✆(714) 776-6200

Gourmet pizza made from the freshest available ingredients and baked in old-style wood-burning ovens is the mainstay at this family-oriented restaurant that serves lunch, dinner, and late-night snacks. Their menu also includes an assortment of Italian entrées.

Next door, you'll find Napolini, the restaurant's pizza-by-the-slice, quick-service option.

 ## TRAVEL TIP

When the Disneyland Resort is crowded—during the peak vacation times, for example—make lunch or dinner reservations at any of the more formal or theme-oriented restaurants within Downtown Disney to avoid long waits. You can make dinner reservations at any Downtown Disney restaurants (except the Rainforest Café) by calling ✆(714) 781-3463 up to sixty days in advance.

Rainforest Café, $$/$$$
✆(714) 772-0413
🖱*www.rainforestcafe.com*

This location of the popular chain of award-winning theme restaurants offers a theme-dining experience, complete with animals, lush trees, waterfalls, large saltwater fish tanks, and even an indoor lightning and rainstorm that starts the robotic elephants trumpeting and the gorillas beating their chests.

Rainforest Café is one of the most popular family-oriented dining destinations in Downtown Disney, in part because of its awesome atmosphere, but also because of its extensive menu, which boasts more than 100 items. The restaurant is open for breakfast, lunch, and dinner. Sandwiches, burgers, soups, salads, steaks, chicken dishes, and vegetarian dishes are available.

When it comes to dessert, the house specialty is the Volcano, a chocolate fudge brownie topped with vanilla ice cream and with so much caramel and hot fudge poured on top that it runs down the sides, making the whole confection look like an erupting volcano. This huge dessert is delicious and big enough for two (or more) people.

As with any theme-dining experience, be prepared to exit the dining room through a gift shop that offers a selection of toys and gifts, all with a rain forest and wildlife theme.

Ralph Brennan's Jazz Kitchen, $$/$$$

✆(714) 776-5200

✐*www.rbjazzkitchen.com*

Ralph Brennan's brings a little Bourbon Street atmosphere to Anaheim, and if you're a jazz music fan or enjoy fine Louisiana cuisine, this is the place to stop for lunch, dinner, or a late-night snack. Specialties here include Gumbo Ya-Ya, blackened chicken, and shrimp Creole, served while you enjoy live music.

In the morning, the Jazz Kitchen Express next door serves chicory coffee and beignets (New Orleans–style donuts drenched in powdered sugar), and all day long, you can pick up a quick bowl of gumbo or jambalaya and a little bread pudding for dessert.

Tortilla Jo's, $$/$$$

✆(714) 535-5000

✐*www.patinagroup.com/tortillajos*

This casual Mexican restaurant belongs to the same parent group as nearby Catal. Menu items include the expected burritos and tacos, along with tortas (Mexican sandwiches) and main dishes such as Arroz con Pollo, Carne Machaca, Carnitas, and Chile Verde. The outdoor seating area overlooks Downtown Disney, and their drink menu includes over 100 kinds of tequila. The convenient taqueria offers authentic cinnamon-sugar churros (delicious Mexican-style doughnuts) and warm Mexican chocolate.

Guest Services

All of the usual amenities, including pay telephones, restrooms, and ATM machines can be found throughout Downtown Disney. The Walt Disney Travel Company (the travel agency owned and operated by the Walt Disney Company) has an office in this area to assist guests in making (or changing) their travel arrangements.

≡ FAST FACT

In Downtown Disney, the First Aid center is located between Ralph Brennan's Jazz Kitchen and Island Charters clothing store.

For international travelers, the Travelex Currency Exchange is located around the corner from the AMC Theatres and Compass Books & Café.

For additional information about the guest services available in Downtown Disney, visit the information kiosks near the main east and west entrances.

CHAPTER 15

Beyond Disneyland: Exploring the Rest of Anaheim

IN ADDITION TO ITS world-famous theme parks, Anaheim is also the home of theaters, shopping centers, museums, sports and recreation facilities, an ice-skating rink, hundreds of restaurants, and other tourist attractions. This chapter details some of the best family-oriented attractions located in the Anaheim area, including nearby Buena Park.

An Overview of Anaheim

For more than fifty years, Anaheim has been a popular vacation, convention, and tourist destination, thanks mainly to the Disneyland Resort and the other theme parks and attractions.

Located about twenty-eight miles southwest of downtown Los Angeles and ninety miles from San Diego, Anaheim is the second-largest city in Orange County. The year-round tourist traffic, however, makes it seem bigger than it is.

Before becoming a tourist destination, Anaheim was California's wine capital. In the late 1880s, blight wiped out all the vineyards, shutting down the area's wine industry forever. After that, Anaheim became an orange-growing center and thrived as an agricultural community until just after World War II.

For information about special events happening in Anaheim during your visit, go to the Anaheim Orange County Visitor and

Convention Bureau Web site at *www.anaheimoc.org* or call them at (714) 765-8888.

Knott's Southern California Resort and Soak City

✉8039 Beach Boulevard, Buena Park

✆(714) 220-5200

✐*www.knotts.com*

Not quite in Anaheim proper, but close enough in adjacent Buena Park, Knott's Southern California Resort is just ten minutes' drive away from the Disneyland Resort. The Knott's complex includes Knott's Berry Farm theme park, Knott's Soak City water park, a shopping area, and the nearby Radisson Resort hotel.

In 1920, decades before Walt Disney founded Disneyland in Anaheim, the Knott family moved to Buena Park and started a twenty-acre farm on rented land. Within eight years, the family built Cordelia Knott's tearoom, established a berry farm, and opened a plant nursery, enabling them to purchase ten acres of the land they previously rented.

In 1932, Walter Knott began growing a new type of berry, a cross between a red raspberry, a blackberry, and a loganberry that he called a "boysenberry." In 1934, to help support the family during the Depression, Cordelia Knott started serving chicken dinners in her tearoom. A few years later, the couple opened a full-service restaurant.

Over the years that followed, the family opened a souvenir shop and saloon near their restaurant as guests came from all over to taste Cordelia's famous chicken and her delicious pies.

For the Knott family, it was a good idea that just kept growing. In 1952, they purchased a narrow-gauge railroad and built tracks for the train to run around the farm. In 1955, Cordelia and Walter attended the grand opening of Disneyland, where they got the idea to transform their property into a theme park. By 1968, the park contained several rides and began charging an admission fee. Since then, Knott's Berry Farm has grown into a full-size theme park for the entire family.

Cordelia died in 1974 at the age of eighty-four; Walter followed in 1981, just shy of his ninety-second birthday, leaving a legacy for people of all ages to enjoy. In 1997, Ohio-based Cedar Fair, L.P., the company that runs Ohio's Cedar Point amusement park, acquired Knott's Berry Farm.

At the turn of the twenty-first century, Cedar Fair added the Knott's Hotel nearby to encourage out-of-towners to make longer visits. Their package deals include theme park tickets, free meals, and parking. These packages might turn out to be a good bargain if you want to visit the park anyway. (866) 752-2444, (714) 995-1111, *www .knottshotel.com.*

Knott's Berry Farm Theme Park

Knott's Berry Farm theme park is open every day (except Christmas). Call (714) 220-5200 or visit the Web site at *www.knotts.com* to get the hours during your visit. You can find the ticket prices for this park in Chapter 6.

Knott's Berry Farm theme park falls between the mostly gentle adventures at the Disney parks and the roller coaster–oriented buzz of Six Flags Magic Mountain. There's also a large kids-only area (offering more than twenty rides for young people) and a slew of family-oriented attractions and shows suitable for the entire family.

 JUST FOR PARENTS

Many of the thrill rides at Knott's have height or weight restrictions, making them off-limits for smaller children. To avoid disappointment and potential tearful scenes, measure your youngsters before you leave home and go over the restrictions listed here with them.

While Knott's Berry Farm is known for its rides, it also offers a wide range of theme-oriented shops, dining options, shows, and activities for people of all ages. Throughout the park, you'll see artisans and craftspeople such as woodcarvers, glassblowers, candle makers, blacksmiths, gemologists, and silversmiths showcasing their skills and creations and giving live demonstrations. These demonstrations are both informative and entertaining, especially for adults.

Weather at Knott's will be the same as at nearby Disneyland. You can get some tips on theme park attire in Chapter 2, but if you're going to the Soak City water park, be sure to bring dry clothing and towels.

As soon as you arrive, pick up a free copy of the Knott's Berry Farm map. It's available at all the ticket counters, at Guest Relations, and at many of the shops. Also pick up a separate show schedule.

TRAVEL TIP

Get acquainted with the park's layout and choose a place to meet in case your group splits up. The fountain near the Grand Entrance area of the park is an easy-to-find, central meeting location.

To get a bird's-eye view of Knott's, go directly to the Sky Cabin ride. This family-oriented attraction will take you on a three-minute flight up one of the tallest towers in the park. You'll ride in an enclosed cabin that rotates slowly, giving you an excellent view of the entire park.

Knott's Berry Farm is divided into several unique themed areas, including Ghost Town, Indian Trails, Camp Snoopy (the kids' area), Fiesta Village, the Boardwalk, and Wild Water Wilderness. Each area offers its own set of rides, attractions, shops, dining options, and unique things to see and do.

FAST FACT

Knott's Berry Farm's areas interconnect. The park has a large oval shape. Within the park, however, you'll find many paths to follow and out-of-the-way places to explore. If you're visiting this theme park for the overall experience, be sure to take some time to explore these paths and exhibits.

Camp Snoopy

Camp Snoopy is the kids' section of Knott's Berry Farm, where Snoopy, Good Ol' Charlie Brown, and other characters from the Charles Schulz *Peanuts* comic strip are the mascots. Actually a theme park within a theme park, Camp Snoopy offers more than twenty rides for younger people, including some scaled-down versions of the faster rides found elsewhere in the park. One of the popular attractions in the six-acre Camp Snoopy area is a petting zoo.

 TRAVEL TIP

This is where you're most likely to find Snoopy and friends meeting and greeting guests, so have your camera ready.

Rides in Camp Snoopy include the following:

- **Camp Bus:** A spinning ride in vehicles that bring to mind a yellow school bus. Guests must be able to stand up by themselves; if they're less than 42 inches tall, they must ride with a responsible person.
- **Charlie Brown Speedway:** Drive scaled-down stock cars on a pint-size track. Guests must be at least 42 inches tall to ride

alone. Anyone over 54 inches tall must be accompanied by someone less than 42 inches tall.

- **Flying Ace Balloon Race:** Fly in a sturdy gondola beneath a colorful balloon. Guests less than 36 inches tall must ride with a responsible person.
- **Grand Sierra Scenic Railroad:** A gentle, quarter-mile train ride. Anyone shorter than 46 inches tall must ride with a responsible person.
- **High Sierra Ferris Wheel:** A classic Ferris wheel. Riders must be at least 36 inches tall; if they're less than 48 inches tall, they must ride with a responsible person. Children may not ride in an adult's lap.
- **Huff and Puff:** This ride for the younger set is self-propelled, and all riders must be less than 52 inches tall.
- **Joe Cool's GR8 SK8:** Riders must be between 36 and 80 inches tall.
- **Log Peeler:** This is a mini-scrambler ride. Riders must be between 32 and 48 inches tall.
- **Lucy's Tugboat:** Children under 42 inches tall must be accompanied by a responsible person. Taller kids can ride alone.
- **Red Baron:** A simple flying ride with Snoopy as the World War I Flying Ace. Riders must be between 32 and 54 inches tall.
- **Rocky Road Truckin' Company:** Drive a mini-eighteen-wheeler. Guests must be able to sit up by themselves; if they're less than 42 inches tall, they must ride with a responsible person.
- **Snoopy Bounce:** Riders must be under 54 inches tall and able to stand on their own.
- **Timberline Twister:** A not-very-scary roller coaster. Riders must be between 36 and 69 inches tall.
- **Woodstock's Airmail:** If the littler folks are pestering you to let them go on Supreme Scream, this version of the ride is just their size. Riders must be at least 36 inches tall.

Ghost Town

The Ghost Town area uses an Old West theme, styled after an 1880s California Gold Rush town. Rides here include the following:

- **Butterfield Stagecoach:** Climb aboard a classic horse-drawn stagecoach for a ride around the perimeter of Ghost Town. This is a slow-paced ride, but one that's enjoyable for the entire family. A responsible person must accompany any guest who is less than 46 inches tall.
- **Calico Mine Ride:** This train ride takes guests through the depths of a gold mine. This somewhat fast-paced journey could be considered a mild thrill ride. It's suitable for people over the age of ten, but if they're less than 46 inches tall, they'll have to bring along a responsible person.
- **Calico Railroad:** Take a leisurely train ride around the perimeter of the theme park on a narrow-gauge steam train. A responsible person must accompany any guest who is less than 46 inches tall.
- **GhostRider:** One of the world's best-known wooden roller coasters and the largest project in Knott's seventy-eight-year history when it was built, GhostRider is a double out-and-back coaster that rises 118 feet above the Ghost Town area and is the largest ride in the entire park. It follows 4,533 feet of twisting track that includes a 108-foot initial drop, followed by thirteen additional drops, sudden dips, twists, and banked turns. It's a must for coaster fans, but they must be at least 48 inches tall. Expect long waits at this popular ride.
- **Screamin' Swing:** This air-powered pendulum swing ride sends riders into the air at 60 miles per hour and pulls 3.5 Gs. Guests must be over 48 inches tall.
- **Silver Bullet:** A steel-tracked, boomerang roller coaster with a zero-G roll, two corkscrews, and six inversions, the Silver Bullet offers a smooth ride, and some people say it feels like you're flying. You must be taller than 54 inches to ride.

- **Timber Mountain Log Ride:** This water-based log ride follows a simulated 2,100-foot river. Much of this ride is experienced in the dark as you travel between 8 and 10 feet per second toward a huge splash (and a large drop) at the end. Chances are you'll get wet, so be prepared. A responsible person must accompany any guest who is less than 46 inches tall.

Shows in the Ghost Town include Knott's Wild West Stunt Show, a family-oriented, comical stunt show presented in an outdoor amphitheater several times daily (weather permitting) and musical performances in the Calico Saloon. You may also see just-for-fun gunfights on the street.

RAINY DAY FUN

Almost everything at Knott's is in the open, and even if they decide to stay open during the rain, this is not the place you want to be. California's rainy season is winter. If you're going to Southern California then, check out the other Anaheim attractions that follow as well as those in the rest of Orange County (see Chapter 16) to decide what you might do in case of a downpour.

Fiesta Village

Fiesta Village is one of the larger areas of Knott's Berry Farm. Here, you'll find the greatest collection of rides (most of which are thrill rides), suitable for teens and adults. Here are some of the highlights in this area:

- **Dragon Swing:** Climb aboard a giant pirate ship that rocks back and forth, traveling high into the air. Guests must be at least 42 inches tall to ride, and a responsible person must accompany anyone who is less than 48 inches tall.

- **Hat Dance:** This spinning ride can best be compared to Disneyland's Mad Tea Party. In this case, however, passengers sit inside colorful, oversize sombreros. Guests must be at least 36 inches tall to ride, and a responsible person must accompany anyone who is less than 42 inches tall.
- **Jaguar!** This medium-thrill coaster takes riders through, around, and above the ancient Temple of the Jaguar. This kid-oriented coaster is suitable for young people (over the age of eight). It's far less scary and less turbulent than a full-size coaster. Guests must be at least 48 inches tall to ride.
- **La Revolucion:** This dizzying ride combines a swinging ship-type ride with a spinning vehicle. You'll be lucky to know which way is up. Guests must be at least 48 inches tall to ride.
- **Merry Go Round:** This classic carousel is more than 100 years old and features forty-eight hand-carved wooden animals, including lions, tigers, camels, zebras, and horses. Riders under 46 inches tall must bring a responsible person with them.
- **Montezooma's Revenge:** This high-tech coaster shoots riders through a giant (seven-story) loop, up an incline, and then screams back the way it came. You go from full stop to 55 miles per hour in less than three seconds. Guests must be taller than 48 inches to ride.
- **WaveSwinger:** In a single-person swing, you rise into the air and then fly around in circles, relatively quickly. WaveSwinger is a classic amusement park ride offering a moderate thrill (in terms of the rapid spinning). Guests must be taller than 48 inches, over 6 years old, and weigh less than 230 pounds.

Entertainment in Fiesta Village includes mariachi bands and arcade games.

JUST FOR PARENTS

If your children are too young or too small to experience the thrill rides, the Parent Swap program allows one adult to stay behind (near the exit of a thrill ride) with the kids, while the other adults in their party enjoy the ride. As soon as the first riders come back, the adult who stayed behind with the kids can enter the ride without waiting in line.

The Boardwalk

The Boardwalk offers a wide selection of carnival-style games of skill, with prizes to win, but there's an additional fee of $1 or $2 per game to play. This area features a handful of thrill rides:

- **Boomerang:** This roller coaster was developed in Europe and is one of the most popular thrill rides in the park, so be prepared for a wait. You're strapped into the coaster's train (two people per row), and then in just under two minutes, you'll fly around a 360-degree loop forward, then reverse direction, and ride around in reverse. One minute of this ride is a slow lift, which greatly builds anticipation for the big drop, loop, and corkscrew. The ride is somewhat rough. Guests must be at least 48 inches tall.

- **Perilous Plunge:** Perilous Plunge isn't your typical water-flume ride. In reality, it's just 34 feet shorter than the real-life Niagara Falls waterfall. This ride takes you in a boat-like vehicle 127 feet into the air and then drops you at a 75-degree angle, going 50 miles per hour. The result is a big splash at the bottom. Plan on getting wet! Guests must be at least 48 inches tall.

- **Rip Tide:** This ride sends you 50 feet in the air while turning you head over heels in two directions at the same time. Riders must be between 54 and 76 inches tall and over ten years old.

- **Sky Cabin:** For the ultimate view of the entire park, enjoy this slow-moving journey up one of the park's tallest towers as the totally enclosed cabin spins slowly. The entire journey lasts about three minutes.
- **Supreme Scream:** A freefall-style ride, the Supreme Scream takes you 254 feet straight up and then drops you straight down. During the three-second drop, you travel at 50 miles per hour, but you're not done when you reach the bottom. Instead, you rebound for several more flights up and down, each one a little smaller than the last until it stops. All this happens in just forty-five seconds. The ride's three towers are the tallest structures in Orange County at 325 feet tall. Guests must be at least 52 inches tall.
- **Wheeler Dealer Bumper Cars:** Wheeler Dealer Bumper Cars offers classic bumper car excitement. One adult rides per car. A child can accompany an adult, but space will be tight. Guests must be at least 48 inches tall to ride alone or between 42 inches and 47 inches to ride with an adult.
- **Wipeout:** This flat ride makes up for its lack of ups and downs with lots of turns. Guests must be taller than 48 inches to ride.
- **Xcelerator:** Vehicles on this hydraulically launched coaster are based on the popular 1957 Chevy, and you go from 0 to 82 miles per hour in just 2.3 seconds before making a vertical, twisting drop from a 205-foot tall peak. You'll be glad it all lasts only sixty-two seconds. Riders must be over 52 inches tall.

Entertainment on the Boardwalk includes the Charles M. Schulz Theatre, showing a Broadway-style musical ice show starring Snoopy, the *Peanuts* characters, and a handful of human singers and dancers, all dressed in colorful costumes. For an extra fee, you can also enjoy Laser Invaders, an interactive attraction featuring laser-tag combat. This is a favorite among preteen boys in particular.

Wild Water Wilderness

Wild Water Wilderness houses two major rides, one of which has little to do with water.

- **Bigfoot Rapids:** This whitewater river ride takes six riders at a time in circular rafts that spin as they proceed along the somewhat turbulent river and over small waterfalls. You're going to get wet on this ride, but it's not at all scary. Make sure your belongings are secured so they remain dry. Guests must be at least 46 inches tall.
- **Wilderness Scrambler:** A flat rotating ride, formerly known as Headspin. Guests must be at least 48 inches tall to ride alone or between 42 inches and 48 inches to ride with a responsible adult.

Also in Wild Water Wilderness are Mystery Lodge, a high-tech tribute to Native American culture; and Ranger Station, where young guests can get a close look at spiders, insects, and other creatures and check out sightings of Sasquatch (aka Bigfoot) in the California High Sierras. This is a self-paced, walk-through attraction, but "rangers" are on-hand to answer questions.

═FAST FACT

Located near Reflection Lake is the Church of Reflection, an old church (historic landmark) that is still used by guests as a memorable place to exchange marriage vows. Contact Guest Relations for details.

Indian Trails

Indian Trails showcases the Native American civilizations of the Pacific Northwest, the Great Plains, the Southwest, and the West. Here you'll find handcrafted totem poles, authentic architecture, and a wide range of crafts and other artifacts on display. Indian Trails is a wonderful place to explore during the day or evening to walk off Mrs. Knott's fried chicken and berry pie before returning to the thrill rides. The area will be of particular interest to adults.

Throughout the year, Knott's Berry Farm hosts a wide range of special events, many of which are based on holidays. They include Knott's Christmas Crafts Village, an annual Spring Crafts festival, special summer shows, and activities for kids.

One of the biggest events of the year is Knott's Scary Farm, one of the oldest theme park Halloween events, featuring scary mazes, stage shows, and plenty of gruesome, simulated gore. This interactive haunted theme park experience is great for older kids, teens, and adults. It may be too scary for the little ones, who will be better off visiting Camp Snoopy, which becomes Camp Spooky to celebrate the Halloween season. This popular event often sells out in advance, and tickets cost quite a bit more than normal admission.

Around Christmas, the haunts go away as Knott's becomes Knott's Merry Farm, featuring an arts-and-crafts village, plenty of twinkling lights, and the Mountain Log Ride transformed into a visit with Santa's elves.

Knott's Soak City

Located next to Knott's Berry Farm is Knott's Soak City, a water-based theme park with a separate admission charge offering more than twenty-one water rides and attractions with a 1950s California theme. This park is more suitable for teens and adults, but there are a few kid-oriented rides.

Soak City is a good place to go on a hot day, with a wide range of water slides, a 750,000-gallon wave pool, a special children's pool, and a family funhouse.

Knott's Soak City opens daily between late May and early September and on weekends only through late September. The remainder of the year, the water park is closed. Hours of operation vary. You can find the ticket prices for this water park in Chapter 6.

Knott's California Marketplace

Rounding out the Knott's Southern California Resort complex is a small shopping and dining area called the California Marketplace. Here you'll find Mrs. Knott's Chicken Dinner Restaurant, which serves the fried chicken and pies that made the Knott name famous throughout Southern California. There's also an ice-cream parlor, a fast-food Mexican restaurant, the Farm Bakery, a candy store, and the Berry Market, which sells the Knott's fruit preserves and other gourmet foods. No admission is required to visit this area, and the first three hours of parking are free.

 TRAVEL TIP

If you're planning to dine at Mrs. Knott's Chicken Dinner Restaurant, be prepared for a wait. Locals and tourists like this place, and during peak mealtimes, you can easily wait an hour or longer to be seated.

You'll also find a handful of souvenir, clothing, and other shops within the California Marketplace, including Snoopy Headquarters, which offers toys, clothing, and other souvenirs—all featuring the *Peanuts* comic strip characters.

Getting to the Knott's Resort

From the I-5, I-405, 91, or 22 freeways, take the Beach Boulevard exit in Buena Park and follow the signs to the park's main entrance. The drive between Knott's Southern California Resort and the Disneyland Resort takes about ten minutes, and some non-Disney hotels in Anaheim offer shuttle service to Knott's.

Plenty of parking is available at the resort.

See Chapter 2 for information about how to get to the Anaheim area. Disneyland Resort Express Bus (*www.airportbus.com*, (714) 938-8900) provides shuttle service directly to Knott's from the Orange County Airport.

Other Anaheim Tourist Attractions

In addition to Disneyland, Disney's California Adventure, and Knott's Berry Farm, Anaheim has a lot to offer a traveling family. Here's a sampling of the activities you can enjoy outside of the well-known theme parks:

Adventure City

⊠1238 S. Beach Blvd. between Ball and Cerritos, Anaheim

✆(714) 236-9300

✍*www.adventurecity.com*

Designed especially for kids between the ages of two and twelve, this outdoor, two-acre theme park offers eleven rides and attractions, a snack shop, game area, and some live entertainment. Hours vary by season. Admission is $12.95 for kids and adults, $9.95 for seniors.

 TRAVEL TIP

To receive a free copy of the Official Visitors Guide for Anaheim/Orange County, call ✆(888) 598-3200 or go to ✍*www.anaheimoc.org*.

Anaheim ICE

⊠300 W. Lincoln Ave., Anaheim

✆(714) 535-7465

✍*www.anaheimice.com*

The training facility for the Anaheim Ducks hockey team offers public skating sessions and pickup hockey games.

Anaheim Museum

⊠241 S. Anaheim Blvd., Anaheim

✆(714) 778-3301

✍*www.anaheimmuseum.com*

This museum showcases the history of Anaheim, starting with the German settlers. It will reopen in late 2007 after an extensive renovation.

Flight Deck Air Combat Center
✉1601 S. Sunkist Ave., Hangar A, Anaheim
✆(714) 937-1511
✐*www.flightdeck1.com*

If you haven't gotten enough of flying around on the theme park rides, this place puts you behind the controls of a high-performance military flight simulator. Live instrumentation and full-immersion audio give the feel of an F-18 Hornet going 450 miles per hour a hundred feet off the deck.

Hobby City Doll & Toy Museum
✉1238 S. Beach Blvd., Anaheim
✆(714) 527-2323

On display are more than 5,000 dolls and toys from around the world, including more than 500 Barbie dolls and a half-scale replica of the White House.

Shopping

No matter what you're looking to purchase or what the weather is like, you'll find plenty of malls and shopping centers to explore in the Anaheim area.

Anaheim GardenWalk
✉321 W. Katella, Anaheim
✐*www.anaheimgardenwalk.com*

The first section of this new shopping and entertainment complex near the Disneyland Resort—restaurants along Katella Avenue—will open in late 2007. The rest, including lush gardens and more shopping and dining opportunities, should be done by spring 2008.

Anaheim Indoor Marketplace
✉1440 S. Anaheim Blvd., Anaheim
✆(714) 999-0888, ✆(800) 479-7927
✐*www.anaheimindoormarketplace.com*

This indoor outlet mall/swap meet contains more than 200 shops offering mostly brand-name merchandise at discounts typically ranging 50 to 70 percent below retail. The marketplace is open daily except Tuesdays and is less than a mile from the Disneyland Resort. A free shuttle bus is available by calling ✆(800) 479-7927.

Disney Character Warehouse Outlet

✉243 Orangefair Mall, Fullerton

✆(714) 870-9363

Run by Asset Management & Sales Company, this outlet store sells Disney's excess inventory at up to 80 percent off original prices. To get there from Disneyland, drive north on Harbor Boulevard across Highway 91. Turn right on Orangethorpe and right again on Pomona, which will take you into the shopping center. To save even more, go to the Anaheim–Orange County Visitor and Convention Bureau Web site *www.anaheimoc.org* and search for "Disney character warehouse" to find a 10 percent off, print-at-home discount coupon.

Downtown Disney

Located in the Disneyland Resort, Downtown Disney offers a collection of upscale shops and boutiques, including the Build-A-Bear Workshop, the block-long World of Disney, Christmas-oriented Department 56, and Disney Vault 28. Check out Chapter 14 for details about this unique shopping and family entertainment complex.

Dining

Downtown Disney and Anaheim GardenWalk offer lots of dining options, including Catal Restaurant, Ralph Brennan's Jazz Kitchen, La Brea Bakery, Naples Ristorante e Pizzeria, Rainforest Café, and Tortilla Jo's. Read more about them in Chapter 14.

Each of the Disney hotels offers a restaurant or two, and inside-the-theme-park favorites include Blue Bayou and California Adventure's Golden Vine, which are described in Chapters 8 and 11.

For some down-home, old-fashioned vittles, there's Mrs. Knott's Chicken Dinner Restaurant at Knott's California Marketplace, and you can get a helping of entertainment with your meal at Joey and Maria's Comedy Wedding, Medieval Times, or the Pirates' Dinner Adventure dinner shows.

If you're looking for a nice, quiet dinner after a hectic day at the park, try the place many locals go for a special or romantic occasion: Anaheim White House, (887 S. Anaheim Blvd., (714) 772-1381, *www .anaheimwhitehouse.com*) serving Northern Italian recipes in a beautifully converted 1909 house. Another local favorite, Mr. Stox (1105 E. Katella Ave., (714) 634-2994, *www.mrstox.com*) serves dishes such as Maryland crab cakes, osso buco, prime rib, and salmon in a pretty dining room.

For a livelier atmosphere, the chefs at Benihana Anaheim (2100 E. Ball Road, (714) 774-4940, *www.benihana.com*) put on a show while cooking your food tableside. J. T. Schmid's Restaurant and Brewery (2610 E. Katella Ave., (714) 634-9200, *www.jtschmids.com*) serves gourmet microbrewed beers, steaks, pasta, pizza, and salads.

The California Country Café (1221 E. Katella Ave., (714) 978-8088) and Original Pancake House (1418 E. Lincoln Ave., (714) 535-9815, *www.originalpancakehouse.com*) get high marks among locals for their family-friendly fare.

Evening Entertainment

Besides the usual dinner and a movie, Anaheim offers some long-running dinner theater performances and concerts.

Joey & Maria's Comedy Italian Wedding
✉Anaheim Plaza Hotel, 1700 S. Harbor Blvd., Anaheim
✆(800) 944-5639
✐*www.comedywedding.com*
Everything is larger than life in this dinner comedy show, which is suitable primarily for teens and adults. The Gnocchi and Cavatelli families gather to celebrate a wedding, but neither side is very happy

with the newlyweds' choice of mates. A cast of family members and guests (all named after some kind of pasta) keep things teetering on the brink of disaster. As you eat dinner, you're one of the guests at this elaborate affair.

The Grove of Anaheim

✉2200 E. Katella Ave., Anaheim

☎(714) 712-2700

✎www.thegroveofanaheim.com

This indoor entertainment venue features artists of all kinds, from Chicago and Dinosaur Jr. to Willie Nelson.

Medieval Times Dinner & Tournament

✉7662 Beach Blvd., Buena Park

☎(714) 521-4740

☎(800) 899-6600

✎www.medievaltimes.com

Inside this giant castle just ten minutes' drive from Disneyland, you and your family can step back in time and enjoy a meal while knights in armor participate in an eleventh-century jousting tournament right before your eyes. While the show is highly entertaining and exciting, the "eat with your hands only" food (which includes a bowl of vegetable soup) is just so-so. If anyone in your party is celebrating a birthday, ask to have the king bestow his blessings.

Pirate's Dinner Adventure

✉7600 Beach Blvd., Buena Park

☎(714) 690-1497, ☎(866) 439-2469

✎www.piratesdinneradventure.com

This dinner show features special effects and swashbuckling swordplay around an 18-foot-wide replica of a Spanish galleon anchored in a 250,000-gallon indoor lagoon. All of the action happens while you're enjoying an appetizer buffet and dinner. Like Medieval Times, the food is not as exciting as the show, but at least you'll get silverware here.

Sporting Events

Anaheim is home to the Anaheim Angels professional baseball team and the Anaheim Ducks ice hockey team. If you'd like to see a game, go to *www.angels.mlb.com* or *www.mightyducks.com* for a schedule. You can also buy tickets online through Ticketmaster at *www.ticket master.com/artist/805893* for the Anaheim Ducks or *www.ticketmas ter.com/artist/805892* for the Anaheim Angels.

 **TRAVEL TIP**

You can watch the USA Men's Volleyball Team practice during the week at the American Sports Centers—the largest indoor sports complex in the world. ✉1500 South Anaheim Blvd., Anaheim, *www.americansportscenters.com*.

If you'd rather watch basketballs going through hoops than base-balls or pucks flying, Anaheim's NBA Development League team, the Anaheim Arsenal (*www.nba.com/dleague/anaheim/*) plays at the Anaheim Convention Center.

CHAPTER 16

Orange County: The Real "O.C."

THANKS TO A STRING of television shows set in Orange County including the recent *Laguna Beach* and *The O.C.*, everyone thinks of sun, sand, and surf when you say "Orange County." These cliché characteristics are magnified on the screen, but in large part true. Beyond that cinematic illusion lies the real O. C., a place of pleasures that range from the simple—running barefoot on the beach and eating a dripping, creamy Balboa Bar on a hot day—to the world-class luxury of Dana Point's St. Regis Resort.

An Overview of Orange County

Orange County was a largely agricultural area until Walt Disney chose it as the spot to build his new amusement park in 1955. The Stanford Research Company told Disney that the area would be the center of future growth, and whether their researchers were prescient or simply created a self-fulfilling prophecy, they were right. Orange County is now home to almost 3 million people, according to the 2005 census.

Other than Disneyland, Orange County's forty-two miles of coastline, nine beaches, and three harbors are its most famous features.

≡FAST FACT

Long before the recent television programs discovered Orange County as a filming backdrop, it appeared in the movies. A scene from *Legally Blonde* was filmed at the Old Orange County Courthouse in Santa Ana, portions of the 1930 film *All Quiet on the Western Front* were shot in Newport Beach and Laguna Beach, and Dana Point harbor stood in for New England in *The Perfect Storm*.

Top Tourist Attractions

Things to do in Anaheim are covered in Chapter 15, but there's still plenty to see and do in the rest of "O.C." Here are some of the most interesting attractions.

Artists Village
✉First and Main Streets, Santa Ana
✐*www.aplaceforart.org*
A revitalizing influence in a once-neglected downtown area, Artists Village is a lively arts center featuring artists' galleries, several theater companies, and the Orange County Center for Contemporary Art.

Bolsa Chica Ecological Reserve
✉3842 Warner Avenue, Huntington Beach (Interpretive Center)
✆(714) 846-1114
✐*www.bolsachica.org*
One of the best spots anywhere for birdwatching—half the bird species in the United States have been sighted there—the 300-acre Bolsa Chica Reserve is a great place to get away from the Orange County hubbub. Across the street is Bolsa Chica State Beach.

Bowers Museum of Cultural Art and Kidseum

✉2002 N. Main St, Santa Ana

☎(714) 567-3600

🖰*www.bowers.org*

With more than 70,000 objects in its collection, the Bowers Museum is one of California's largest cultural institutions. Their holdings include a large collection of California Plein Air (this term refers to the act of painting outside rather than in a studio) paintings, California Native American artifacts, and objects from California history. It's open from 10 A.M. to 4 P.M. Tuesday through Sunday except July 4, Thanksgiving, December 25, and January 1. Weekend admission is $19 for adults, $14 for seniors over age sixty-two and students, and free for kids under age five. Weekdays, it's $2 cheaper.

Located in the same place, Kidseum is an indoor, 11,000-square-foot interactive, hands-on center where kids can learn about other cultures through storytelling, puppet shows, and activities.

Crystal Cove State Park

✉8471 Pacific Coast Hwy, Laguna Beach

☎(949) 494-3539

🖰*www.crystalcovestatepark.com*

Originally developed as a South Seas movie set, this beautiful stretch of Orange County sand features a restored historic district, a 1,140-acre underwater diving park, and some of the coast's best tide pools. It's also home to a charming bunch of beach cottages (*www .crystalcovebeachcottages.org*) built from the 1930s to the 1950s.

Crystal Cathedral

✉12141 Lewis St, Garden Grove

☎(714) 971-4000

🖰*www.crystalcathedral.org*

Visitors are welcome at Sunday services held in a soaring glass cathedral. Take a guided tour Monday through Friday.

Discovery Science Center

✉2500 N. Main St., Santa Ana

✆(714) 542-2823

✐*www.discoverycube.org*

Its creators call it "an amusement park for the mind," and this science museum offers more than 100 interactive exhibits covering all aspects of scientific discovery. Kids love to watch an indoor geyser erupt, lie on a bed of 3,500 real nails, or dance on a musical floor. It's easy to find; just look for a ten-story-high cube balanced on one of its points.

RAINY DAY FUN

If it's raining and the kids are so bored that they're figuratively climbing the walls, why not let them climb them literally? Adventure City has a twenty-four-foot indoor rock-climbing tower that's suitable for ages four and up. For even more climbing fun, the Discovery Science Center's Dino Quest includes a climbing wall embedded with fossils, and "The Cube" has plenty of other fun, interactive things for kids to do, too.

The museum is open daily from 10 A.M. to 5 P.M. Admission is $12.95 for adults, $9.95 for seniors over fifty-five years old and kids ages three to seventeen, and free for children age two and under.

Glen Ivy Hot Springs, "Club Mud"

✉25000 Glen Ivy Road, Corona

✆(888) 258-2683

✐*www.glenivy.com*

Technically just outside of Orange County across the Riverside County line, Glen Ivy Hot Springs is a great place to rest and relax for a day in an eleven-acre oasis that includes natural mineral springs and mud baths. They're open daily except Thanksgiving, December

25, and Easter. Admission is $35 per person on weekdays and $48 per person on weekends and includes parking, use of all pools, sauna, steam rooms, Roman Baths, red clay mud bath, towels, and lockers. Spa treatments are available for an extra charge. Guests must be at least sixteen years old to visit and eighteen years old for the spa treatments.

RAINY DAY FUN

If rainy days make you think of England, which then turns your thoughts to afternoon tea, the Ritz Carlton Laguna Niguel (⊠One Ritz Carlton Drive, Laguna Niguel, ✆(949) 240-2000) serves an elegant afternoon tea. In downtown Los Angeles, the Millennium Biltmore Hotel (⊠506 South Grand Ave., ✆(213) 624-1011) is famous for its afternoon teas, and they offer etiquette lessons for children during the holidays.

Huntington Beach Surfing Walk of Fame
⊠Pacific Coast Highway and Main Street, Huntington Beach

Along this surfer's answer to the Hollywood Walk of Fame, you'll find granite stones honoring surfing pioneers, champions, surf culture icons, local heroes, and others who've made a mark on the surfing scene.

International Surfing Museum
⊠411 Olive Avenue, Huntington Beach
✆(714) 960-3483
⊲www.surfingmuseum.org

The collections at this museum include surfboards, surfing memorabilia, music, and films. It's open daily from 12 P.M. to 5 P.M. during summer and on Monday through Thursday only in winter. Admission is $2 for adults, $1 for students, and children under six are free.

Mission San Juan Capistrano

✉26801 Ortega Hwy, San Juan Capistrano

☎(949) 234-1300

✍*www.missionsjc.com*

The remains of this romantic Spanish mission founded more than 200 years ago spread over ten acres. The Great Stone Church stands in ruins, but surrounding it are the beautiful Serra Chapel, Padres' quarters, an industrial area, soldiers' barracks, and cemetery. The mission is open daily from 8:30 A.M. to 5 P.M. except Thanksgiving, December 25, and Good Friday afternoon. Admission is $7 for adults, $6 for seniors over sixty years old, $5 for kids aged five to eleven, and children under three years old get in free.

═FAST FACT

Cliff swallows make their summer home in San Juan Capistrano and spend the winter 6,000 miles south in Argentina. Every year, as if driven by some invisible starter's pistol, the five-inch-long birds leave California around the Day of San Juan (October 23) and return to San Juan Capistrano *en masse* on March 19, Saint Joseph's Day. They collect mud from the nearby river, building their nests under the eaves of the old mission. The entire city celebrates their return with a parade and festival. In fact, the city song is "When the Swallows Come Back to Capistrano" by Leon Rene.

Richard Nixon Library and Birthplace

✉18001 Yorba Linda Blvd., Yorba Linda

☎(714) 993-5075

✍*www.nixonfoundation.org*

No matter what you think of our controversial thirty-seventh president, you'll know more about him when you leave this place than you did when you went in. Besides a number of exhibits that focus on the presidency in general and Nixon's accomplishments in particular, his birthplace is also on the grounds. The library is open from 10 A.M. to 5 P.M. Monday through Saturday, and from 11 A.M. to 5 P.M. on Sunday. It is closed Thanksgiving and December 25. Admission is $9.95 for adults, $3.75 for children aged seven to eleven, and free for kids under seven. Students and seniors aged sixty-two and over get in for $6.95, and members of the military pay $5.95 with ID.

Santa Ana Zoo
✉1801 East Chestnut Ave., Santa Ana
✆(714) 835-7484
✐*www.santaanazoo.org*
Unlike its larger Southern California counterparts, this small zoo is laid-back and easy to visit. Home to at least fifty monkeys (as mandated by its founder) and a bunch of other animals, it's open daily from 10 A.M. to 4 P.M. Admission is $6 for adults, $3 for children and seniors, and free for children under three years old.

Beaches

With 328 days of sunshine per year, Orange County is a terrific place to go to the beach, and it's got more than forty miles of them to choose from.

Balboa Beach
✉Balboa Peninsula, Newport Beach
Stretching the length of Newport Beach's Balboa Peninsula, this popular beach area includes the Wedge, one of the West Coast's best bodysurfing spots. It also boasts a scenic pier. In the summer, it's fun to watch all the local kids taking swimming and surfing lessons here.

Bolsa Chica State Beach
✉Pacific Coast Highway between Golden West Street
  and Warner Avenue, Huntington Beach
✆(714) 846-3460
✐*www.parks.ca.gov*

Besides the Bolsa Chica Ecological Reserve listed under Attractions, this beach is a popular spot for surf fishing and a good place for beginning surfboarders. It runs from Seal Beach to the Huntington Beach Pier.

Huntington City Beach and Huntington Pier

✉Pacific Coast Highway at Main Street, Huntington Beach
✐*www.stockteam.com/hbpier.html*

Centered on the historic Huntington Pier and right across the street from restaurants and shopping, busy Huntington Beach is a great place for making sandcastles, sunning on the sand, and watching surfers. The scenic pier juts 1,853 feet into the Pacific Ocean, making it the subject of countless photographs.

The young surfers who ride the waves here don't tolerate novices, so if you're just learning, you'll be better off to try Bolsa Chica Beach instead. Ironically, the sport that gave "Surf City USA" its name is banned south of the pier in summer.

TRAVEL TIP

If you're a fan of *The O.C.* television show, the Newport Beach Conference and Visitors Bureau offers a map of its locales at ✐*www.visitnewportbeach.com*. It shows the location of the opening credit shots, the characters' favorite hangouts, and where to find the cast's handprints set in cement.

The pier is open from early morning until midnight, and there's a restaurant at the end. If you're here in May, you may enjoy the Duck-a-thon, an annual event when thousands of rubber ducks are launched from the pier, with the first ones arriving back on shore winning prizes for their sponsors.

Huntington State Beach

✉Enter at Magnolia Avenue and Pacific Coast Highway,
  Huntington Beach

✆(714) 536-1454

⌨www.parks.ca.gov

This long, skinny beach wedged between the Pacific Coast Highway and the Pacific Ocean is one of the area's best beaches for volleyball games. With lifeguards on duty, it's also a good place to go swimming. It also has fire rings where you can light a beach bonfire, one of the most stereotypically California things you could do.

≡FAST FACT

Southern California water quality varies widely depending on the season, and some Orange County beaches are subject to "red tide," caused when algae grow very fast, or "bloom," and their pigments give the water a red color. Although generally not harmful, the condition is unsightly. Heal the Bay (⌨*www.healthebay.org*) summarizes data and grades each beach on its water quality in both wet and dry weather.

Main Beach, Laguna

✉Broadway and Ocean Avenues at Pacific Coast Highway, Laguna Beach

⌨*www.lblg.org/beach/main.htm*

People watching is a popular pastime on this beach often seen on the television series *Laguna Beach*. It's also a good place for beach volleyball, swimming, and bodysurfing, but surfboarding is not permitted in summer. A pretty boardwalk paralleling the oceanfront offers a good place to watch all the fun without getting sand in your shoes, and when you're tired of the beach scene, downtown Laguna is just a few steps away.

Beach Cities

Orange County residents have always known that their home has some of the most beautiful beach communities anywhere. Any of these beach towns would make a great place to spend a day or two, and if you're ready to get away from the Disney madness, you may enjoy moving to a hotel nearer the sand. Hotels in this upscale resort area tend to be more expensive than near the Disneyland Resort. Key to rates for hotels listed here (double occupancy):

$: $90 to $129 per night
$$: $130 to $199 per night
$$$: $200 to $299 per night
$$$$: Over $300 per night

Huntington Beach

Known as "Surf City USA," Huntington Beach is the center of Orange County surf culture. With public beaches lining its entire western boundary, Huntington is a great place for a day at the beach that could be the stuff of anyone's California beach fantasy. Add an evening bonfire with roasted hot dogs and marshmallows if you like, and if you're here around Christmas, don't miss a chance to see the over-the-top lighted displays around Huntington Harbor.

═══FAST FACT

Huntington Beach holds the official trademark "Surf City USA," according to the U.S. Patent and Trademark Office, but that doesn't keep rival Santa Cruz (south of San Francisco) from disputing their claim, while applying for their own trademark as "Original Surf City, USA." Coincidentally, Surf City (without the USA) is also the name of communities in New Jersey and North Carolina.

A few of the best places to stay in Huntington Beach include:

- Best Western Regency Inn, ✉19360 Beach Boulevard, ✆(714) 962-4244, ✐*www.bestwestern.com*, $
- Hilton Waterfront Beach Resort, ✉21100 Pacific Coast Hwy, ✆(714) 845-8000, ✐*www.hilton.com*, $$$
- Hyatt Regency Huntington Beach Resort & Spa, ✉21500 Pacific Coast Highway, ✆(714) 698-1234, ✐*www.huntington beach.hyatt.com*, $$$

Newport Beach

The city of Newport Beach covers twenty-five square miles and has only six miles of oceanfront, but all its best tourist spots center on the beach and the islands of Newport Harbor. The best place to start exploring is on the Balboa Peninsula just off Pacific Coast Highway.

From the Balboa Fun Zone, a harbor cruise on the *Pavilion Paddy* or the *Pavilion Queen* (*www.catalinainfo.com*) is the best way to get acquainted with Newport Harbor and to slow down to its unhurried pace. You'll pass cottages so small you'd have to go outside just to change your mind and million-dollar mansions divided by sibling squabbles. If you suddenly get a feeling of déjà vu, never fear. You're not hallucinating, just remembering a movie or television program—perhaps the original *Treasure Island* or an episode of *Gilligan's Island*?

A few minutes on the four-car ferry from the Balboa Peninsula takes you to Balboa Island, one of seven artificial islands cradled between the mainland and the peninsula. In the beginning, these islands seemed like just another real estate scam, as watery, lots-to-be: waterfront $15, inland $10, and only $5 down. James Cagney won one of them in a poker game. An eccentric countess bought another, and only those with her permission could be her neighbors. One has streets named for jewels. Yet another was designed to be a racetrack.

Today, the seven islands of Newport Harbor are real. Cradled inside Balboa Peninsula, they are some of the most expensive real estate in Southern California. Those $10 and $15 lots now cost $1.5 million and up, and they are surrounded by one of the world's largest small yacht harbors. It's a quiet, relaxed place where you're more likely to meet the harbor patrol than the highway patrol, and sun-blond kids zip around on bicycles like a scene from a Norman Rockwell painting.

Once planned to be a racetrack, Balboa Island now teems with cottages arranged in neat rows, American flags flying outside. It's a short walk from the ferry landing to Marine Avenue, the island's only shopping area, where you'll find a variety of goods, from handmade kites to resort wear. Along this homey main drag, you can buy one of Newport Beach's most famous culinary treats, the Balboa Bar, a block of ice cream on a stick, coated to order with chocolate and rolled in the topping of your choice.

 RAINY DAY FUN

If you're stuck in the rain, a visit to the toy store may be the answer. The local chain named Toy Boat * Toy Boat * Toy Boat (which is its official name and also a tongue-twister—try saying it three times fast) carries classic toys and beach gear. You'll find them in Newport Beach at ⊠1827 Westcliffe Drive and ⊠21111 Newport Coast Drive, and at Fashion Island shopping center.

If you want to stay in Newport Beach, these are a few of the nicest spots:

- Balboa Bay Club & Resort, ⊠1221 West Coast Highway, ✆(888) 445-7153, ✍*www.balboabayclub.com*, $$$
- Bay Shores Peninsula, ⊠1800 West Balboa Blvd., ✆(800) 222-6675, ✍*www.thebestinn.com*, $$

- Fairmont Newport Beach, ✉4500 MacArthur Boulevard, ✆(800) 257-7544, *www.fairmont.com/newportbeach*, $$$
- Holiday Inn Express Newport Beach, 2300 West Coast Highway, ✆(949) 722-2999, *www.ichotelsgroup.com*, $$
- Newport Dunes RV Park, ✆(800) 765-7661, ✉1131 Back Bay Drive, *www.newportdunes.com* is sometimes called the "Ritz of RV Parks" for its luxurious amenities, but you don't have to drive a Winnebago or an Airstream to stay there. Just book one of their twenty-four cottages and you can enjoy the same ambiance as the folks in the $2.5-million Featherlite Vantare Platinum Plus super-RV down the way.

Laguna Beach

The coastline grows irregular in Laguna Beach, and the mountains edge closer to the sea, creating a dramatic landscape that has attracted tourists since the late nineteenth century. Artists first discovered this scenic spot in the early 1900s, and by the 1920s, it had become an artist's colony.

≡FAST FACT

The beautiful, life-size mural of a gray whale and her calf on the wall of the Hotel Laguna at ✉425 South Coast Highway is the work of artist Wyland, the first of ninety marine-themed murals he has created worldwide. In Laguna Beach, you can visit his gallery down the street from the mural at ✉509 South Coast Highway.

Today, Laguna is still one of Orange County's art centers, hosting the annual Festival of Arts, Pageant of the Masters, and Sawdust Art Festival.

Laguna Beach is also a good place for shopping and fine dining, and a late-afternoon walk along the beachside boardwalk is a popular activity.

- Casa Laguna Inn, ✉2510 South Coast Highway, ✆(800) 233-0449, ✐*www.casalaguna.com*, $$$
- Holiday Inn Laguna Beach, ✉696 South Coast Highway, ✆(949) 494-1001, ✐*www.ichotelsgroup.com*, $$
- Laguna Riviera Beach Resort, ✉825 South Coast Highway, ✆(949) 494-1196, ✐*www.lagunariviera.com*, $
- Montage Resort and Spa Laguna Beach, ✉30801 South Coast Highway, ✆(866) 271-6953, ✐*www.montagelaguna beach.com*, $$$$

Dana Point

Nineteenth-century explorer and author Richard Henry Dana called this spot one of the most romantic in California when he sailed here in his ship *The Pilgrim*, and little has changed in that regard during the ensuing two hundred years. Dana Point is focused on the sea, with a large artificial harbor. Fishing excursions and winter whale-watching trips are among the most popular activities.

≡FAST FACT

Richard Henry Dana, for whom Dana Point is named, is the author of *Two Years Before the Mast*, a book recounting his time spent at sea, exploring the California coast almost a decade before the 1849 Gold Rush brought the world to California's doorstep.

Dana Point is also home to some of the county's most luxurious accommodations, as well as some more affordable spots:

- Holiday Inn Express Dana Point, ✉34280 Pacific Coast Highway, ✆(949) 248-1000, ✐*www.ichotelsgroup.com*, $
- Ritz-Carlton Laguna Niguel, ✉1 Ritz Carlton Drive, ✆(949) 240-2000, ✐*www.ritzcarlton.com*, $$$$

- St. Regis Monarch Beach Resort and Spa, ✉1 Monarch Beach Resort Drive, ☎(949) 234-3200, *⌨www.stregismonarch beach.com*, $$$$

San Clemente

One of Orange County's oldest and southernmost towns, San Clemente gained instant fame when former U. S. president Richard M. Nixon made his home, Casa Pacifica, the "Western White House."

Created by developer Ole Hanson in 1929, San Clemente was envisioned as a Spanish village by the sea, filled with red-tile-roofed white stucco homes that still contribute to its charming appearance.

≡FAST FACT

Visitor's Bureau representatives like to quote the county's 312 days of sunshine, but June gloom is something they'd rather not talk about. This weather phenomenon is characterized by cloudy skies, created when an ocean cloud layer hangs onshore all day long. On the average, about half the days in May and June are affected, and the closer you stay to the beach, the more likely you are to experience it.

Located at the southern end of the Los Angeles megalopolis, San Clemente is lightly visited, but well worth a day's excursion for shopping on Avenida del Mar, strolling on the pier, or building a sandcastle. You can also visit Hanson's home, Casa Romantica, which is now open to the public. The beach here is popular with surfers and scuba divers.

San Clemente is also one of the most affordable places to stay in Orange County:

- Best Western Casablanca Inn, ✉1601 North El Camino Real, ☎(949) 361-1644, *⌨www.bwcasablanca.com*, $

- Hampton Inn & Suites, San Clemente, ✉ 2481 South El Camino Real, ✆(949) 366-1000, ✍*www.hamptoninnsanclemente.com*, $$
- San Clemente Inn, ✉ 2600 Avenida Del Presidente, ✆(949) 492-6103, ✍*www.sanclementeinn.com*, $

Shopping

Most of Orange County shopping centers on larger shopping malls, and some of them are so big and popular that they're practically a tourist attraction in themselves.

The Block at Orange

✉20 City Boulevard W., Orange

✆(714) 769-4000

✍*www.theblockatorange.com*

One of Orange County's most popular destinations, the sleek, trendy Block at Orange includes more than 100 shops and restaurants in an outdoor shopping plaza. Besides a big lineup of clothing and accessory shops, bookstores, and food outlets (including Jody Maroni's Sausage Kingdom, a longtime Venice Beach favorite), you'll find a Bose Factory Outlet and the Burke Williams Day Spa. Non-shoppers (or those who've shopped until they dropped) can entertain themselves (or be entertained) at the Vans Skate Park, visit the enormous, thirty-screen AMC movie theater, or bowl at Lucky Strike Lanes.

The mall is located about a ten-minute drive from Disneyland and is accessible by the Anaheim Resort Trolley.

The camp

✉2937 Bristol St., Costa Mesa

✆(714) 444-4CMP

✍*www.thecampsite.com*

The camp is a must for the person who loves the outdoors, with retailers such as Patagonia and Cyclewerks, as well as other shops and activities, all in a natural compound setting. Besides shopping, you can get certified for scuba diving here, take a yoga class, or enjoy some vegan cuisine.

Fashion Island

✉Pacific Coast Highway and Newport Center Drive,
   Newport Beach
✆(949) 721-2000
✍www.shopfashionisland.com

One of Orange County's premier shopping destinations for more than thirty-five years, this beautiful, outdoor mall is home to Orange County's only Bloomingdale's and Neiman Marcus stores, along with over 35,000 square feet of retail space housing 200 other shops and exclusive boutiques, restaurants, and cafés. Residents and visitors alike enjoy the open-air ambiance and architecture, and the custom-made Venetian carousel is a local favorite.

Laguna Beach

✍www.lagunabeachinfo.org

Laguna Beach's charming downtown offers plenty of chances to shop. You'll find a wide variety of stores here, including antique shops, clothing boutiques, specialty gift shops, and some excellent art galleries. The best shopping area extends along Pacific Coast Highway and up Forest Avenue.

Orange County Market Place

✉88 Fair Drive, Costa Mesa
✆(949) 723-6616
✍www.ocmarketplace.com

Held every weekend at the Orange County Fairgrounds, the Market Place features more than 1,100 vendors strung along over four miles of aisles, selling everything you can imagine (and some things you never thought of) in a swap meet–style atmosphere. Admission is $2 for adults; children under twelve years old get in free.

South Coast Plaza

✉3333 Bristol Street, Costa Mesa

✆(800) 782-8888

✐*www.southcoastplaza.com*

Some people call this mall Orange County's equivalent of Rodeo Drive. One of the country's largest retail centers, covering over 128 acres, South Coast Plaza has no less than nine anchor stores and 300 shops. The Jewel Court between Nordstrom's and Saks Fifth Avenue is home to many of the same shops found on the famous Beverly Hills drive including Gucci, Versace, Hermès, Tiffany, and Van Cleef and Arpels. It also has two carousels.

More than just a shopping center, South Coast Plaza is a popular tourist destination that has its own hotel (Westin South Coast Plaza). The Orange County Performing Arts Center is next-door. South Coast Plaza also puts on a sumptuous Christmas display, including two Santas, one at each end of the huge complex.

Annual Events

Sometimes, one of the most enjoyable aspects of travel is mixing with the locals at festivals and other events. These are some of Orange County's best annual events that may be of interest to visitors.

Festival de las Golondrinas

✉San Juan Capistrano

✆(949) 493-1976

✐*www.swallowsparade.com*

A romantic legend says that the swallows return to Mission San Juan Capistrano from Goya, Argentina, every year on March 19, and it's a good reason to celebrate. Festivities include a celebration at the mission, a parade, a street fair, and a market.

Glory of Easter

✉12141 Lewis St, Garden Grove

☎(714) 971-4000

🖱*www.crystalcathedral.org*

Similar to their Christmas extravaganza the Glory of Christmas (described later), this Crystal Cathedral show features an Easter theme.

Grunion Run

For a fun, fishy good time, head for the Orange County beaches when the grunion run. Spring and summer nights, a few nights after the full and new moons, thousands of six-inch-long, female grunion fish come ashore at high tide to lay their eggs and the males aren't far behind. The resulting spectacle is a unique California beach sight. You can even go fishing with your bare hands (and without a license), although it may be hard to figure out what to do with the little critters once you've got them. Bolsa Chica State Beach and Doheny State Beach are two of the best places to watch. You can find out when the grunion runs are expected at *www.dfg.ca.gov/mrd/gruschd.html*.

Orange County Fair

✉88 Fair Drive, Costa Mesa

☎(714) 708-1500

🖱*www.ocfair.com*

Held annually in July and August, the Orange County Fair is one of the area's most popular events. Originally a showcase for farm products and livestock, today's fair retains a small-town feel but also includes concerts by headliner groups such as Paul Simon, Hootie and the Blowfish, and LeAnn Rimes, along with the expected product showcases, rides, and foods.

The fairgrounds are also home to many other events and attractions, including Centennial Farm, a four-acre working farm, and annual markets, expositions, and festivals.

Orange County Performing Arts Center

✉600 Town Center Drive, Costa Mesa

✆(714) 556-2787

☜www.ocpac.org

With a new facility that opened in mid-2006, designed by award-winning architect Cesar Pelli, the home of the South Coast Repertory Theater and Orange County Philharmonic also mounts touring productions and art exhibits.

Pageant of the Masters

✉650 Laguna Canyon Road, Laguna Beach

✆(800) 487-3378

☜www.foapom.com

A most unusual artistic pageant and an Orange County fixture for more than seventy years, the Pageant of the Masters features "living pictures," recreations of famous paintings with real people posed in the scenes. Clever tricks of lighting, makeup, and design conspire to fool the eye, making three-dimensional humans appear as flat as the paintings they mimic. The associated juried art show, called the Festival of Arts, features some of the finest works you'll find anywhere.

The festival is held every July and August, and tickets to this popular event sell out long before it starts.

Sawdust Art Festival

✉935 Laguna Canyon Road, Laguna Beach

✆(949) 494-3030

☜www.sawdustartfestival.org

Started as a revolt against the local art "establishment," the Sawdust Festival has become one of the country's best art festivals, with more than 200 local artists participating, giving demonstrations, and offering their works for sale. Intentionally different from other art shows and spurning their stuffy air, the Sawdust Festival includes handmade artists' booths as creative as their artwork.

The summer festival runs from July through September, and the Winter Fantasy Festival happens in late November and early December.

Toshiba Tall Ships Festival
✉Dana Point
☎(949) 496-2274
🖰www.tallshipsfestival.com

Held in September, the largest tall ship gathering on the West Coast features living-history demonstrations, Polynesian dancers, tall ship cruises, sea chantey concerts, a pirate's encampment, and dramatic sunset cannon battles. General admission is $6 for adults and $4 for children over three years old, and there's an extra charge for special cruises and activities.

U.S. Open of Surfing
✉Huntington Beach Pier, Huntington Beach
☎(310) 473-0411
🖰www.usopenofsurfing.com/home.php

Since Jack Haley won the inaugural U.S./West Coast Surfing Championships at Huntington Beach in 1959, Surf City USA has hosted annual surfing competitions, including this six-star event held in July, which attracts more than 600 of the world's top surfers.

Christmas in Orange County

Orange County may seem like an unlikely place to celebrate an old-fashioned Christmas, but a heart of Norman Rockwell lurks beneath its sun, surf, and sand exterior, making this one of the best places in California to celebrate the holiday season.

Glory of Christmas
✉12141 Lewis St, Garden Grove
☎(714) 54-GLORY
🖰www.crystalcathedral.org/glory_christmas/index.cfm

This annual presentation is a bit like an old-fashioned church Christmas pageant but with an orchestra accompaniment, live animals, elaborate sets, and flying angels.

The Glory of Christmas runs from Thanksgiving through the end of December. Tickets cost $30 to $40, except for $18 discount nights (Tuesday through Thursday).

Huntington Beach Cruise of Lights

✉Huntington Beach

✆(714) 840-7542, ✑*www.cruiseoflights.org*

Homeowners whose properties line Huntington Beach waterways go all out at Christmas, decorating not just their front yards but the backside of their homes facing the water. Locals take to the waterways in their own boats to see the display that includes dancing penguins, fabulous light displays, and star-spangled extravaganzas. For a week each December, the Huntington Harbor Philharmonic Committee offers narrated boat cruises so landlubbers can join the fun. This beautiful cruise is a holiday highlight and local favorite. The proceeds from ticket sales to the Cruise of Lights go to the nationally recognized youth music education programs that the Huntington Harbor Philharmonic supports.

Newport Beach Harbor Parade

✉Newport Beach

✆(949) 729-4400, ✑*www.christmasboatparade.com*

Another local pleasure, the Newport Beach Harbor Parade is a chance for as many as 100 local boat owners to deck their watercraft out in lights and holiday themes and drive them around for everyone to see. It's a tradition that's been going on for almost a hundred years. You can view the parade for free anywhere along its route (which is described at their Web site), or reserve a table at a waterside restaurant and watch the show. The parade runs for a week in mid-December. Local boat charter companies offer visitors a chance to be in the parade instead of just watching.

CHAPTER 17

The Stars Shine in Los Angeles County

MUCH OF THIS BOOK is dedicated to the Southern California theme parks, but there's a lot more to see and do in the Southland than ride roller coasters and meet cartoon characters. It would take an entire book to describe everything the Los Angeles area has to offer, but this chapter highlights some of the family-oriented favorites.

An Overview of Los Angeles County

One of California's original twenty-seven counties, Los Angeles is one of the nation's largest counties, encompassing 4,081 square miles. With a 2005 population of almost 10 million people, 28 percent of California residents, it's the most populous county in the United States, home to more people than all but eight states.

The greater Los Angeles metropolitan area encompasses five counties—Los Angeles, Orange, Ventura, and parts of Riverside and San Bernardino Counties—that together make up a metropolis that almost half of Californians call home. This place is so densely populated in many places that a sign beside the road is the only visible clue that you've crossed a city or county boundary.

≡ FAST FACT

Many popular Los Angeles–area attractions can be found in Hollywood. Although the Hollywood area has a name and an identity, it is actually a district of the city of Los Angeles. Neighboring West Hollywood, however, is a separate, incorporated city.

Besides its mainland cities and areas that include Hollywood, West Los Angeles, and Long Beach, Los Angeles County also includes San Clemente and Santa Catalina Islands.

Top Tourist Attractions

In addition to Six Flags Magic Mountain and Universal Studios Hollywood (of which you will read more in Chapters 18 and 19, respectively), the Los Angeles area teems with all kinds of things to do and see. These are some of the most popular, organized by area:

Hollywood

When people say "Hollywood," they sometimes have a vague idea of what the area really is, if it exists at all, thinking more of the film industry than a specific place. Nevertheless, they often head for Hollywood Boulevard looking for Hollywood magic, and in recent years, the venerable boulevard has become a capsule of film industry cachet. Along Hollywood Boulevard, centered on its intersection with Highland, you'll find the following:

Hollywood & Highland
✉ 6801 Hollywood Boulevard
✆ (323) 467-6412
✎ *www.hollywoodandhighland.com*
A $615 million family-entertainment destination, Hollywood & Highland occupies 1.3 million square feet. Reached from the

boulevard via steps along a winding, mosaic-paved path inlaid with short quotes from figures in Hollywood history, the central courtyard is surrounded by an arch and columns that pay tribute to D. W. Griffith's classic 1916 film *Intolerance*. Beyond the courtyard is an oversize casting couch that makes a perfect spot to take an "I was there" photograph with the Hollywood Sign in the background.

The complex also includes more than seventy upscale retail shops and restaurants and the Renaissance Hollywood Hotel.

The Kodak Theatre
✉ 6801 Hollywood Boulevard
✆ (323) 308-6300
🖎 *www.kodaktheatre.com*

The Academy Awards ceremonies returned to Hollywood when this theatre was finished in 2002. When it isn't staging the star-studded awards spectacular, the Kodak Theatre hosts a mix of Broadway shows, music concerts, and live nationally televised specials. On most days, you can also take a guided tour. Tour prices are $15 for adults and $10 for seniors, children over twelve, and students. Children under age three are free.

Traveling south along Hollywood Boulevard, you'll find these points of interest:

Hollywood Walk of Fame
✉ Hollywood Boulevard from Gower to La Brea
  and along Vine Street from Yucca to Sunset
🖎 *www.hollywoodchamber.net*

Since the Walk of Fame began in 1960, more than 2,000 brass-and-terrazzo stars have been embedded in the Hollywood sidewalks, memorializing people from all aspects of the entertainment industry. Some visitors enjoy walking along and reading the names they recognize, but if you want to find a specific star, visit the Walk of Fame Web site ahead of time to find out where it's located.

≡FAST FACT

Each time a new honoree receives a star on the Walk of Fame, a special dedication ceremony is held. The star cannot be placed unless the celebrity shows up in person, making this one of the most reliable ways to see a superstar. To find out if one of these fun events will take place during your visit, go to the Walk of Fame Web site or call ✆(323) 469-8311.

Mann's Chinese Theatre

✉6925 Hollywood Boulevard

✆(323) 464-6266

⌨*www.manntheatres.com/chinese*

Built in 1927 as Grauman's Chinese Theatre, this beautiful, Chinese-themed motion picture theater is a famous landmark for many reasons. Hollywood's biggest motion pictures have held their premieres here since the days of Douglas Fairbanks and Mary Pickford, but perhaps even more famous are the cement handprints and footprints that adorn the forecourt. Celebrities who have left their mark in Mann's cement include Clint Eastwood, Clark Gable, Tom Hanks, Jack Lemmon, Walter Matthau, Marilyn Monroe, and Jane Russell (whose inscription reads, "Gentlemen Prefer Blondes"), Eddie Murphy, Paul Newman, Joanne Woodward, and *Star Wars* robots R2-D2 and C-3PO. Besides the standard handprints, footprints, and signatures, you'll also find an imprint of Roy Rogers's horse Trigger's shoe, Whoopi Goldberg's dreadlocks, and Jimmy Durante's nose.

When a gala "red carpet" premiere event isn't taking place, the theater is open to the public, showing first-run films. You can take a guided tour or buy a ticket to the show—a peek at its interior is worth the price of admission, no matter what's playing.

RAINY DAY FUN

Going to the movies on a rainy day isn't a new idea, but in Hollywood, you can give it a different twist. Take in a film at the Mann's Chinese Theatre or the El Capitan (✉6838 Hollywood Blvd., *http://disney.go.com/disneypictures/el_capitan*) or tour the Egyptian Theatre (✉6712 Hollywood Blvd., *www.americancinematheque.com*) to get a glimpse of film-going's golden age.

Hollywood Wax Museum
✉6767 Hollywood Boulevard
☎(323) 462-8860
www.hollywoodwax.com

If you want to see movie stars and other celebrities modeled in wax, this is the place for you.

RAINY DAY FUN

On a rainy day in Hollywood, take the kids to the El Capitan Theatre where a family-friendly movie is always playing. Owned by the Disney Company, the theater also features a live mini-musical featuring Disney characters such as Buzz Lightyear. Before or afterward, Disney's Soda Fountain and Studio Store next door is also a big hit with the kids.

Guinness Book of World Records Museum
✉6764 Hollywood Boulevard
☎(323) 463-6433
www.guinnessattractions.com

Filled with the one-of-a-kind exhibits the Guinness Book of World Records is famous for, the museum is open from 10 A.M. to midnight. Admission is $12.95 for adults and $6.95 for kids aged six to twelve.

Musso and Frank Grill

✉6667 Hollywood Boulevard

✆(323) 467-7788

Around for more than eighty years, Musso and Frank is Hollywood's oldest restaurant. The last survivor of Hollywood's famous eateries, it serves old-fashioned dishes rarely seen on today's menus—corned beef and cabbage, Postum (but no espresso), jellied consommé, and it has been a favorite of stars and celebrities since Ernest Hemingway and William Faulkner sat at the bar and Charlie Chaplin dined at table number one. While it's a bit expensive for the kind of food it serves, it's a Hollywood tradition that deserves a look.

Ripley's Believe It or Not! Museum

✉6780 Hollywood Boulevard

✆(323) 466-6335

✐*www.ripleys.com*

Another Hollywood standby, the Ripley museum is filled with the odd, weird, and truly strange stuff they're famous for. Get $2 off adult admission and $1 off child's admission with coupons on their Web site.

RAINY DAY FUN

The Ronald Reagan Presidential Library houses a fascinating collection of presidential memorabilia. Located north of Los Angeles in Simi Valley, the library is open every day except Thanksgiving, Christmas, and New Year's Day. Admission costs $12 for adults, $9 for seniors over sixty-two years old, $3 for children ages eleven to seventeen, and anyone under eleven years old is free. ✉40 Presidential Drive, Simi Valley, ✆(800) 410-8354, ✐*www.reaganlibrary.com*

Hollywood Bowl

✉2301 North Highland Ave.

✆(323) 850-2000

✍www.hollywoodbowl.org

The Los Angeles Philharmonic's outdoor home is by far the city's most enjoyable outdoor performance venue. Concertgoers in the know bring a picnic to enjoy before the show begins. and most concerts allow you to bring in alcoholic beverages. Special events include the July 4th Fireworks Spectacular and the JVC Jazzfest. Ticket prices range from $1 to $5 each in the uppermost benches to over $100 for a garden box seat.

Hollywood Heritage Museum

✉2100 North Highland Avenue

✆(323) 874-4005

✍www.hollywoodheritage.org

When producer Emile Lasky and director Cecil B. DeMille arrived in Hollywood in 1913 looking for a place to turn their hit play *The Squaw Man* into a motion picture, they leased a barn at Selma and Vine Streets to use as their studio. They were so successful that in 1914, they formed Paramount Studios. The barn was moved to the new studio location, where it stayed until 1979, when it was rescued from demolition and moved to its current location. Today it houses a museum that focuses on silent films and the early film industry. The museum is open on weekends only. Admission is $5 for adults, $3 for seniors and students, and $1 for children aged three to twelve.

Hollywood Forever Cemetery

✉6000 Santa Monica Boulevard

✆(323) 469-1181

✍www.hollywoodforever.com

Known as "The Resting Place of Hollywood's Immortals," the cemetery, which has been around since the late 1800s, is the last resting place of many Hollywood founders and early stars, including Cecil B. DeMille, Jayne Mansfield, Rudolph Valentino, and Douglas Fairbanks.

You can pick up a map at the shop near the entrance and learn more about those interred there at the LifeStory theaters located throughout the park.

The Hollywood Sign

Hollywood is filled with signs and billboards, but the largest is the world-famous Hollywood sign, which stands 50 feet tall and 450 feet across. It has been a Hollywood landmark for more than seventy-five years. The sign was originally built as an advertisement for Hollywoodland, a 1920s Beachwood Canyon real-estate development. It can be seen from many locations in the Hollywood area and makes an excellent backdrop for a family photo, but it is not accessible to the public.

Beverly Hills

Justifiably famous for its opulence and as the home of many early film stars, Beverly Hills provides some nice glimpses of the rich and famous lifestyle.

Rodeo Drive

www.rodeodrive.com

Rodeo Drive is known for its beyond-upscale shops, boutiques, galleries, and restaurants. It's not uncommon to find Rolls Royces, Mercedes Benzes, Lamborghinis, and Lotus Elans parked at the metered spots along Rodeo Drive, which may give you a clue about the price levels at the shops they're visiting. The street is only about three blocks long, but it's a fun place to walk, and you won't be alone, even if you're just window-shopping. Almost any time, more gawkers than real shoppers stroll the sidewalks here. Architecture buffs may enjoy seeing the Anderton Court Shops (322 N. Rodeo Drive), designed by Frank Lloyd Wright.

Where Rodeo runs into Wilshire Boulevard is the Regent Beverly Wilshire Hotel, better known as the *Pretty Woman* hotel for its pivotal role in the film starring Julia Roberts and Richard Gere.

☂ RAINY DAY FUN

On a rainy day, Museum Row on Wilshire Boulevard near the Los Angeles County Museum of Art offers a museum for almost any taste, from classic art to fossilized woolly mammoths to arts and crafts.

Beverly Hills Trolley Tour

For a modest $5 per adult and $1 per child, the Beverly Hills trolley tour takes you past many interesting sights. Guides won't tell you who lives where now, but they have plenty of stories from days gone by. For more information, go to *www.beverlyhills.org* or call (310) 285-2438.

Surprisingly, the parking lots around Rodeo Drive (whose entrances look more like high-priced hotel driveways than simple parking lots) are free, and they even provide valet parking.

≡ FAST FACT

Bijan (✉420 Rodeo Drive) prides itself on being one of the world's most expensive stores in the world, and you need an appointment just to shop there. During a typical visit, a customer will spend over $100,000.

West Hollywood and Sunset Strip

The heart of the city's gay and lesbian community is also a gathering place for wannabe trendsetters and the truly trendy they emulate. Along Santa Monica Boulevard, you'll find great shopping and dining opportunities.

Melrose Avenue

Melrose Avenue between Highland Avenue and La Cienega Boulevard is one of West Hollywood's better-known streets, boasting cutting-edge boutiques and clothing stores, as well as cafés and restaurants. It's easy to spend a few hours walking along the street and exploring the one-of-a-kind shops. Several secondhand clothing stores on Melrose sell clothing worn by famous celebrities, including Decades (8214 Melrose Avenue).

Sunset Strip

Also in West Hollywood is the famous Sunset Strip. The 1.5-mile-long section of Sunset Boulevard between Doheny Drive and N. Crescent Heights Boulevard is a lively nightspot, lined with famous clubs such as Whisky-A-Go-Go, the Roxy, and the Viper Room.

For more information about activities in West Hollywood, visit *www.weho.org*.

Griffith Park

Griffith Park is the country's largest urban park, with more than 4,000 acres of natural terrain. It's also the home of the Hollywood Sign, located on Mount Lee. Other attractions in Griffith Park include the following:

Los Angeles Zoo
✆ (323) 644-4200
✎ *www.lazoo.org*

The 113-acre zoo receives over 1.4 million visitors per year. You may remember seeing it during the opening sequence from the television sitcom *Three's Company.* From crocodiles to elephants, exotic birds to primates, and bears to lions, the zoo showcases more than 1,000 animals and features a special children's zoo. The Los Angeles Zoo is open daily, except Christmas. Admission costs $10 for adults, $5 for children, and $7 for senior citizens.

Griffith Park Observatory
☎(213) 473-0800

✐*www.griffithobs.org*

Also film-famous from the ending scene of the James Dean film *Rebel Without a Cause*, the Griffith Park Observatory features outer space–oriented exhibits, a planetarium, and other public astronomy programs. The Griffith Observatory is open six days a week (closed Monday). Admission is free.

Other attractions in Griffith Park include the Autry National Center, formerly known as the Museum of Western Heritage ((323) 667-2000, *www.autrynationalcenter.org*); Travel Town ((323) 662-9678); and the Griffith Park & Southern Railroad ((323) 664-6788, *www.gprah.com*).

Santa Monica
Favorite Santa Monica tourist spots include the Santa Monica Pier (and its seaside amusement park) and the Third Street Promenade.

Santa Monica Pier
☎(310) 458-8900

✐*www.santamonicapier.org*

The Santa Monica Pier is home to Pacific Park, one of California's few remaining seaside amusement parks, but its most famous occupant is the beautiful, historic carousel featured in many films, including *The Sting* and *Titanic*. The view from the pier is awesome, and the area is well worth exploring for an hour or so, especially if the weather is nice. There's a nearby beach and parking is available. Admission is free (but the rides charge admission), and the pier is open all year.

Third Street Promenade
✐*www.downtownsm.com*

A short walk from the pier, the Third Street Promenade offers lots of shopping, an outdoor pedestrian mall, and a nearby indoor mall. With several restaurants, a street closed to automobile traffic, street performers, and two movie theaters, Third Street is a popular, lively spot on weekend evenings.

Long Beach

It's easy to find Long Beach. Just go south on I-605 until it ends. Besides being home to the Los Angeles area's busiest harbor, Long Beach offers a few things you may enjoy:

The *Queen Mary*
✉1126 Queen's Highway
✆(562) 435-3511
🖰*www.queenmary.com*

The RMS *Queen Mary*, once the world's fastest ship, has docked in Long Beach for more years than she sailed the Atlantic. On board, you'll find tours and displays about her years as a luxury liner and a troop carrier, along with a special Ghosts and Legends Tour, and an after-hours Paranormal Shipwalk. You can even spend the night in one of the staterooms at Hotel Queen Mary. General admission costs $22.95 for adults, $19.95 for seniors and military, and $11.95 for children aged five to eleven. First Class Passage tickets, which include a self-guided shipwalk tour, a guided tour of the ship's World War II history, a behind-the-scenes tour, and the Ghosts and Legends tour cost $27.95 for adults, $24.95 for seniors and military, and $16.95 for kids ages five through eleven.

Aquarium of the Pacific
✉100 Aquarium Way
✆(562) 590-3100
🖰*www.aquariumofpacific.org*

This large aquarium is home to more than 12,000 marine animals representing over 550 species. Permanent exhibits focus on marine life in the Pacific Ocean.

Museums of Note

The Los Angeles area is home to more museums than almost any other place in the country. These are a few of the most popular and well noted, but if you have a special interest, you'll find a complete list at *http://gocalifornia.about.com/od/calamuseums*.

The Getty
✉1200 Getty Center Drive, Los Angeles
✆(310) 440-7330
🖎*www.getty.edu*

It's hard to say which is better at the Getty Center: Richard Meier's architecture or the collections housed inside. If you want to visit and figure it out for yourself, it's open daily except Mondays, January 1, July 4, Thanksgiving, and December 25. The center is also open late on Friday and Saturday nights. Admission is free, but there's an $8 parking charge.

Getty Villa
✉17985 Pacific Coast Highway, Pacific Palisades
✆(310) 440-7300
🖎*www.getty.edu*

The original Getty Museum is housed in an authentically reconstructed Roman villa filled with an impressive antiquities collection. The Getty Villa is open Thursday through Monday except January 1, July 4, Thanksgiving, and December 25. Admission is free, but advance reservations are required and parking costs $8.

George C. Page Museum at the La Brea Tar Pits
✉5801 Wilshire Boulevard, Los Angeles
✆(323) 934-7243
🖎*www.tarpits.org*

There aren't any dinosaurs here, but kids who like the large reptiles will also like the woolly mammoths, saber-toothed cats, dire wolves, and other creatures once captured and fossilized in the tar pits that still bubble away on the front lawn. The museum is open daily. Admission is $7 for adults, $4.50 for children thirteen to seventeen years old, and $2 for kids aged five to twelve.

Los Angeles County Museum of Art

✉5905 Wilshire Blvd., Los Angeles

✆(323) 857-6000

✐*www.lacma.org*

The city's premier art museum occupies several pavilions, each with a different theme. It hosts many outstanding traveling exhibits and offers free Friday night concerts. The museum is open daily except Wednesdays, Thanksgiving, and Christmas. Admission costs $9 for adults, $5 for students and seniors, and anyone under seventeen years old gets in free.

Norton Simon Museum

✉411 W. Colorado Blvd., Pasadena

✆(626) 449-6840

✐*www.nortonsimon.org*

One of the world's most distinguished art collections, the Norton Simon holds works dating from the fourteenth through twentieth centuries, including a noted Vincent Van Gogh collection. The Norton Simon is open daily except Tuesday. Admission is $8 for adults and $4 for seniors. Anyone under age eighteen gets in free.

Petersen Automotive Museum

✉6060 Wilshire Blvd., Los Angeles

✆(323) 930-2277, ✐*www.petersen.org*

Exhibits and dioramas in this four-story museum feature more than 150 rare, classic cars and other conveyances. The museum is closed on Mondays, except when Monday is a major holiday. It's also closed on Thanksgiving, Christmas, and New Year's Day. Admission costs $10 for adults and $5 for students, seniors, and military. Kids aged five through twelve get in for $3, and kids under five years old get in free. Parking in their lot costs $8.

Some of Los Angeles's more unusual museums include the Museum of Jurassic Technology (9341 Venice Blvd., Venice Beach, (310) 836-6131, *www.mjt.org*), and the Bunny Museum (1933 Jefferson Drive, Pasadena, (626) 798-8848, *www.thebunnymuseum.com*).

Shopping

Besides Santa Monica's Third Street Promenade, Rodeo Drive, and Melrose Avenue, shoppers may enjoy the Beverly Center (8500 Beverly Boulevard #501, Los Angeles, *www.beverlycenter.com*) at the edge of Beverly Hills and Hollywood. In the Los Angeles Fashion District ((213) 488-1153, *www.fashiondistrict.org*), over 1,000 shops sell directly to the public at a discount. Stores are open Monday through Saturday, and a few open on Sundays as well.

A veritable cottage industry has sprung up in Los Angeles, selling clothing items worn by stars in movies and television programs and castoffs from celebrity closets. Some of the most popular shops include It's A Wrap (3315 W. Magnolia Blvd., Burbank, (818) 567-7366, *www.itsawraphollywood.com*), which sells movie and television props as well as costumes, and Star Wares (5341 Derry Avenue, Suite D, Agoura Hills, (818) 707-8500, *www.starwares.com*), which sells by appointment at their store and through their Web site.

Sporting Events

The downtown Staples Center is a 900,000-square foot sports and entertainment facility with a 20,000-seat capacity that hosts more than 230 sports, entertainment, and other events annually. The indoor stadium is home to professional sports teams, including the Los Angeles Lakers (basketball), Los Angeles Kings (ice hockey), Los Angeles Clippers (baseball), Los Angeles Avengers (football), and Los Angeles Galaxy (soccer). It's also one of the city's most popular concert arenas. 1111 South Figueroa Street, Los Angeles, (877) 305-1111 General Information, (213) 742-7340 Box Office, *www .staplescenter.com*.

The Los Angeles Dodgers play near downtown in Dodger Stadium (1000 Elysian Park Avenue, *http://losangeles.dodgers.mlb .com*). When there's no game going on, you can take a behind-the-scenes tour. Tours cost $15 for adults and $10 for military, seniors over fifty-five years old, and children fourteen years old and younger.

Sightseeing and Studio Tours

If you have a few hours to spend and want to see all the sights Los Angeles, Hollywood, and the surrounding areas are famous for, consider taking a sightseeing tour.

Starline Tours

✆(800) 959-3131

✎*www.starlinetours.com*

Starline offers eighteen different Los Angeles tours. The two-hour movie stars' homes tour ($37 for adults/$27 for children) is a favorite among tourists, as is the five-hour Grand Tour of Los Angeles. If you're staying in the Los Angeles area, Starline Tours will pick you up at your hotel at no additional charge.

VIP Tours

✆(800) 438-1814

✎*www.viptoursandcharters.com*

VIP offers several tours, using fourteen-passenger vans and a fleet of mini-buses and motor coaches. The Los Angeles City Tour and Movie Stars Homes, for example, is a four-hour tour that takes you to key L.A. destinations—including Beverly Hills, Rodeo Drive, Mann's Chinese Theatre, and the Walk of Fame—past a handful of television and movie studios, and to many celebrity homes. They offer morning, midmorning, afternoon, and midafternoon departures seven days a week. The tour cost is $65 (adults) and $48 (kids). Call the company directly or visit the Web site for information about other tours.

If you want an entertaining overview of motion picture production, take the Studio Tour at Universal Studios Hollywood. If, however, you want to actually explore a working studio, take one of these tours instead.

TRAVEL TIP

You can purchase maps showing the stars' homes from street vendors in Hollywood and Beverly Hills, but don't expect to use them to find Brad Pitt mowing the lawn or Julia Roberts walking the twins. Most stars don't live in this part of town (or anywhere in the Los Angeles area), and the maps seldom give the stars' current home addresses. At best, these maps will send you to a home originally built by a celebrity or where someone famous may have once lived.

NBC Studios Tour
✉3000 West Alameda Avenue, Burbank
✆(818) 840-3537
✐*www.nbc.com*

The NBC tour is a seventy-minute walking tour through a working television studio complex, the only network television studio open to the public in Los Angeles. You'll see a special effects demonstration, visit working sets, and walk through makeup, wardrobe, and dressing room facilities. There's also a souvenir shop selling NBC show merchandise. Admission is $7 for adults, $3.75 for children, and $6.25 for senior citizens.

Paramount Studios Tour
✉860 North Gower Street, Los Angeles
✆(323) 956-1777
✐*www.paramount.com*

Paramount is the only working studio left in Hollywood, and it's steeped in history. On the tour you'll see many famous locations, find out how Charles Bronson chose his stage name on the Paramount lot, and see where shows such as *Star Trek Enterprise* (as well as the other *Star Trek* television shows and movies), *Entertainment Tonight*, and feature films are produced. The tour is $15 per person, and reservations are required. Kids under ten are not permitted. The two-hour walking tour is given on weekdays only.

Sony Pictures Studio Tour

✉10202 West Washington Boulevard, Culver City

☏(323) 520-8687

✐*www.sonypicturesstudios.com*

At the Sony Studio, you'll see where game shows such as *Jeopardy!* and *Wheel of Fortune* are filmed and walk past other popular television show and movie sets. On a two-hour walking tour, you'll also pass the stage where *The Wizard of Oz* was filmed. Tours are given Monday through Friday. Tickets are $25 per person, and all visitors must be at least twelve years old.

Warner Bros. Studios Tour

✉3400 Riverside Drive, Burbank

☏(818) 972-8687

✐*www2.warnerbros.com/vipstudiotour/*

The VIP tour (which is actually their standard tour) visits the Warner Bros. Museum, several production facilities, and the back lot. Longer Deluxe tours include visits with working professionals and lunch. Tours operate on weekdays only. Admission for the VIP Tour is $30, the Deluxe Tour is $150, and reservations should be made in advance. Children under eight years old are not permitted on the tour. This is the most informative studio tour and includes the most behind-the-scenes activity in terms of working soundstages where television shows (like *ER*) and movies such as *Ocean's 13* are made.

TRAVEL TIP

One of the most enjoyable ways to get a peek at how popular television shows are created is to watch one being filmed. Audiences Unlimited (☏(818) 753-3470, ✐*www.tvtickets.com*) offers free tickets to sitcoms and game shows. To be in the audience for the *Jay Leno Show*, *Dr. Phil*, *The Price Is Right*, *Wheel of Fortune*, and other talk and game shows, check with TV Tickets at ✐*www.tvtix.com*.

Beaches

Los Angeles County's beaches are the stuff of song and screen, featured in thousands of films.

Santa Monica Beach

Santa Monica Beach, near the Santa Monica Pier, is a popular spot in summer, and a nice place to watch the sunset.

Venice Beach

Venice Beach and Boardwalk will look familiar even if you haven't been there. This beach is where the *Baywatch* television series was filmed, and where the show's signature yellow lifeguard trucks still patrol the beaches. The waterfront promenade, running alongside a beautiful beach area, is filled with street performers, shops, and souvenir stands. Venice is definitely a tourist destination that's worth visiting during the summer months and during the daylight hours. It's a good place for walking, inline skating, or bike riding, and inline skates and bike rentals are available. There are also numerous cafés and fast-food places along the beachfront. In addition to shopping, the main activity here is sunbathing and people watching, especially at legendary Muscle Beach.

RAINY DAY FUN

If you get stuck near the beach on a drizzly day, head for the airport, but don't jump on a plane and flee for sunnier places. Instead, head for the Encounter Restaurant, the flying saucer–shaped building that you've seen dozens of times, an icon of Los Angeles. The kitschy, Jetsons-style interior is fun, the food is quite good (and they even have a special Space Cadet menu for kids), and you can sit at the bar and watch the airplanes come and go. ✆(310) 215-5151, ✐www .encounterlax.com.

Nearby in Venice, you'll find what's left of the sixteen miles of canals that gave the city its name when it was founded by real-estate developer Abbot Kinney. Stroll along the canals in the area bordered by Washington, South Venice Boulevard, Pacific Avenue, and Ocean Avenue.

South Bay Beach Towns

The South Bay beach towns—Manhattan Beach, Hermosa Beach, and Redondo Beach—face the Santa Monica Bay south of LAX, strung along a sidewalk locals call the Strand. The beach scene is fun to watch, and a walk here takes you past beach volleyball players, sunbathers, and surfers. Each town has a different feel. Try Manhattan Beach for a lively, upscale shopping and dining atmosphere, Hermosa Beach for a funkier, surfer culture, or head to the Redondo Beach Pier for a meal and an after-dinner stroll along the sand. Polly's on the Pier at the Redondo Marina is the area's best (and possibly most popular) breakfast spot, but you won't mind waiting with all the goings-on to watch.

Nightlife

Along Sunset Boulevard, Wilshire Boulevard, Hollywood Boulevard, and various other locations throughout Hollywood and the Los Angeles area, you'll find some of the world's trendiest nightclubs. As with any trend, the hot place to be seen in L.A. changes quickly, so ask your hotel's concierge to recommend the best clubs to visit. Most clubs have a dress code, and you must be either eighteen or over twenty-one to get in. Some offer live entertainment, while others feature some of the country's best-known DJs.

No matter what type of music you enjoy or what crowd you like to party with, chances are there's an L.A. club to satisfy your desires. Los Angeles for Visitors (*http://golosangeles.about.com*) lists the city's best nightclubs by type. You can also pick up a free copy of the LA Weekly (*www.laweekly.com*) at any hotel or newsstand for information about the club scene and a detailed calendar of events for the entire Los Angeles County area.

≡FAST FACT

Tonight Show host Jay Leno often performs at the Comedy & Magic Club in Hermosa Beach on Sunday nights, trying out new material for his show. ⊠1018 Hermosa Ave., Hermosa Beach, ✆(310) 372-1193 *www.comedyandmagicclub.com.*

The world's most famous comedy clubs, where virtually all of the biggest names in comedy have gotten their start, can be found in and around the Los Angeles County area. The Comedy Store—(323) 650-6268, *www.thecomedystore.com*—on Sunset Boulevard has launched top comics' careers since 1972, and on occasion, a Comedy Store alumnus shows up unannounced to try out new material. There's also The Improv (323) 651-2583, the Laugh Factory (323) 656-1336, and more than twenty-five other comedy clubs in the area. Most have shows every night and cater to an adult (18+ or 21+) crowd.

Getting Around

The Los Angeles metropolitan area is the antithesis of the oft-maligned small town so tiny that it posts both city limits signs on the same pole. From the time you enter the Los Angeles area near Oxnard until you break free of the urban sprawl south of South Clemente, the drive across the never-ending city—on a good day with light traffic—takes more than two hours.

Most Angelenos get around by automobile, contributing to the city's legendary bad traffic. A map is essential to getting around Los Angeles, and before you go somewhere, it's best to plot not only your primary route but also a backup in case of traffic jams. Radio station KFWB 980 FM is a good source of traffic reports, but you'll need to know the lingo: "looky-loos" are people who slow down to gawk at an accident, a "sig alert" is any incident that closes at least one lane of traffic for thirty minutes or more, a "carbecue" is a car on fire, and

"TMC" means too many cars, something you may hear more often than you'd like.

RAINY DAY FUN

If it's raining (or even if it isn't) and it's Sunday (or the first Saturday of the month), take a Metro Art Tour to see the public art at the Metro Line stations. Tours meet at 10 A.M. at the street-level entrance to the Hollywood Boulevard Metro Station and at the information booth in downtown's Union Station. ✆(213) 922-2738, *www.mta.net.*

Los Angeles freeway signs can be maddening to a newcomer. You need to know the freeway's names (not just their numbers), and knowing what cities you're driving toward may help you navigate. These are some common names: Santa Monica Freeway (I-10), Hollywood Freeway (170), San Diego Freeway (I-405), Pasadena Freeway (110 north of downtown), Harbor Freeway (I-110 south of downtown). The I-5 is often called the Golden State or Santa Ana Freeway.

To avoid some of the traffic, try the Metropolitan Transit Authority (MTA) Metro rail (*www.mta.net*). It can take you downtown, to Hollywood, Wilshire Boulevard, Long Beach, Pasadena, and other places.

CHAPTER 18

Six Flags Magic Mountain

SIX FLAGS MAGIC MOUNTAIN is the Los Angeles area's extreme theme park with no fewer than sixteen monster coasters guaranteed to zip, whip, flip, and rattle you. It's located in Valencia north of the Los Angeles metro area, about sixty miles from Disneyland, a one- to two-hour-plus drive depending on traffic.

An Overview of Six Flags Magic Mountain

✉26101 Magic Mountain Parkway, Valencia

✆(661) 255-4100

✐*www.sixflags.com*

Six Flags's world-class coasters and other rides make it particularly suited to teens and adults. However, Bugs Bunny World, its kids' area based on the Looney Tunes cartoons, contains plenty of rides designed for younger people, including a kids-only roller coaster.

You'll also find Six Flags Hurricane Harbor in the same place. The large water park contains water slides, a wave pool, a lazy river, and three large activity areas. Hurricane Harbor charges a separate admission fee, but you can also buy an all-inclusive (discounted) ticket. See Chapter 6 for details.

Six Flags Magic Mountain opens seven days per week during the spring and summer. However, unlike the Disney theme parks, it is open only on weekends and holidays the rest of the year. See Chapter 6 for a summary of admission prices.

To get to Magic Mountain from Anaheim, take the Interstate 5 freeway (I-5) north toward Sacramento. Exit at Magic Mountain Parkway and follow the signs to the entrance. From Hollywood and Universal City, take US 101 north, transferring to the 170 freeway north to connect with I-5.

Once you arrive at Magic Mountain, you'll find free day kennels for your pet near the parking lot and several picnic areas where you can enjoy food you bring to the park. You can't bring food from outside into the park itself and dining options there are minimal, so you may want to pack a picnic and eat it here.

When you pay for parking, you'll receive a full-color park map and guide. Reviewing the map before entering the park will help you get around and chalk out a plan to see everything. Each ride's height restrictions are also listed in the free booklet, as is information about shows and dining options.

The walk between the parking lot and the entrance can take more than fifteen minutes. You may want to take the tram and save your legs for walking later. Expect to spend up to fifteen minutes to get through the security screening before you get inside.

Magic Mountain Rides and Attractions

During peak times, Magic Mountain gets very crowded, with seemingly endless lines forming for the newest and most extreme rides. Even when the park isn't too crowded, you could still wait between an hour and ninety minutes for each ride, and longer for the newer ones.

Most rides and attractions that make up Magic Mountain are outdoor-based, and Valencia is in an area that gets hotter than the coastline. Chapter 2 gives some general guidelines about theme park attire. Dress for comfort and wear sunblock and sunglasses, especially in summer. Bring a glasses case or find some other way to keep your spectacles or sunglasses from falling off when you go feet-over-head on those roller coasters. Find a way to keep your hat on, too.

TRAVEL TIP

By purchasing an optional FastLane ticket, you can avoid lines. Each ticket affords four opportunities to bypass the line at the major attractions. The ticket can be applied to four people on the same ride, one person on four different rides, or any other combination. Only a limited number of FastLane tickets are sold daily, so buy them as early in the day as possible.

Like most modern amusement parks, Magic Mountain is divided into themed areas, and all of them offer plenty of fast rides and other attractions. While Magic Mountain isn't nearly as big as Disneyland, it's still easy to wear yourself out walking around. To save on shoe leather, explore one area at a time before moving on to the next. If your group includes a mix of ages, you may want to split up, with the young kids enjoying Bugs Bunny World while the coaster-cravers head for their favorites.

A free tram circles the park and offers an alternative to walking, but you may have to wait to board it. The Orient Express people mover also travels directly from Six Flags Plaza to the top of Samurai Summit.

 JUST FOR PARENTS

Many of the park's big, fast rides restrict age or height and are not suitable for smaller children. For most of the faster rides, guests must be at least 42 inches tall and some have a minimum of 54 inches. Measure your youngsters before you leave home so they know what they can go on, and check the signs posted near each ride's entrance to be sure the restrictions have not changed.

Baja Ridge

Baja Ridge is home to some of Magic Mountain's biggest, meanest coasters.

Revolution

Opened during America's bicentennial in 1976, Revolution shoots you along 3,457 feet of track at speeds up to 55 miles per hour. The ride lasts about two minutes, and during that time, you'll go through a 90-foot-high vertical loop and feel positive G-forces up to 4.4. Each train holds twenty riders (in five cars, with passengers sitting in pairs). Guests must be at least 48 inches tall.

≡FAST FACT

Revolution was the world's first giant looping coaster and was inspired by the old-fashioned wooden coasters of yesteryear.

Viper

For over eleven years, Viper has thrilled people of all ages. It takes you 188 feet into the air, and then sends you speeding at 70 miles per hour along its 3,830 feet of track. The ride lasts two minutes and is famous for its 140-foot-tall vertical loop, once the world's tallest. Each train holds twenty-eight people, sitting in pairs. As with most coasters, the best seats are always in the front. Guests must be at least 54 inches tall.

X

Taking the ride dubbed as the first "4th dimensional thrill," X riders fly, flip, spin, and rotate 360 degrees forward, backward, upside down, and head first. It's the closest thing possible to flying through the air at high speeds.

Riders are strapped into the ride in a standing position (each car holds twenty-eight passengers—seven rows, four people across).

They will ultimately glide along the ride's 3,610 feet of twisting track at speeds up to 76 miles per hour. To kick off the excitement, there's a 200-foot drop right at the start.

Be prepared for long waits to ride X. Your best hope of avoiding them is to head for it first thing in the morning. On weekdays, when it's less crowded, the lines are a bit shorter. However, Magic Mountain often runs the ride at less than full capacity then, and waits up to two hours are still typical. X is so popular that its waiting line closes long before the whole park does. Guests must be at least 48 inches tall.

Bugs Bunny World

A giant tree marks the entrance to Bugs Bunny World, a six-acre mini-park. Its seventeen kid-oriented rides include gentler roller coasters, a carousel, a pint-size train, and other rides suited to smaller children. Looney Tunes cartoon characters appear in this area to greet guests, pose for pictures, and sign autographs. If you're visiting Magic Mountain with kids less than twelve years old, this is where they'll have the most fun.

You'll find also the Warner Bros. Kids' Club Stage in Bugs Bunny World (featuring live entertainment) and Looney Tunes Lodge, a fun place filled with thousands of foam balls.

Colossus County Fair

Colossus County Fair has an old-fashioned, county-festival feel, but its rides are better described as state-of-the-art. The Magic Mountain Metro System (which is the transit system within the park) stops at Colossus County Fair.

Buccaneer

Riders climb aboard a land-based version of an old-fashioned pirate ship that "sails" out of control during a wild adventure cruise. An adult must accompany guests shorter than 48 inches tall.

Circus Wheel

The Circus Wheel ride is all about spinning and twisting. It's a traditional amusement park ride that's moderately rough. Minimum height to ride alone is 42 inches tall.

Colossus

This coaster takes riders 125 feet into the air for a 2.5-minute ride at speeds over 62 miles per hour. Riders on the dual-track wooden roller coaster fly over fourteen hills, one that drops 115 feet. Guests must be at least 48 inches tall.

═FAST FACT

Colossus is a traditional wooden coaster that opened back in 1978. It is, however, the tallest and fastest wooden dual-track coaster on the West Coast. Since it debuted, the ride has undergone several changes, including adding new lighter cars that increased its maximum speed and reprofiling the track.

Cyclone 500

For an additional fee, you can strap yourself into a go-cart and race around a nearly mile-long track. Each car holds a driver and (optional) passenger. Guests must be at least 58 inches tall.

Goliath

The name says it all—Goliath is big...very big...and very fast. Riders reach a top speed of 85 miles per hour as they race along the 4,500 feet of track. The three-minute ride includes a near-vertical (61-degree) drop into a 120-foot-long underground tunnel. The very high G-forces that it produces can induce harrowing near-blackouts. The highest point is 255 feet. Guests must be at least 48 inches tall.

JUST FOR PARENTS

If your smaller kids are pestering you to let them ride Goliath, take them instead to Goliath Jr. They may also enjoy Daffy's Adventure Tours, the Canyon Blaster, and other rides in Bugs Bunny's World as well as the Sky Tower.

Scream

Cars sit on top of the track in this floorless coaster, and the riders' feet dangle. After an initial 128-foot vertical loop, there's a heartline spin (the train twists, but the riders' hearts stay in a more-or-less straight line), and a dive loop. Minimum height to ride is 54 inches.

Swashbuckler

A spinning swing set lifts guests high into the air, then it goes around, and around, and around—fast. It's best to avoid Swashbuckler if you're prone to motion sickness. Guests must be at least 42 inches tall.

 TRAVEL TIP

Many of the Six Flags Magic Mountain rides are not for smaller kids, expectant mothers, anyone with a heart or back condition, or people who suffer from other physical ailments that might be aggravated by high speed, G-forces, jerks, or hanging upside down. If you suffer from motion sickness, stay off the rides that induce it or bring your favorite remedies. If you have questions or concerns about a specific ride, consult the signs posted outside its entrance or ask a park employee.

THE EVERYTHING FAMILY GUIDE TO DISNEYLAND

Entertainment in Colossus County Fair includes Center Ring Games and the Boardwalk Arcade, where for an extra fee you can play skill- and luck-based carnival games, video games, and pinball machines. Magic Moments Theater features family-oriented shows with nonstop visual laser effects year-round. The loud music and sound effects accompanying Magic Moments' visual effects may be too intense for younger children.

Cyclone Bay

Cyclone Bay is literally packed with exciting rides, and you may feel like you've been hit by a cyclone by the time you're done.

Déjà Vu

Whether you're traveling forward or backward along 1,203 feet of track, you're in for major excitement. Seated ski lift–style, you'll find yourself traveling up to 65 miles per hour through seemingly end-less twists and turns. Guests must be between 54 inches tall and 75 inches tall.

Dive Devil

This ride nicely combines the excitement of skydiving and hang gliding as you're hoisted 150 feet into the air (strapped in a harness) and dropped. You'll ultimately reach sixty miles per hour as you ride alone or strapped together with up to three people. An extra fee is required to go on Dive Devil, but it's the closest you'll get to skydiving without actually jumping out of an airplane. Guests must be at least 48 inches tall.

Jet Stream

Enjoy what starts off as a calm and relaxing log flume water ride, but don't think you'll be dry for long. The trip ends with a dramatic 57-foot plunge and a giant splash. An adult must accompany guests less than 42 inches tall.

Thrill Shot

It could be called "slingshot" because it flings you into the air so fast you'll be subjected to 2.5 Gs on the way up. It requires an additional fee, and you have to be at least 52 inches tall.

Cyclone Bay entertainment includes Sharkey's Shooting Gallery (an old-fashioned shooting gallery but with electronic rifles) and Cyclone Bay Arcade and Games (additional fee).

Gotham City Backlot

Gotham City Backlot refers to the *Batman* films, and it is home to the Batman ride and show, along with other rides.

Atom Smasher

A spinning, twirling, fast-paced ride. Minimum height is 42 inches.

Batman: The Ride

While suspended below the track, riders sit in ski lift–style chairs and travel at more than 50 miles per hour along a 2,700-foot track. Batman originally opened in 1994 and features hairpin turns, vertical loops, a corkscrew, and a "one-of-a-kind heartline spin with a zero gravity force producing a feeling of weightlessness." Guests must be at least 54 inches tall.

Grinder Gearworks

Riders are lifted into the air and spun so fast that they get plastered against the wall, while leaning at a 45-degree angle as it spins. Guests must be at least 42 inches tall.

Gotham City entertainment includes the Batman & Robin Live Action Show, a stunt show based on the popular *Batman* movies. The family-oriented program features an elaborate set and impressive special effects, including lasers and pyrotechnics (which may frighten young children). You'll get a good view no matter where you sit, but on busy days, it's a good idea to get there twenty to thirty minutes before showtime to be sure you get in. During off-peak periods, the show may not be presented.

High Sierra Territory
High Sierra Territory goes to California's mountains for inspiration. The Magic Mountain Metro System stops here.

Freefall
What goes up must come down. That's the basic concept behind this classic theme park ride that lifts riders up a ten-story tower and then drops them at 55 miles per hour. The actual drop lasts about two seconds, but it feels much longer. Guests must be at least 42 inches tall.

Goldrusher
Goldrusher is an out-of-control runaway mining train. It travels at 35 miles per hour and lasts about 2.5 minutes. It's somewhat less wild than a traditional coaster but still offers plenty of excitement. Guests must be at least 48 inches tall.

Goliath Jr.
For young people who enjoy fast rides but aren't old enough for the park's large coasters, Goliath Jr. takes riders a mere 10 feet into the air and travels at only ten miles per hour. The ride lasts about ninety seconds. Riders must be shorter than 54 inches tall.

Granny Gran Prix
The electronically powered re-creations of antique cars make a good ride for parents to take with their children and preteens. Guests must be at least 48 inches tall to ride alone or 42 inches if accompanied by an adult.

Sierra Twist
Riding in a sled-shaped vehicle, you'll spin around while zipping down the track. Guests must be at least 42 inches tall.

Log Jammer
For a water-based log ride that's a bit wet and wild, check out Log Jammer. It's not as fast and furious as some of the other Magic

Mountain rides, but certainly offers its own entertainment. An adult must accompany guests less than 42 inches tall.

Yosemite Sam Sierra Falls

A whitewater rafting simulation ride, Yosemite Sam takes you on a twisting and turning journey along a river. Be prepared to get a bit wet, although the ride is much tamer than many offered within the park and drier than Roaring Rapids or Tidal Wave. Guests less than an adult must accompany 42 inches tall.

Entertainment in High Sierra Territory includes Just Wingin' It, a free-flight show featuring beautiful exotic birds from around the world, and Wile E. Coyote Critter Canyon petting zoo.

TRAVEL TIP

The Golden Bear Theater hosts concerts and special events throughout the year. For details on events during your visit, contact Guest Relations or check the signs located near the theater entrance. The amphitheater holds 3,200 guests.

Entertainment at Rapids Camp Crossing includes Mining Town Games and the Mining Town Arcade.

Movie District

The Movie District is the complement to Gotham City and home of Batman's nemesis in *Riddler's Revenge*.

The Riddler's Revenge

Since 1998, *Riddler's Revenge* has offered yet another destination for coaster fanatics seeking the ultimate adventure. The ride is based around Batman's archenemy Riddler. It's a fast-moving coaster, where riders stand up for the entire journey as they travel along 4,370 feet of track at speeds up to 65 miles per hour. The ride includes six inversions, one 360-degree vertical loop, one 360-degree oblique loop, and two over-the-top diving loops, plus two 150-foot-long barrel rolls. Guests must be at least 54 inches tall.

Roaring Rapids

The first constructed whitewater rafting ride, Roaring Rapids offers a splashing good time, but it is far less scary than some of the park's other rides. You will get wet on Roaring Rapids, so you may want to ride during the warmer part of the day. People over ten years old will enjoy Roaring Rapids, but they must be at least 42 inches tall.

 **TRAVEL TIP**

Roaring Rapids, Jet Stream, Tidal Wave, and the tamer Yosemite Sam Sierra Falls are great rides for cooling off on a particularly hot day or when you need to take a break from flying around on steel rails. Wear lightweight clothing that dries quickly or bring a change with you.

Sandblasters

This is a traditional bumper car ride. Guests must be at least 42 inches tall.

Spin Out

As you spin, the floor drops out below you. Riders must be over 36 inches and under 75 inches tall.

Tidal Wave

Have you ever wondered what it would be like to travel down a 50-foot waterfall? Get on Tidal Wave and you'll find out. The ride ends with a splash! Guests must be at least 42 inches tall.

Samurai Summit

Samurai Summit, the "mountain" in Magic Mountain, features a quiet Japanese garden with flowers, a stream, and panoramic views. It may well be the quietest spot in the park.

The Magic Mountain Metro System stops at Samurai Summit. You can also get there on the Orient Express people mover from Six Flags Plaza.

Ninja

For ninety seconds, you'll race along nearly a half-mile of track while traveling at 55 miles per hour. The trains swing freely from side to side (with 180 degrees of movement) as it goes around sharp turns, drops, and twists. Guests must be at least 42 inches tall.

Sky Tower

For the ultimate aerial view of Magic Mountain, Sky Tower takes you up twenty-eight stories and spins slowly around. Then it brings you calmly back to ground level. It's the perfect family-oriented ride.

Superman The Escape

Superman flings you into the air, going from a standstill to almost 100 miles per hour in about seven seconds. When it first made its debut at Magic Mountain in 1997, Superman held the world's record for tower height (415 feet), speed (100 miles per hour), and time spent weightless (6.5 seconds). You'll feel like Superman as you fly in the air, but you may wish your stomach were made of steel if you go on it too soon after eating. Guests must be at least 48 inches tall.

Tatsu

Tatsu flies at more than 62 miles per hour through plunges, spirals, loops, curves, and dives, including a 263-foot change in elevation from top to bottom. The three-and-a-half minute ride takes you over 3,602 feet of track and through the whole park.

Six Flags Plaza

The six flags refer to the ones that once flew over the state of Texas, where the Six Flags Corporation got its start. You'll find a few rides and attractions around the plaza.

Grand Carousel

Originally built in 1912 and fully restored, the carousel is the perfect attraction for young people and adults alike who want to enjoy a classic amusement park ride. An adult must accompany guests shorter than 42 inches tall.

Palace Games features skeeball, games of skill, classic arcade games, and pinball machines. There's an additional fee to play.

Six Flags Hurricane Harbor

www.sixflags.com/parks/hurricaneharborla
Hurricane Harbor features enough towers, falls, pools, and coves to satisfy anyone's urge for water fun. Its attractions include Tornado, a six-story-high funnel that sends riders in four-person rafts down a 132-foot-long course. Six Flags Hurricane Harbor water park is open weekends only beginning in mid-May. It is open every day from late May through early September, and returns to weekends-only through September. See Chapter 6 for a summary of admission prices.

Magic Mountain Events

Presented on selected dates between late May and early September, Looney Tunes Nights feature a live-action musical parade starring popular Looney Tunes characters and popular DC Comics superheroes. The parade concludes with a fireworks presentation over Six Flags Plaza (a display visible from anywhere in the park where you can see the Sky Tower).

Throughout the year, Six Flags Magic Mountain hosts special events, including a July Fourth Fireworks Spectacular that's one of Southern California's most impressive displays. During most of October, the theme park transforms into a Halloween Fright Fest, with special attractions and events. In late summer, the park hosts Festival Latino (a Latino culture festival).

Dining at Magic Mountain

Inside the park there are dozens of fast-food purveyors and two sit-down restaurants: Mooseburger Lodge in the High Sierra area and the Laughing Dragon Pizza Company in Samurai Summit. Other food options—and the areas of the park you can find them in—include:

- **Buongusto Deli** (Cyclone Bay): Panini sandwiches and Italian ices
- **Carousel Grill** (Colossus County Fair): Hot specialty sandwiches including Philly cheesesteaks and grilled chicken clubs
- **Chicken Plantation** (Six Flags Plaza): Fried chicken, fish and chips, and more.
- **Colossus Cookery** (Colossus County Fair): Cheeseburgers, fries, soft drinks, and more
- **Eduardo's Grill** (The Movie District): Tacos, burritos, nacho platters, and soft drinks
- **Food, Etc.** (Colossus County Fair): Food court serving sushi, pasta, pizza, tacos, nachos, taco salad, submarine sandwiches, turkey legs, salads, cookies, and desserts
- **Goliath Goodies** (Colossus County Fair): Churros, fresh fruit, and cold beverages
- **Katy's Kettle** (Rapid's Camp Crossing): Cheeseburgers, chicken-strip meals, fries, and soft drinks
- **Laughing Dragon Pizza Co.** (Samurai Summit): Gourmet pizza, pasta, and salads
- **Los Cuates Mexican Grill** (Cyclone Bay): Authentic Mexican fare including tacos, burritos, and soft drinks
- **Mooseburger Lodge** (High Sierra Territory): Sit-down restaurant featuring burgers, barbecue, and entertainment

- **Panda Express** (Baja Ridge): Chinese food
- **Paradise Picnic Pavilion** (High Sierra Territory)
- **The Pizza Vector** (Gotham City Backlot): Pizza
- **Plaza Ice Cream Co.** (Six Flags Plaza): Ice cream, coffees, and cookies
- **Plaza Cafe** (Six Flags Plaza): Sandwiches, drinks, and specialty coffees
- **Smoothies Etc.** (Colossus County Fair): Smoothies and French fries
- **Snack'n Shack** (High Sierra Territory): Icees, ice cream, and soft drinks
- **Surfside Grill** (Cyclone Bay): Chili dogs, chili fries, soft drinks, and Icees
- **Suzette's Bakery** (Six Flags Plaza): Funnel cakes, soft drinks
- **Wascal's** (High Sierra Territory): Cheeseburgers, chicken-strip meals, fries, and soft drinks
- **Waterfront Commissary** (The Movie District): Cheeseburgers, fries, chicken-strip meals, and individual pizzas

Dining options near Magic Mountain are very limited, and consist mostly of fast food.

Lodging Near Magic Mountain

It is possible to enjoy Magic Mountain in a single day. However, if you're traveling with kids who spend a lot of time in Bugs Bunny World and you want to do other things, too, if you're with thrill-seekers who don't mind standing in line for ninety minutes for two minutes' exhilaration, or if you plan to also play at Hurricane Harbor, you may want to break up your visit to make it a two-day excursion.

If you decide to do this, look into buying a season or combination ticket. You may also want to choose a nearby hotel to minimize the time you spend in Los Angeles traffic.

Near Six Flags Magic Mountain, there are a handful of hotels, motels, and RV parks including:

Hilton Garden Inn

✉27710 The Old Road, Valencia 91355

☎(661) 254-8800

🖰*www.hiltongardeninn.com*

Holiday Inn Express

✉27513 Wayne Mills Place, Valencia

☎(661) 284-2101

🖰*www.ichotelsgroup.com*

Hyatt Valencia

✉24500 Town Center Drive, Valencia

☎(661) 799-1234

🖰*http://valencia.hyatt.com*

Best Western Valencia Inn

✉27413 N. Tourney Road, Valencia 91355

☎(661) 255-0555

🖰*www.bestwestern.com*

Castaic RV Park

✉31540 Ridge Route Road, Castaic 91384

☎(661) 257-3340

Valencia Travel Village RV Park

✉27946 Henry Mayo Road, Hwy 126, Valencia 91355

☎(661) 257-8047

CHAPTER 19

Universal Studios Hollywood

LOCATED IN UNIVERSAL CITY and just north of Holly-wood, the place it's named for, Universal Studios Hollywood is one of the world's best-known working motion picture and television studios. Although the facility continues to be a working studio, it's also one of Hollywood's most popular theme parks.

An Overview of Universal Studios Hollywood

✉100 Universal City Plaza, Universal City

☎(800) 864-8377

🖱*www.universalstudioshollywood.com*

With rides, shows, and attractions based on blockbuster motion pictures and popular television shows, Universal Studios Hollywood allows you to experience your favorite movies in a whole new way. Universal is a family-oriented theme park, combining quasi-thrill rides, movie-themed shows, attractions, dining, and shops.

Universal Studios Hollywood is divided into three main areas: the Upper Lot, the Lower Lot, and the studio. Adjacent to the theme park and accessible without an admission ticket, you'll find Universal CityWalk, a dining and shopping complex, and the Gibson Amphitheater, a popular concert venue.

Operating hours for Universal Studios Hollywood theme park are from 8 A.M. to 10 P.M. during the summer, Thanksgiving, Easter, and Christmas, and 9 A.M. to 7 P.M. during all other times. Call or check their Web site to find out their hours during your visit. Ticket prices are summarized in Chapter 6.

≡FAST FACT

If you've been to Universal Studios Florida, you may notice that the Hollywood theme park is somewhat smaller than the one in Florida. However, the working studio section in California is bigger. After all, this place was originally (and still is) a busy major motion picture studio.

Universal Studios Hollywood is located between Hollywood and the San Fernando Valley, just off the Hollywood (US 101) Freeway. Take the Universal Center Drive or Lankershim exit and follow the signs.

If you're staying in Anaheim, you can visit Universal Studios Hollywood without renting a car. If you buy a full-price admission ticket, you'll get free round-trip shuttle bus transportation between Anaheim and Universal. The shuttle bus operates seven days a week and leaves both locations several times a day. While it's not as flexible as driving on your own, the price is right and you don't have to worry about driving hassles.

The Studio Tour

The Studio Tour (sometimes called the Backlot tour) is Universal's most unique attraction. Visitors ride in an open-sided tram through the working part of Universal Studios to get a look at Hollywood history, see sets from well-known movies, and even come across a few surprises. The Backlot tour is suitable for people of all ages.

Departing every few minutes throughout the day, the fifty-five-minute tour, narrated by Whoopi Goldberg (on video) gives a fun-filled (albeit scripted) look at how a major motion picture studio operates.

You'll see famous movie sets (from *Jurassic Park III*, *Psycho*, *Back to the Future*, and *The Grinch*), pass working soundstages, and learn a bit about the studio's history. You might even glimpse a famous celebrity at work, but don't count on it.

≡FAST FACT

Universal's back lot is home to more than 500 famous sets from movies and television shows. In the years since Universal Studios opened in 1912, they have produced over 8,000 movies, countless television shows, infomercials, television commercials, and music videos.

The Studio Tour also offers a few surprises as your tram enters areas designed just to entertain visitors. You'll experience an earthquake (Hollywood style), get caught in a simulated flood, and get perilously close to the *Jaws* shark.

🧳 TRAVEL TIP

Especially in the evening, be sure to bring a jacket. The trams are open and constantly moving, so if the temperature drops, you will be cold if you're not dressed appropriately. Seats in the last row are directly over the engines, making them a real "hot seat" on warm days but a cozy spot when it's chilly.

The Studio Tour entertains, and it gives a cursory look at studio operations, but if you're truly interested in a behind-the-scenes look at how a studio works, you may want to try the other studio tours

THE EVERYTHING FAMILY GUIDE TO DISNEYLAND

described in the previous chapter. Alternatively, if you can afford it, Universal offers a special VIP Experience tour. Besides theme park admission and front-of-the-line access to all rides and attractions, the package includes a personalized studio and back lot tour where you visit working soundstages (instead of looking at them as you ride past in the tram), see studio facilities not open to the general public, and explore the props department.

The Upper Lot

The Universal Studios Hollywood theme park area is divided into two main areas: the Upper Lot and the Lower Lot. It's easy to travel between these two areas by taking a series of escalators, and the journey takes about five minutes. An elevator is also available. The Upper Lot holds most of the park's attractions, including the following.

Back to the Future...The Ride

Although it has been around for a few years now, Back to the Future continues to be an extremely popular attraction, so be prepared to wait to ride it. Fortunately, the waiting area is mostly covered, so you'll stay out of direct sun or rain. Inside, a video preshow featuring Doc Brown and Biff from the *Back to the Future* movie trilogy sets the stage for your travels. After the preshow, smaller groups watch an additional four-minute video that continues the background story. Finally, you board the time-traveling vehicle, Doc Brown's latest invention. The ride combines a flight simulator, surround audio, and an Omnimax movie shown on an eighty-foot-tall projection screen. The vehicle jumps and jolts, and although there are no real drops, it feels as if there are. Guests must be at least 40 inches tall.

The Blues Brothers

A twenty-minute show presented several times a day in an outdoor stage area, the live musical performance stars the Blues Brothers, Jake and Elwood, who perform popular musical numbers.

Fear Factor Live

An audience participation show based on the popular reality series, Fear Factor Live pits contestants against each other as they attempt stunts and face up to creepy creatures.

Hollywood Ticket Office and TV Audience Ticket Booth

Universal Studios, along with all the other nearby studios and television networks, offers free tickets to see tapings of popular sit-coms, game shows, and other programs. Pick up tickets for these events, as well as shows at the Gibson Amphitheatre here.

Nickelodeon Blast Zone

This kids-only attraction is a colorful, interactive play area complete with shooting fountains and other water-based activities to enjoy on hot days. Children like this attraction a lot, and they're going to be completely soaked when they're done, so dress them in something that dries quickly or bring a change of clothing. Besides the water play, you'll find the Wild Thornberrys Adventure Temple (containing over 25,000 foam balls and other activities) and Nick Jr. Backyard (designed for kids under the age of six), which are totally dry areas for children to explore. This is the place to meet characters from Nickelodeon's most popular shows.

Shrek: 4-D

Shrek, Donkey, and Fiona take off on a new adventure in a 3-D show with some "fourth-dimension" surprises.

Terminator 2: 3-D

If you saw the *Terminator 2* motion picture, you know it was jam-packed with nonstop special effects and plenty of action. This twenty-minute 3-D movie, shown in a custom-built theater contin-ues the story. The show combines three-dimensional filming with lasers, live actors, robots, indoor pyrotechnics, and state-of-the-art sound effects. Your adventure begins outside, with a visit to

Cyberdyne Corporation headquarters, where Kimberly (the director of corporate affairs) provides a brief presentation about the new Skynet system. Stand near the middle of the room for the preshow and be sure you can see the Cyberdyne logos on the large video monitors overhead. The movie portion of the attraction transports guests to the year 2029 and reunites Arnold Schwarzenegger, Linda Hamilton, Edward Furlong, and director James Cameron for an exciting adventure. The entire attraction takes place in an air-conditioned building. The waiting area to enter the ride, however, is outdoors (but covered).

Due to the violent subject matter (and the loud explosions), it may not be suitable for young kids. If it were shown in traditional theaters, it would have a PG-13 rating.

Universal's Animal Actors

A twenty-minute show features animal trainers and a cast of animals you've seen on popular television shows and movies. Exotic birds, trained monkeys, snakes, and famous dogs are among the animals that perform in a show that's both extremely cute and enjoyable. The show appeals to small children in particular, but it is suitable for all ages. It's presented in a large theater so there's seldom a wait—assuming you arrive about fifteen minutes before showtime. Showtimes are posted in front of the theater, on information boards throughout the park, and in the printed park schedule available from the ticket booths. The theater is covered, so you'll be sheltered from direct sunlight or light rain.

Van Helsing Fortress Dracula

Based on the vampire-hunter motion picture, this self-paced, walk-through attraction re-creates sets and props from the movie, creating an experience that's a bit like a classic carnival fun house, but with much better effects. Like the movie, the attraction is not suitable for young kids.

WaterWorld

Based very loosely on the *WaterWorld* motion picture, the fifteen-minute, high-energy live show features exciting motorboat stunts and extreme Jet Ski action. They combine with pyrotechnics and other special effects that create realistic explosions designed to keep you at the edge of your seat. The loud explosions may frighten young children, but most kids aged five and older, teens, and adults will enjoy the show. When the park is crowded, arrive at the theater at least fifteen minutes before the posted showtime to ensure getting a seat, and pay attention to your hosts, who will help you locate the seats that are going to get wet. It's up to you to decide whether you want to sit in them or not.

The Lower Lot

The Lower Lot is separated from the Upper Lot by a series of escalators, so long that audio entertainment is provided to keep you from getting bored on the way. About halfway between the two areas, where you switch escalators, a large terrace offers a wonderful view of the Universal Studios' soundstages and back lot. You can also see the Warner Bros. Studios in the distance. Attractions and rides in the Lower Lot include the following.

Revenge of the Mummy—The Ride

Based on the movies *The Mummy* and *The Revenge of the Mummy*, this attraction takes you to the ancient land of Egypt on a thrill-packed roller coaster. This indoor roller coaster employs both backward and forward motion and is full of special effects and shocks at every turn. This fast-paced and turbulent ride combines Animatronics, projected CGI computer graphic effects, original motion picture footage (starring Brendan Fraser), and motion-simulator technology to create a totally new type of theme park experience. Designed for teens and adults, Revenge of the Mummy is designed to take you on a trip inside an ancient tomb, where you'll experience firsthand many of the horrors seen in the movie. Not only is this ride scary due to its fast and turbulent element (like a high-tech roller coaster), it also creates the feeling that you're inside a horror film, complete with mummies, scarab beetles, and fireballs.

The coaster has no inversions or extreme heights, but it is filled with several drops that lead to some substantial airtime. Because the coaster is in the dark and filled with many psychological elements to induce that spooky, creepy-crawly feeling, parents may want to consider whether their children can handle this ride even though Universal categorizes it as a "family ride." Guests must be at least 48 inches tall to ride Revenge of the Mummy.

Backdraft

Based on the movie directed by Ron Howard (who also narrates), Backdraft offers a behind-the-scenes look at how the film was created. It combines a documentary-style movie with live demonstrations. The theme, of course, is fire, and in the finale, the theater heats up as live (but controlled) explosions happen just a few feet in front of you. Backdraft is entertaining, but you'll also learn a lot about the nature of fire and develop a newfound respect for firefighters and the many challenges they face as they enter burning buildings. Backdraft is not suitable for young children.

Jurassic Park—The Ride

Showcasing life-size and lifelike robotic dinosaurs, this boat ride through Jurassic Park, the prehistoric theme park from the motion picture series, mimics the film's story. The first part of your river journey will be quiet, peaceful, and rather beautiful. That is, until an angry T-Rex starts coming close. Then, things start getting a little hairy. Just when you think you're safe, grab your personal belongings before you take an 85-foot plunge into total darkness to end your adventure. The exciting and somewhat scary ride ultimately ends with a big splash, and it's nearly impossible to stay dry. Before you go on, find a way to protect your valuables from the water and stow your glasses and sunglasses. The nearby gift shop sells inexpensive, waterproof ponchos that can help keep you dry. As you go down the massive drop at the end, cameras take your photo, which you can purchase as a souvenir from the gift shop. Guests must be at least 46 inches tall.

Lucy: A Tribute

Displays in this mini-museum chronicle the life of actress and comedienne Lucille Ball. It's a self-paced, walk-through attraction that features props, costumes, and countless photos from Lucy's career. The up-close and personal look at a Hollywood legend appeals to anyone who is a fan of the *I Love Lucy* shows and Ball's work.

Special Effects Stages

This attraction includes three stages, each one illustrating how sound, visual, and other Hollywood blockbuster special effects are created.

Dining and Shopping in Universal Studios

Most dining options at Universal Studios are best described as fast food or snacks, but you'll find full-service restaurants where you can sit down and relax located in CityWalk, a two-minute walk from the main gate.

Restaurants inside the park include:

- **Cyber Grill.** Features flame-broiled Angus burgers, topped with apple-wood smoked bacon, served underneath a mound of fries
- **Doc Brown's Chicken.** Great fried chicken and more
- **Dodger Dogs.** Features the famous hot dogs from Dodger Stadium
- **Flintstone's Drive-In.** Features the Bedrock jumbo turkey leg, smoked, roasted, and served with a tangy BBQ sauce, and Nathan's hot dogs, a Coney Island favorite
- **Hollywood Cantina.** South-of-the-border fare including beans and rice, marinated chicken, and burrito grandes loaded

with traditional carne asada or marinated chicken, beans, and rice

- **Hollywood Grill.** Delicious grilled items including Philly cheesesteaks
- **Jurassic Café.** Features such delicacies as oven-roasted half chicken, and extra chunky clam chowder, served in a La Brea Bakery sourdough bowl
- **Louie's Pizza & Pasta.** Try their famous 20-inch pizzas loaded with homemade sauce and four cheeses, or Louie's Original Rolled Lasagna with Italian cheeses and sausage
- **Mel's Diner.** Features Angus steak burgers with an original secret sauce, grilled chicken sandwiches, and more
- **Panda Express.** Wide variety of Asian foods and fresh sushi rolls made every morning, including California rolls

You'll find a gift or souvenir shop outside most major rides and attractions in Universal Studios Hollywood, selling toys, themed clothing, and other souvenirs.

TRAVEL TIP

Don't be surprised if you run into Charlie Chaplin, the Phantom of the Opera, Woody Woodpecker, Frankenstein, Groucho Marx, Hercules, Xena the Warrior Princess, Laurel and Hardy, Marilyn Monroe, Dracula, the Blues Brothers, the Wolfman, the Mummy, or Nickelodeon characters anywhere in the park.

When a roving photographer takes your picture, they give you a receipt. Take that receipt to Hollywood Photographs to view the photo and buy one for a souvenir if you want it.

To see and do just about everything in Universal Studios on a day with average crowds in the park, plan to be there all day.

Universal CityWalk

When you're ready to break for lunch or have a nice sit-down dinner, head out the gate and into CityWalk. Restaurants here include Bubba Gump Shrimp Co. (a seafood restaurant themed after the movie), Buca di Beppo (Italian), Hard Rock Café, the Wolfgang Puck Café (gourmet pizza), and Tony Roma's (ribs and steaks).

Once the theme park closes, you'll find nightclubs still open in the CityWalk area. Adults-only clubs such as B. B. King's Blues Club, Howl at the Moon dueling piano bar, and the Rumba Room offer full-service bars, music, and plenty of dancing, but they may have strict dress codes that require a change from your T-shirt-and-shorts theme park attire, and they charge admission.

CityWalk features more than thirty one-of-a-kind stores and kiosks selling interesting specialty items. You'll also find ongoing live entertainment, talented street performers, and other attractions here.

If all the movie-themed activity leaves you hankering to see the latest blockbuster film, try the huge, state-of-the-art, eighteen-screen Universal Studios Cinemas. There's also a 3-D IMAX theater with a six-story-tall screen. For movie show times, call (818) 508-0588.

Gibson Amphitheatre

Gibson Amphitheatre (formerly called Universal Amphitheatre) is one of Hollywood's largest indoor concert venues, where big-name recording artists perform regularly. Call (818) 622-4440, or go to their Web site at *www.hob.com/venues/concerts/Gibson* to get a schedule.

Lodging Near Universal

In Universal City and nearby Burbank, there are a handful of hotels including:

Best Western Media Center
✉3910 W. Riverside Drive, Burbank
✆(818) 842-1900, ✐*www.bestwestern.com*

Beverly Garland's Holiday Inn

✉4222 Vineland Avenue, North Hollywood

☎(818) 980-8000, ☎(800) 238-3759, ✑www.beverlygarland.com

Coast Anabelle

✉2011 West Olive Ave., Burbank

☎(818) 845-7800, ☎(800) 426-0670, ✑www.coasthotels.com

The Graciela Burbank

✉322 North Pass Avenue, Burbank

☎(818) 842-8887, ☎(888) 956-1900, ✑www.thegraciela.com

Hilton Burbank Airport

✉2500 Hollywood Way, Burbank

☎(818) 843-6000, ✑www1.hilton.com

Hilton Universal City at Universal Studios

✉555 Universal Terrace Pkwy, Universal City

☎(818) 506-2500, ✑www1.hilton.com

Holiday Inn Express

✉3241 Cahuenga Blvd, Los Angeles

☎(323) 845-1600, ☎(888) 465-4329, ✑www.ichotelsgroup.com

Marriott Courtyard

✉2100 Empire Avenue, Burbank

☎(818) 843-5500, ☎(800) 321-2211, ✑www.marriott.com

Safari Inn

✉1911 West Olive Avenue, Burbank

☎(818) 845-8586, ☎(800) 782-4373, ✑www.coasthotels.com

Sheraton Universal Hotel

✉333Universal Hollywood Drive, Universal City

☎(866) 716-8130, ✑www.sheraton.com/universal

Sportsmen's Lodge Hotel

✉12825 Ventura Blvd., Studio City

☎(818) 769-4700, ☎(800) 821-8511, ✑www.slhotel.com

You could also stay in Hollywood or other parts of Los Angeles and drive to Universal Studios. The Metro Red Line Train goes there from Hollywood.

CHAPTER 20

Exploring San Diego

SAN DIEGO IS CALIFORNIA'S oldest city and its second-largest after Los Angeles. Although new tourist attractions seldom open here, it's still a wonderful place to go with nearly perfect weather much of the year and a nice array of things to do.

San Diego is a popular destination for anyone looking to relax at a resort or play golf, and it boasts a number of family-oriented tourist attractions such as SeaWorld, LEGOLAND, and two popular zoos. You'll also find beautiful beaches, museums, shopping, and countless other indoor and outdoor activities suitable for the entire family.

An Overview of San Diego

San Diego is less than ninety miles away from the Disneyland Resort in Anaheim, a straight drive south on Interstate Highway 5. You can also take a bus or train from Anaheim or Los Angeles to San Diego, but once you're in San Diego, having a car will certainly be helpful.

If you're only making a one-day side trip to San Diego and your Anaheim-area hotel offers a good rate and meets your needs, you could easily stay put. However, if you plan to spend more than a day in San Diego, you'll be better off changing hotels and avoiding all the extra driving.

If you're looking to stay at a world-class resort, you'll have several to choose from in the San Diego area, but there are also many affordable hotels and motels suitable for families. Determine your accommodation needs using the information in Chapter 4; then follow the tips in Chapters 2 and 3 to help you get a nice room at a good rate. Most San Diego visitors stay downtown (especially if they're attending a convention) or in the area called Hotel Circle near the intersection of I-8 and I-5.

If you need information for your San Diego visit beyond what's presented in this chapter, you can find information about the city's most popular sights at *http://gocalifornia.about.com/od/casdmenu/* or contact the San Diego Convention and Visitors Bureau at (619) 236-1212 or *www.sandiego.org*. They also offer free publications and discount coupon books.

San Diego Zoo and Wild Animal Park

When it comes to zoos and wildlife, San Diego offers animal aficionados two of the most incredible zoos in the world, both of them run by the same nonprofit organization, the San Diego Zoological Society. Each of these attractions will provide at least one full day's worth of entertainment that's suitable for the entire family.

The San Diego Zoo
⊠2920 Zoo Drive, San Diego
✆(619) 234-3153
✐*www.sandiegozoo.org*
Open every day, including all holidays. See Chapter 6 for prices.

Located in Balboa Park near downtown San Diego, the 100-acre San Diego Zoo is home to more than 4,000 rare and endangered animals. Its grounds also hold a prominent botanical collection featuring more than 700,000 exotic plants. Some of the most popular creatures here include black-and-white pandas and the largest collection of koalas outside Australia.

☂ RAINY DAY FUN

It seldom rains hard in San Diego, and animals are sometimes more active when it's cool and damp outside. Bring rain gear and enjoy them. On the few really rainy days, the bus tour will keep you dry, and you can focus on the indoor exhibits such as the nursery, reptiles, and other indoor areas.

When you first arrive at the San Diego Zoo, pick a place to meet in case your group gets separated or splits up on purpose. The Flamingo Lagoon near the entrance is a good spot, and you can watch the colorful orange birds while you wait. Walk there together so everyone knows where it is.

The majority of the San Diego Zoo's animals live in natural habitats, including the following.

Absolutely Apes

Red-haired orangutans and black siamangs, both indigenous to the same Asian rain forest ecosystem, share a jungle habitat. It offers them plenty of places to climb and swing, just as they would in their home forests.

Children's Zoo

The petting zoo and animal nursery are a big hit with adults as well as kids.

Flamingo Lagoon

More than seventy of the large, coral-colored birds make their home in the lagoon, and they've been a favorite since the zoo first opened in 1916.

Giant Panda Research Station

One of the zoo's most popular areas ever since giant pandas Basi and Yuan Yuan took up residence in 1987, the panda viewing area has been expanded to allow more and better views of the current residents. When a newborn panda is on hand, lines grow quite long and the exhibit may close periodically to keep the mother and baby from getting too stressed.

Gorilla Tropics/Scripps Aviary

A simulated rain forest is home to the zoo's gorilla family, a troop of bonobos (pygmy chimpanzees), white-fringed colubus monkeys, and a flock of free-flying birds who roost in the aviary.

Ituri Forest

The equatorial rain forest setting is designed to mimic the real Ituri in the Democratic Republic of Congo. Swamp monkeys and river otters are the exhibit's most entertaining creatures. They play together, with the monkeys trying to grab the otters' tails or hitch a ride on their backs. Their companions include hippos, guenons, and monkeys.

Kopje

A variety of unusual animals live in a replica of an East African kopje (a little hill or rocky island in the middle of grassland). The lions live with klipspringers, dwarf mongooses, and Bateleur eagles.

Monkey Trails & Forest Tales

A forested canyon is home to golden-bellied mangabeys, Schmidt's guenons, large and colorful mandrills (all of them monkeys), exotic birds, pygmy hippos, and a clouded leopard, as well as many other creatures.

Polar Bear Plunge

This chilly environment houses not only polar bears, but also other Arctic animals such as Siberian reindeer, Pallas's cats, and diving birds. You can watch the polar bears swimming underwater as well as on dry land. You'll see a herd of reindeer in the exhibit behind the white bears, just as you might in the wild, but they're safely separated by a protective moat. The diving ducks are also fun to watch.

Rain Forest Aviary

The path through this free-flight aviary leads down from the tree-tops to the forest floor, and along the way, you will see hundreds of Asian tropical birds.

Reptile Mesa

An amazing collection of slithery pythons, cobras, boas, tortoises, rattlesnakes, and gila monsters live here, along with Galapagos tortoises and other reptiles.

Sun Bear Forest

Energetic Bornean sun bears—named for the yellow patch on their chest—are zoo favorites, climbing trees and looking great for all the photos that get snapped while they're in action.

Tiger River

Malayan tigers live in this rain forest environment, where they have a flowing river and waterfall. They share their home with long-snouted Malayan tapirs and web-footed fishing cats.

Wings of Australasia

You'll see a colorful collection of over 100 birds native to Australasia (Australia, New Guinea, Tasmania, and the surrounding islands), including wrinkled hornbills and Micronesian kingfishers.

Elsewhere in the zoo, you'll find elephants, giraffes, zebras, koalas, and many more creatures to enjoy. Daily shows feature sea lions or explore predators and prey.

Zoo visitors can take a thirty-five-minute guided bus tour to get oriented, and the Skyfari Aerial Tram can be a great shortcut across the park as well as a way to see what the place looks like from above.

JUST FOR PARENTS

The San Diego Zoo allows you to get close to many exotic animals not found in other zoos and offers a variety of animal experiences. However, the animals are kept in a somewhat artificial setting compared to the San Diego Wild Animal Park, where several species live together in groups on spread-out areas, more as they do in the wild. If you have time to see only one of the parks, choose the experience you think you and your children will like best.

For a special (albeit simulated) adventure, try the ENTCO Wild Earth Safari Ride, an interactive experience that takes a driver and photographer on a quest for that "perfect" picture.

If you're in the area when one is scheduled, the overnight Safari Sleepovers are quite popular and a lot of fun. During these fun events, you and the kids aged four and up can enjoy special activities, sleep overnight at the zoo, and enjoy breakfast the next morning before you leave. When evaluating the cost of these special events, don't forget that you will not need a hotel room for the night.

Allow a full day to see everything at the zoo, or if you have less time, pick the most interesting areas and skip the rest. Plenty of walking is required and almost all of the exhibits are outdoors.

The San Diego Zoo and the Wild Animal Park are about thirty miles apart, and if you try to see them both in the same day, you'll end up seeing nothing at either one.

The San Diego Wild Animal Park

✉15500 San Pasqual Valley Road, Escondido

✆(619) 234-6541 or ✆(760) 747-8702

✍*www.sandiegozoo.org*

Open daily, including all holidays. See Chapter 6 for prices.

Of all the zoos in America, this one is among the most spectacular in terms of visual appeal, home to 3,500 animals representing more than 400 species.

When you arrive at the Wild Animal Park, pick a place for your group to meet in case you get separated or decide to split up. Just like in the San Diego Zoo, the flamingo lagoon is a good place to meet.

RAINY DAY FUN

Much of the Wild Animal Park is in the open. The Wgasa Bush Railway cars have a roof (but no sides) and may be dry enough if it's not raining too hard. If it's raining hard, you may be better off heading somewhere else.

Most of the animals at the Wild Animal Park don't live in cages, but in habitats where many species roam freely together, as they would in the wild. Guests travel through these areas in an open-sided tram, with a tour guide to explain what you're seeing. The fifty-five-minute Wgasa Bush Line Railway tour (included in your admission) is a highlight, but it's not the only thing to do at the Wild Animal Park. Exhibits include:

African Aviary

This open aviary boasts rare species seldom seen in the wild, prehistoric-looking African open-billed storks, and a host of other feathered creatures.

Condor Ridge

Besides exhibiting North America's biggest flying bird (the California Condor), this area is home to big-horned sheep and thick-billed parrots.

Heart of Africa

Okapis, warthogs, giraffes, and cheetahs are just some of the eleven species of mammals and twenty species of birds found here.

Lion Camp

A thick glass window keeps you safe from the lions, but you can watch them close-up.

Lorikeet Landing

Buy a cup of nectar for $2 before you enter this fun exhibit. The next thing you know, your hand, shoulders, and arms will become a perch for a handful of hungry lorikeets (colorful birds a little bigger than a parakeet).

Elephant Overlook

The park has four Asian elephants and four African elephants, and this overlook puts you in the middle so you can watch them all.

Hidden Jungle

Inside this glass-walled greenhouse, you can get a look at smaller creatures such as butterflies, small birds, and insects.

Kilimanjaro Safari Walk

A two-mile walking trail gives you a chance to slow down and see some of the animals in the East Africa Field Exhibit.

Other areas to visit in the Wild Animal Park include the Petting Kraal and Animal Care Center. If you're hungry, you'll find places to eat in Nairobi Village.

The Wild Animal Park also offers a wide range of special activities, including bird and elephant shows, and their animal encounters provide a chance to see some of the animals up-close and learn about them from their trainers.

You and your kids may enjoy one of the park's sleepovers, when the family can stay in the park after closing time, enjoy special activities, sleep in a safari tent, and have breakfast before leaving the next day, or if you'd like to stay late but would rather sleep somewhere else, their Roar and Snore programs offer an after-hours look at the park.

Besides all of this, you can get a bird's-eye view of the park in a helium-filled balloon, take a photo safari, get close to the cheetahs, and ride an animal-themed carousel. Special programs for adults only include behind-the-scenes tours and visits to the animal conservation center and veterinary center. For more information about these tours and activities, call the Wild Animal Park or visit their Web site.

SeaWorld San Diego

✉500 SeaWorld Drive, Mission Bay
✆(619) 226-3815, ✆(800) 257-4268
🖰*www.seaworld.com*

Killer whales, dolphins, sea lions, walruses, and other sea creatures are all on display at SeaWorld San Diego. The most popular attraction here, especially for kids, is the killer whale show featuring the famous Shamu. Visitors can interact with some of the creatures, watch them in exhibits, see them perform, and enjoy shows and rides. SeaWorld is open year-round. See their Web site or call for hours. Chapter 6 summarizes prices.

RAINY DAY FUN

You get wet at some of the shows and rides anyway, so unless it's raining hard, you'll still have fun. On rainier days, bring a raincoat and focus on the indoor shows and exhibits.

Rides and attractions at SeaWorld include the following:

Aquarium de la Mer

Seahorses, the giant Pacific octopus, beautiful lionfish, swell sharks, and delicate moon jellyfish all live in this saltwater aquarium.

California Tide Pool

In this pool, you can find out what starfish and sea urchins feel like and learn more about the California coastal environment.

Forbidden Reef

One of the most enjoyable of SeaWorld's interactive exhibits gives visitors a chance to touch and feed bat rays and see moray eels in their underwater caverns.

Freshwater Aquarium

Species on display include four-eyed fish, electric eels, and freshwater stingrays.

Journey to Atlantis

The water ride uses the lost continent of Atlantis as its theme. It's part watery flume ride and part roller coaster, and it features not one but two drops. You're almost guaranteed to get wet.

Manatee Rescue

Rehabilitated manatees live in an artificial river; you can watch them float and paddle around from an underwater viewing area. This is one of the few places outside Florida you can see the endangered creatures.

Rocky Point Preserve

A two-part attraction, Rocky Point features an area where you can feed bottlenose dolphins and then visit an underwater viewing area to watch California sea otters at play. An interactive, educational exhibit surrounds it.

Shamu's Happy Harbor

A play area for kids, this harbor is on dry land. It includes a water maze, slides, a climbing net, and sand castle building.

Shark Encounter

A 57-foot-long acrylic tube runs through the middle of the sharks' watery world, giving a great chance to see them at close range.

Shipwreck Rapids

Ride a giant, raft-like inner tube through a turbulent river. Each tube carries nine passengers on a five-minute simulated journey around a tropical island. The splashing you'll get on this ride is especially welcome on a hot summer day.

Skyride

This six-minute ride goes out across Mission Bay and back, and there's no extra fee to go on it.

Skytower

On a clear day, you can see up to 100 miles in every direction from the top of this 265-foot-tall tower.

Wild Arctic

The simulated ride over Arctic terrain includes foggers, misters, and simulated snow to make it feel realistic.

World of the Sea Aquarium

Here you'll find warm-water fish from around the world and a display simulating what divers see off the San Diego coast.

For Wild Arctic, Shipwreck Rapids, Skyride, and Journey to Atlantis, guests must be at least 42 inches tall to ride. Children less than 56 inches tall need to bring a responsible person with them to go on the Skytower.

The most popular SeaWorld show by far is Believe (the Shamu Show), a choreographed program that shows the close relationship between the killer whales and their trainers.

SeaWorld also presents a wide range of other live entertainment. Dolphin Discovery features bottlenose dolphins and pilot whales doing tail-walks, jumps, and backflips. Clyde and Seamore's Risky Rescue is a humorous program featuring a couple of cute critters, and Pet's Rule! features a flock of familiar animals in a show that proves that pets do rule.

Cirque de la Mer (summers only) is a live acrobatic circus presented on the water, and R. L. Stine's Haunted Lighthouse is a fun interpretation of an old fisherman's tale, presented in 4-D (3-D with a few effects thrown in). In the summer, SeaWorld hosts live concerts featuring national recording artists, as well as fireworks displays.

For unique opportunities to interact with the animals, SeaWorld offers a Dolphin Interaction Program (touch, feed, and practice behaviors with the dolphins), Trainer for a Day Program (feeding, health care, and behavior interactions), and Wild Arctic Encounter (white whales, walruses, seals, and polar bears). Their Behind-the-Scenes Tour takes visitors into two working areas of the park, the Saving a Species Tour includes an opportunity to hand-feed an endangered animal, and the Animal Spotlight Tour gives visitors a chance to interact with dolphins and feed moray eels and sea turtles. Of course, each of these great things to do requires an extra fee.

Special dining opportunities at Sea World include Breakfast with Shamu and Dine with Shamu, which offer seating right next to Shamu's pool. If you choose the summer Showtime Picnic, your meal will be delivered to you while you wait to see the Shamu show. Call ahead for reservations.

Busch Entertainment Company (part of Anheuser-Busch) owns SeaWorld, and besides all the sea creatures, you'll find a team of their legendary Clydesdale horses on display.

Plan on spending most of a day at SeaWorld, even if you don't plan on doing everything.

LEGOLAND

✉One LEGOLAND Drive, Carlsbad
✆(760) 438-5346
🖱*www.legoland.com*

LEGOLAND's schedule varies by season, and they are closed midweek during the off-season. Check their Web site or call to find out their schedule when you plan to visit. See Chapter 6 for a summary of admission prices and options.

Based on the immensely popular LEGO building-block toy products, LEGOLAND is a kid-oriented theme park. It's specially designed for younger children aged three to twelve, with over forty rides and attractions. LEGOLAND is an hour's drive south of Disneyland and a half-hour trip north of SeaWorld.

One of LEGOLAND's most charming characteristics is that many of the rides and all of the sculptures in the park look as if they've been created from oversize LEGO blocks.

☂ RAINY DAY FUN

On a rainy day, you can head for the indoor play areas, but expect everyone else to be in there, too. You could also buy a big bag of LEGOblocks from one of the shops and go back to your hotel for some building fun.

LEGOLAND covers 128 acres and expertly mixes education, adventure, and fun in this first park of its kind in the United States. In fact, there are only three other LEGOLAND parks in the world: the original park in Billund, Denmark; LEGOLAND Windsor outside of London; and LEGOLAND Deutschland in Günzburg, Germany (near Munich).

LEGOLAND combines hands-on interactive attractions, family rides, and shows with restaurants, shopping, and landscape features. Thirty million bricks were used to create the 5,000 models that decorate the park, adding to its charm and delight. For kids who enjoy building with these blocks, this park will be a life-size inspiration.

LEGOLAND structures their height restrictions differently than other theme parks. They often limit riders to a minimum height just as other parks do, but they may also list a second, shorter height to ride, but only if a taller person goes along. For example, riders must be 48 inches tall to ride Safari Trek alone, but if they are at least 34 inches tall, they can ride with a "taller companion" who is over 48 inches tall. The companion doesn't have to be an adult but does have to meet the taller height requirement listed. The following descriptions refer to this as a "taller companion."

JUST FOR PARENTS

Even though LEGOLAND was designed for smaller children, many of the rides still have height restrictions. If your children are less than 52 inches tall, measure them before they go so you'll all know which rides they can go on. If you're traveling with very small children, the LEGOLAND Web site includes a special section called "What 2 Do When You're 2."

Dino Island

The highlight at Dino Island is the Coastersaurus, a railed roller coaster that flies around a bunch of life-size LEGO brick dinosaurs. Kids can also dig for "dinosaur remains" in a giant sandbox. Bring your own sand toys or rent them.

Explore Village

Explore Village provides a lot of soft adventure in a whimsical garden setting. You'll also find shops and live entertainment shows in Explore Village. The kids will like watching Ristorante Brickolini's pasta machine turn flour and eggs into pasta before their eyes, although they may prefer to eat one of their wood-fired pizzas.

Amusements in this area include:

Fairy Tale Brook

A lovely ride in a leaf-shaped boat through favorite childhood fairy tales, recreated with LEGO bricks. No minimum height, but anyone shorter than 48 inches must ride with a taller companion at least 48 inches tall.

LEGOLAND Express

Kids ride in a colorful train. No minimum height but those shorter than 34 inches tall must ride with a taller companion at least 36 inches tall.

Playtown

A play area geared for the park's youngest guests (preschoolers). It includes buildings, slides, and fire and police stations.

Safari Trek

The LEGO creations here are the animals of Africa, and riders take a safari drive to see them. Minimum height is 34 inches, and anyone less than 48 inches tall must bring along a taller companion.

Water Works

An interactive water play area.

Fun Town

A kid-size town in the center of LEGOLAND, Fun Town offers several rides and attractions, including:

Adventurers' Club

Search for the Seven Keys as you travel on a mysterious journey where you'll meet inhabitants of the Amazon rain forest, ancient Egypt, and the Arctic.

Flight Squadron

Ride in spiffy biplanes, in a LEGO interpretation of a traditional carnival ride. Minimum height is 34 inches, but anyone shorter than 48 inches must bring a taller companion.

Fun Town Fire Academy

The whole family will have fun racing to the fire in a LEGO fire truck and pumping enough water to put out the simulated blaze. Minimum height is 34 inches, and anyone less than 48 inches tall needs a taller companion.

Kid Power Towers

The self-propelled ride takes you to the top of a tower where you can see the entire park and all the way to the ocean. It's capped with an exhilarating free-fall to the bottom. The kid-oriented thrill ride is suitable for kids over 40 inches tall, but if they're shorter than 48 inches, they need a taller companion.

Skipper School

Learn boating skills as you navigate through the "skipper's" watery course. The ride is very popular, but lines are shorter first thing in the morning or late in the day. Minimum height is 34 inches, and anyone shorter than 48 inches needs a taller companion.

Sky Cruiser

The vehicles look like snazzy pedal cars, but it's actually a tame roller coaster. The popular ride is less busy right after the park opens or late in the day. Minimum height is 36 inches, but anyone shorter than 48 inches needs a taller companion.

Sky Patrol

Maneuver your own LEGO helicopter on a semi-thrill ride for pint-size pilots, who fly straight up and back down. Minimum height is 34 inches; anyone shorter than 48 inches needs a taller companion.

Volvo Driving School

A "real-life" driving experience for children aged six through twelve, who drive a real electric car through a controlled course that simulates city streets.

Volvo Jr. Junior Driving School

If your three- to five-year-old is dying to drive, too, they can follow a more controlled path but still get to "drive" their LEGO cars.

You'll find live entertainment (and learn about fire safety at the same time) at Fun Town Stage. You can also take a tour through a simulated LEGO factory to see how the bricks are made and then stock up LEGO bricks by the pound in the LEGO clubhouse.

Pirate Shores

Pirate Shores is LEGOLAND's water play area that features:

Soak–N-Sail

The play area sports all kinds of gadgets pumping and spraying water, and occasionally gives visitors a surprise soaking. Kids must be 36 inches tall to enjoy the water slides.

Splash Battle

Riders drive a boat-shaped vehicle equipped with water cannons that they can fire at spectators and other riders. Minimum height is 36 inches; but up to 44 inches tall, riders need a taller companion.

Swabbies Deck

The smaller set can get wet in gentler water play with water jets, fountains, and squirt cannons.

Treasure Falls

A mini-flume ride with a 12-foot drop. Check with the park for height requirements.

Knights' Kingdom

This area re-creates the time when kings and queens reigned supreme. The main structure in this area is a castle. Rides include:

Enchanted Walk

A nature stroll through a landscaped setting, exhibiting LEGO models of animals native to the San Diego area.

Knights' Tournament

Riders can select how much they want to be twisted and turned as they ride at the end of giant, six-passenger robotic arms. This ride is for the bigger kids, who must be at least 49 inches tall and need a taller companion if they're shorter than 55 inches.

Royal Joust

On this gentle ride, youngsters ride LEGO-themed horses through an enchanted forest. Riders must be at least 36 inches tall, younger than twelve years old, and weigh less than 170 pounds.

The Dragon

The kid-oriented roller coaster is housed in the castle. Merlin the Magician is the host on a ride down to a cave, where a fire-breathing dragon guards the crown jewels. Minimum height is 40 inches, but those less than 48 inches tall need a taller companion.

The Hideaways

An outdoor playground area that contains rope climbs, cargo nets, and slides.

You'll find food in Knights' Kingdom at the Knights' Table Barbecue and Granny's Apple Fries. Kids will also enjoy playing with the thousands of LEGO bricks at the Builder's Guild.

Miniland USA

Miniland USA will appeal to guests of all ages. Here, dozens of LEGO Master Builders show their skill by recreating five areas of the United States, constructed one-twentieth of life size using 20 million bricks. You'll see famous landmarks from Washington D.C.; New Orleans; New York City; Florida; San Francisco; and Southern California. There's also an animated New England harbor scene. You can see even more LEGO creations in the Block of Fame, a 3-D art gallery, and watch the Master Builders at work in the Model Shop.

The only ride in Miniland is the Coast Cruise, a floating tour through the heart of the park that provides a prime viewing opportunity for many of the LEGO models such as the Eiffel Tower, Sydney Opera House, Mt. Rushmore, the Taj Mahal, and the Statue of Liberty in front of the New York City skyline. There's no minimum height for this ride, but riders less than 48 inches tall need a taller companion.

≡FAST FACT

LEGO building blocks are one of the most successful toy products in history, currently sold in more than 138 countries throughout the world. Thus far, over 300 million children and adults have bought LEGO bricks, resulting in several billion hours of creative play.

Imagination Zone

This is the place to find some of the more exciting rides at LEGO-LAND. They include:

aquazone Wave Racers

Riders are sure to get wet on this simulated Jet Ski ride, especially if their younger siblings or mischievous parents are manning one of the spectator-driven water cannons. Minimum height is 40 inches, and anyone shorter than 52 inches has to bring a taller companion.

bionicle Blasters

Riders combine their arm-power to make the vehicles in this ride spin. Minimum height is 42 inches, and anyone shorter than 52 inches needs a taller companion.

LEGO technic Test Track

Guests ride a roller coaster in life-size versions of LEGO technic vehicles. Kids must be at least 42 inches tall to ride and need a taller companion if they're shorter than 52 inches.

LEGO Show Place shows a thirteen-minute-long, 4-D movie that spins tales of sorcerers and magicians, and there are a lot of opportunities for interactive play at bionicle Evolution, Build & Test, and Maniac Challenge.

You'll also find a handful of paid activities at LEGOLAND, including a kid-size golf course, water balloon battles, panning for treasure, and wall climbing. The kids can get a temporary airbrush tattoo and have their face painted, and have their portrait or caricature drawn.

To see everything, be prepared to spend one full day at LEGO-LAND. If your kids want to enjoy the water play at Pirate Shores, be sure to bring a change of clothes so they aren't wet and miserable.

Other Top Tourist Attractions

LEGOLAND, SeaWorld, and the zoos are the most spectacular family-oriented attractions in San Diego. However, plenty of other area attractions may interest your family. Downtown San Diego offers many things to see and do, all within walking distance of each other:

Gaslamp Quarter
✉410 Island Avenue, San Diego
✆(619) 233-5227
✐*www.gaslamp.org*

The historic downtown district features restaurants, galleries, shops, and jazz bars. This is a wonderful place to walk around in the evening before catching a bite to eat. However, most of the restaurants are expensive, and the quality of food and service sometimes doesn't measure up to the price.

Petco Park and the San Diego Padres
✉100 Park Blvd., San Diego
✆(619) 795-5000
✐*http://sandiego.padres.mlb.com*

The local major league baseball team plays in a beautiful, new downtown ballpark, and when there's no game on, you can take a behind-the-scenes tour.

San Diego Maritime Museum
✉1492 N. Harbor Drive, San Diego
✆(619) 234-9153
✐*www.sdmaritime.org*

The outdoor museum includes a fine collection of ships, including the *Star of India*, the world's oldest active ship.

Seaport Village
✉840 W. Harbor Drive, San Diego

✆(619) 235-4014

✑*www.seaportvillage.com*

At Seaport Village, you can dine at one of four sit-down restaurants or select something from one of thirteen sidewalk eateries. You can also ride an antique carousel, walk along the waterfront, or browse through the one-of-a-kind shops.

USS *Midway*
✉910 N. Harbor Drive, San Diego

✆(619) 544-9600

✑*www.midway.org*

A former aircraft carrier, the *Midway* offers a lot to see, and many of its docents are former crewmen who can tell you what it was like to serve on the ship. People are often surprised by how much they like the *Midway*, so don't dismiss it just because you weren't in the military or think you don't like boats.

 **RAINY DAY FUN**

On a rainy day in downtown, head for the water. You'll find a batch of fun family activities below decks at the *Star of India* and there's a lot to do on the lower levels of the USS *Midway*.

Around town, you'll find plenty more to do, including:

Balboa Park
Headquarters: ✉1549 El Prado, San Diego

✆(619) 239-0512

✑*www.balboapark.org*

The cultural heart of San Diego is set on 1,200 acres of land, located just north of downtown. In a short walk through the park, you'll find fifteen museums, several theaters including the Tony Award–winning Old Globe, gardens, a carousel, and the famous San Diego Zoo. On summer nights, everyone likes the outdoor concerts at the Spreckels Organ Pavilion. The Prado restaurant here is considered one of San Diego's best.

RAINY DAY FUN

Any of the Balboa Park museums make a good place to escape the precipitation, but the kids may like the Reuben H. Fleet Science Center, San Diego Air & Space Museum, or the Model Railroad Museum best.

Admission to the Balboa Park grounds is free, but most museums charge an entrance fee. If you plan to spend a lot of time in Balboa Park, visiting a half dozen or more museums, you may save money by getting a Passport to Balboa Park. The passport costs $35 for adults and $19 for children aged three through twelve; it is valid for seven days.

You can buy a passport at the visitor center or at the box office of any participating museum. For more information, call (619) 255-0217.

Centro Cultural de la Raza
✉2125 Park Blvd. San Diego
✆(619) 235-6135
✍*www.centroraza.com*

Dedicated to Mexican, Indigenous, Chicano, and Latino art and culture, the museum holds special exhibits and dance programs featuring their resident company, Ballet Folklorico en Aztlan. Open Tuesday through Sunday, noon through 4 P.M.

Japanese Friendship Garden

✉Near the Spreckels Organ Pavilion, Balboa Park

✆(619) 232-2721

☞*www.niwa.org*

Balboa Park's lovely tea garden started out as a small teahouse during the 1915–1916 Panama-California Exposition. Today, it spreads over nine acres and includes both traditional and modern teahouses, a cherry tree grove, and an outdoor theater.

It is open Labor Day to Memorial Day, Tuesday through Sunday from 10 A.M. to 4 P.M. In summer, the garden is open until 5 P.M. on weekdays. Entrance is $3 for adults, $2.50 for seniors over fifty-five years old, $2 for students and military with ID, and free for children age six and under.

Marston House

✉3525 Seventh Ave.

✆(619) 298-3142

☞*www.sandiegohistory.org*

The classic 1905 Arts and Crafts–style home built for local merchant George W. Marston sits amidst English and California-style gardens. Inside, it's furnished with original furniture and a collection of pottery and Native American baskets. It's open Friday, Saturday, and Sunday for guided tours at 10 A.M., 11 A.M., 1 P.M., 2 P.M., and 4 P.M., except Thanksgiving, December 25, and January 1. Admission is $5 for adults, $2 for ages six to seventeen, and $4 for students, seniors, and military.

Mingei International Museum

✉1439 El Prado

✆(619) 239-0003

☞*www.mingei.org*

The word *mingei* means "arts of the people," and the Mingei Museum is dedicated to promoting and understanding world folk art and mounting displays of traditional and modern creations. It is open from 10 A.M. through 4 P.M. Tuesday through Sunday, except on national holidays. Admission is $6 for adults and $3 for children ages six through seventeen and students with ID.

Museum of Photographic Arts
✉1649 El Prado
✆(619) 238-7559
✑*www.mopa.org*

An unusual institution devoted to the photographic arts, the museum holds a collection of more than 4,000 works focusing on modern and contemporary works. Hours are 10 A.M. through 5 P.M. Monday through Sunday, and Thursdays until 9 P.M., except Thanksgiving, December 25, January 1, and July 4. Admission is $6 for adults, $4 for students, seniors, and military, and free for anyone under twelve years old. Everyone gets in free on the second Tuesday of the month.

Museum of San Diego History
✉1649 El Prado
✆(619) 232-6203
✑*www.sandiegohistory.org*

The place to go to learn about San Diego history, this museum holds a large collection of artifacts, costumes, and artworks, along with a notable collection of historic photographs. It is open every day 10 A.M. to 5 P.M. except Thanksgiving, December 25, and January 1. Admission is $5 for adults, $4 for seniors over age sixty-five, military, and AAA members, $2 for children ages six to seventeen, and free for kids under age five.

Reuben H. Fleet Science Center
✉1875 El Prado
✆(619) 238-1233
✑*www.rhfleet.org*

San Diego's science museum features more than 100 interactive exhibits and the city's only IMAX Dome Theater. The center is open daily from 9:30 A.M. to 5 P.M. Gallery admission is $7 for adults, and

$6.25 for kids ages three through twelve and seniors over sixty-five. You'll pay extra to see an IMAX film.

San Diego Air & Space Museum

✉2001 Pan American Plaza

✆(619) 234-8291

✎*www.aerospacemuseum.org*

The Air & Space Museum chronicles aviation history with a collection of more than sixty aircraft and space vehicles. One of their most important holdings is the only *Apollo* space capsule actually flown in space and exhibited west of the Rockies. Open daily 10 A.M. to 4 P.M. and to 5 P.M. Memorial Day through Labor Day, the museum is closed Thanksgiving, December 25, and January 1. Admission is $10 for adults over eighteen years old and $5 for youth ages six to seventeen, and $8 for seniors over sixty-five and students with valid ID. Active military gets in free with ID. Everyone gets in free on the fourth Tuesday of the month.

San Diego Art Institute (SDAI): Museum of the Living Artist

✉1439 El Prado

✆(619) 236-0011

✎*www.sandiego-art.org*

The institute features works by San Diego artists, with a new show opening every four to six weeks. Open 10 A.M. to 4 P.M. Tuesday through Saturday, and 12 to 4 P.M. on Sunday. Admission is $3 for adults and $2 for seniors, military, and students with ID.

San Diego Automotive Museum

✉2080 Pan American Plaza

✆(619) 231-2886

✎*www.sdautomuseum.org*

The Automotive Museum holds a collection of more than ninety classic automobiles, including Frank Sinatra's 1967 Austin Petrol Hire Car and Russell Crowe's Harley-Davidson. Open daily 10 A.M. to 5 P.M., the museum is closed Thanksgiving, December 25, and January 1; it closes at 2 P.M. the day before each of these holidays. Admission is $8 for adults ages sixteen through sixty-four, $6 for seniors sixty-five and over and military with ID, $5 for students with ID, $4 for youth ages six through fifteen, and free for children under six.

San Diego Hall of Champions Sports Museum
✉2131 Pan American Plaza
✆(619) 234-2544
☞www.sdhoc.com

The multisport museum features memorabilia and exhibits celebrating sports from surfing and skateboarding to basketball and football. It is open daily 10 A.M. to 4:30 P.M. Admission is $6 for adults, $4 for seniors and military, $3 for children seven to seventeen years old, and free for children six and under.

San Diego Model Railroad Museum
✉1649 El Prado
✆(619) 696-0199
☞www.sdmrm.org

The world's largest operating model railroad museum features four enormous scale-model layouts of Southwestern U. S. railroads in O (1/48th actual size), HO (1/87th actual size), and N (1/160th actual size) scales. Kids will enjoy the interactive Lionel train gallery. The museum is open Tuesday through Friday 11 A.M. to 4 P.M., and Saturday and Sunday 11 A.M. to 5 P.M. On Tuesday and Friday nights, visitors can watch the local model railroad clubs work on the exhibit. Admission is $6 for adults, $5 for seniors sixty-five and older, $3 for students with ID, and $2.50 for active military with ID. Children under fifteen get in free when accompanied by an adult.

San Diego Museum of Art
✉1450 El Prado
✆(619) 232-7931
☞www.sdmart.org

The San Diego region's oldest and largest art museum holds a fine selection of European old masters, nineteenth and twentieth century American art, and large Asian and Latin American art collections. The museum is open 10 A.M. to 6 P.M. Tuesday through Sunday and 10 A.M. to 9 P.M. on Thursdays. Admission is $10 for adults, $8 for seniors over sixty-five and military, $7 for students with ID, and $4 for youths ages six to seventeen. Children less than five years old get in free.

San Diego Museum of Man

✉ 1350 El Prado

✆ (619) 239-2001

✑ www.museumofman.org

Housed in Balboa Park's most recognizable building, the San Diego Museum of Man is devoted to anthropology. Their collections include Maya monuments, rare Egyptian tomb artifacts, and Peruvian mummies. The museum is open daily 10 A.M. to 4:30 P.M. except Thanksgiving, December 25, and January 1. Admission is $8 for adults, $6 for seniors over sixty-five years old and active military with ID, and $4 for ages six through seventeen. Children less than six years old get in free.

San Diego Natural History Museum

✉ 1788 El Prado

✆ (619) 232-3821

✑ www.sdnhm.org

The Natural History Museum focuses on Southern California and Baja California. Exhibits may include topics such as fossils, dinosaurs, or animals, and the museum also shows films in a 300-seat, giant screen theater. The museum is open daily 10 A.M. to 5 P.M. except Thanksgiving and December 25. Admission is $11 for adults, $9 for seniors over age sixty-two, $7 for active military, youth ages thirteen through seventeen, and students with ID. You'll pay $6 for children aged three through twelve. Kids under age two get in free.

Timken Museum of Art

✉1500 El Prado

✆(619) 239-5548

✑*www.timkenmuseum.org*

The Timken Museum is home to the Putnam Foundation Collection of European Old Master paintings, American paintings, and Russian icons. Their holdings include works by Rembrandt, Rubens, Fragonard, Bierstadt, and Pieter Bruegel the Elder. The Timken is open Tuesday through Saturday 10 A.M. to 4:30 P.M., Sunday from 1:30 P.M. to 4:30 P.M. except major holidays, and the month of September. Admission is free.

Veterans Museum & Memorial Center

✉2115 Park Boulevard

✆(619) 239-2300

✑*www.veteranmuseum.org*

Located in the historic Naval Hospital Chapel on Inspiration Point, the Veterans Museum honors the men and women of the Armed Forces, Coast Guard, and Wartime Merchant Marine. Exhibits include artifacts, documents, photographs, memorabilia, and artwork from the Civil War to the present. The center is open Tuesday through Saturday 9:30 A.M. to 3 P.M.

WorldBeat Center

✉2100 Park Boulevard

✆(619) 230-1190

✑*www.worldbeatcenter.org*

The WorldBeat Center focuses on the cultures of indigenous Americans, African-Americans, and the African Diasporas. They teach a variety of classes, sponsor exhibitions, and host concerts. Hours and admission vary.

There's enough to do in Balboa Park to keep you busy for a long time, but there are also a lot of fun things to do in the rest of the city.

Belmont Park
✉3146 Mission Boulevard, #F, San Diego
☎(858) 228-9283
🖰*www.belmontpark.com*
This classic seaside amusement park includes a selection of shops, restaurants, a wooden roller coaster, and the Plunge swimming pool.

Cabrillo National Monument
✉1800 Cabrillo Memorial Drive, San Diego
☎(619) 557-5450
🖰*www.nps.gov/cabr*
The location overlooking San Diego Bay and the Pacific Ocean is an excellent place for whale watching from land. You'll also find not one but two lighthouses, tide pools, and a monument honoring Juan Cabrillo's landing in San Diego back in 1542.

Hotel del Coronado
✉1500 Orange Avenue, Coronado
☎(619) 435-6611
🖰*www.hoteldel.com*
Even if you can't afford to stay in San Diego's best-known hotel, you can enjoy visiting. The internationally renowned resort hotel has hosted twelve U.S. presidents, countless celebrities, and one resident ghost. In addition to sightseeing and shopping, a self-guided tour is available.

Mission San Diego de Alcala
✉10818 San Diego Mission Road, San Diego
☎(619) 281-8449
🖰*www.missionsandiego.com*
The first Spanish mission in California was founded in 1769 near today's Old Town, but a few years later, it moved to the current location, where you'll find the rebuilt mission church, a museum, a working archaeological site, and landscaped gardens that are all open to the general public.

Mission Bay

In addition to providing a home to SeaWorld, this 4,600-acre park offers beautiful picnic areas, seventeen miles of oceanfront beaches and trails, plus areas for boating and swimming.

Old Town State Historical Park

✉ San Diego Avenue at Twiggs Street, San Diego

☎ (619) 220-5422

🖱 *www.parks.ca.gov/?page_id=663*

A favorite of tourists and locals alike, Old Town commemorates the area's earliest European settlement. Five original adobes reflect ordinary life in San Diego from 1821 to 1872. Old Town is the site of the Whaley House, one of the best-known haunted houses in America. It's also home to a number of specialty boutiques offering unique international collectibles, and several international restaurants.

Not in San Diego proper, but an easy drive nearby, these spots may tickle your fancy, tweak your curiosity, or even float your boat.

ARCO Olympic Training Center

✉ 2800 Olympic Parkway, Chula Vista

☎ (619) 656-1500

🖱 *www.usoc.org*

Thousands of Olympic hopefuls train here every year, and guided tours are offered daily.

Birch Aquarium at Scripps

✉ 2300 Expedition Way, La Jolla

☎ (858) 534-3474

🖱 *www.aquarium.ucsd.edu*

A jewel of a small aquarium, Birch features beautiful, intimate displays and great ocean views. Admission is $11 for adults, $9 for seniors over sixty, $8 for college students, and $7.50 for ages three to seventeen.

🌂 RAINY DAY FUN

The Birch aquarium can keep the kids (and the adults, too) busy for hours on a rainy day. If you're there on the third Saturday of the month, you can participate in special family activities, too.

Carlsbad Flower Fields
✉5704 Paseo del Norte, Carlsbad
☎(760) 431-0352
🖰*www.theflowerfields.com*

Fifty acres of colorful, rose-shaped ranunculus flowers draw thousands of visitors every March and April.

Del Mar Fairgrounds
✉2260 Jimmy Durante Boulevard, Del Mar
☎(858) 793-5555
🖰*www.dmtc.com*

The thoroughbred horseracing season runs through the summer, and the San Diego County Fair is held in June, usually closing on July 4.

Palomar Observatory
✉Highway of Stars, Palomar Mountain
☎(760) 742-2119
🖰*www.astro.caltech.edu/palomar*

For astronomy buffs, the observatory houses the continental United States' largest telescope. Free tours are offered daily.

Quail Botanical Gardens
✉230 Quail Gardens Drive, Encinitas
☎(760) 436-3036
🖰*www.qbgardens.org*

Stroll through the lush gardens and view exotic plants from all over the world.

San Diego Sightseeing Tours

If you have a limited amount of time to spend in San Diego, an organized tour can give you a quick overview of the city. A harbor cruise is also a great way to learn more about San Diego's history.

San Diego Trolley Tours

☎(619) 298-8687

✐*www.trolleytours.com*

Their two-hour tour showcases more than 100 local points of interest. The trolleys travel through San Diego and Coronado on a continuous loop, so you can select a few of your favorite destinations and get off to explore attractions, shopping, and dining at your own pace—and then get back on again. You can start the tour at any one of nine stops.

 TRAVEL TIP

One benefit of a guided tour is that you don't need a car and you don't have to worry about getting lost. Once you get the overview of what's available in San Diego, you can explore on your own and at your own pace, revisiting the attractions that were the most interesting.

Throughout the trolley ride, you'll enjoy colorful anecdotes, humorous stories, and historical information, all combined in a fast-paced two-hour narrative that both entertains and educates.

Seal Tours

☎(619) 298-8687

✐*www.sealtours.com*

Seal Tours offers a ninety-minute ride around town in an amphibious vehicle that takes you on land and sea. Tickets are $30 for adults and $15 for children.

Harbor Tours

Much of San Diego's history centers on the water, especially its long association with the Navy. Harbor tours run from the waterfront in two legs, each an hour long; one leg goes out toward Point Cabrillo and the other goes south past the Coronado Bridge. You can choose to do one or both. San Diego Harbor Excursion ((619) 234-4111, (800) 442-7847, *www.sdhe.com*) is a locally owned company that provides a dedicated narrator on every trip. Hornblower offers similar cruises ((888) 467-6256, *www.hornblower.com*). With either company, one-hour cruises cost about $17 for adults, $15 for seniors, and $8.50 for children. The full two-hour tour will cost $22, $20, and $11, respectively.

Old Town Ghost Tours

www.oldtownsmosthaunted.com

For a spooky good time, join ghost hunter Michael Brown in Old Town for a child- and family-friendly ghost hunt. Brown doesn't guarantee that you'll see a ghost, but he does know about some scary spots. Adult tickets are $19, and kids six to twelve are $10.

San Diego Beaches

With over seventy miles of beaches, San Diego has plenty of sandy spots. Some beaches attract surfers and divers, while others are remote getaways. To find out about beach conditions during your visit, call (619) 221-8824.

A few of San Diego's most enjoyable beaches include:

Coronado Beach

The long, flat beach that runs behind the scenic Hotel del Coronado is a great place for a walk or run. Its clean sand and gentle waves also make it a good place to take the kids. It's busy right behind the hotel, but gets quiet just a short walk away.

La Jolla Cove
The pretty little cove just below the cliffs in lovely La Jolla offers some great tide pools and a sheltered place to sun.

La Jolla Shores
A long stretch of flat sand makes this beach a great place for snapping some afternoon photos, taking romantic walks, building sandcastles, and having picnics.

Mission Beach
On the stretch of sand that separates Mission Bay from the Pacific Ocean, this beach features a nice boardwalk and Belmont Park, a classic seaside amusement park.

Windansea Beach
One of California's beach icons, famous for the Polynesian-style shack that surfers first built here in 1940, Windansea became famous in Tom Wolfe's novel *The Pumphouse Gang*. It's still a popular place for surfing, but it is not for beginners.

Imperial Beach has a pretty boardwalk and an annual sandcastle contest, but the poor water quality there makes it a bad choice for beach play.

Shopping

If you're looking to take home souvenirs or just enjoy the sport of shopping, your options are plentiful in the San Diego area, and just across the border, Tijuana offers a bargain-lover's paradise.

These are some of the best places to shop in San Diego. Most are open seven days a week.

 RAINY DAY FUN

Going shopping may sound like a good idea on a rainy day, but some San Diego shopping malls have open roofs. If you're looking for a place to get in out of the rain, ask your hotel's concierge or front desk for recommendations.

Bazaar Del Mundo

✉4105 Taylor Street, San Diego

✐*www.bazaardelmundo.com*

Located near Old Town State Historic Park, Bazaar del Mundo's shops sell items from Mexico and other international locations. You'll find the Laurel Burch Gallerita here, as well some nice Mexican restaurants.

Fashion Valley Shopping Center

✉7007 Friars Road, San Diego

✆(619) 297-3381

✐*www.simon.com*

Fashion Valley is an outdoor shopping center that has 150 stores, an AMC movie theater, and restaurants that include P. F. Chang's, California Pizza Kitchen, and the Cheesecake Factory.

Hillcrest

Go north on University Avenue from downtown and you'll find the Hillcrest area, a lively neighborhood popular with San Diegans but less known among tourists, where you can find some nice boutique shops and reasonably priced, good restaurants.

Horton Plaza

✉324 Horton Plaza, San Diego

✆(619) 239-8180

✍*www.westfield.com/hortonplaza*

Downtown San Diego's multilevel mall spans seven blocks with 150 stores, a food court, a fourteen-screen movie theater, and the San Diego REPertory Theatre.

Mission Valley Center

✉1640 Camino del Rio N., #1290, San Diego

✆(619) 296-6375

One of San Diego's largest open-air shopping centers, Mission Valley contains more than 150 stores, including Nordstrom Rack, Loehmann's, Macy's, and an AMC twenty-screen movie theater.

Plaza del Pasado

✉Juan and Calhoun Streets

✆(619) 297-3100, ✍*www.plazadelpasado.com*

Located near Old Town State Historic Park, Plaza del Pasado (Plaza of the Past) is home to shops, restaurants, and historic attractions.

Seaport Village

✉849 W. Harbor Drive, San Diego

✆(619) 235-4014, ✍*www.seaportvillage.com*

With its waterfront dining and shopping, this San Diego landmark has something for every member of the family.

Nearby communities also offer some great shopping in the San Diego area. Here are a few of the best:

La Jolla

Prospect Street in downtown offers a wide range of boutiques, art galleries, and shops to browse in, and it's a nice place for dinner, too.

Coronado

Besides the shops at the Hotel del Coronado, Orange Avenue is lined with a good selection of small, local shops, and it has a nice, laid-back ambiance.

TRAVEL TIP

Bargaining is not only acceptable in Tijuana, it's expected. Know the going price of anything you want to buy before you go, take cash, and shop around. When you're ready to buy, ask the price, but try not to appear too eager, and then wait for the shopkeeper to reduce his or her price several times before making a firm counteroffer.

Tijuana

Most shoppers head for the shops along Revolución Avenue, but the Arts and Crafts Market at Calle Segunda (2nd Street) and Via Negrete offers better bargains and a more laid-back environment. To be sure you can get back into the United States with no hassles, bring along proof of citizenship or residency, or your passport and visa if you're from another country.

Useful Phone Numbers

THE FOLLOWING USEFUL PHONE NUMBERS will help you plan the ultimate vacation to Disneyland or to any of the tourist attractions and theme parks described in this book. Refer to Chapter 2 for airline and car-rental company telephone numbers. Chapter 4 contains Disneyland-area hotel information, and Chapter 14 supplies phone numbers for Downtown Disney shops and restaurants.

GENERAL NUMBERS

Amtrak: ☎(800) USA-RAIL

Greyhound: ☎(800) 231-2222

Pacific Coast Gray Line: ☎(714) 978-8855 or ☎(800) 828-6699

Prime Time Shuttle: ☎(800) 733-8267

Super Shuttle: ☎(800) 554-3146

Transportation Safety Administration (TSA): ☎(866) 289-9673

Walt Disney Travel Company: ☎(800) 225-2024

ANAHEIM AND ORANGE COUNTY

Adventure City: ☎(714) 236-9300

Anaheim ICE: ☎(714) 535-7465

Anaheim Indoor Marketplace: ☎(714) 999-0888 or ☎(800) 479-7927

Anaheim Museum: ☎(714) 778-3301

Anaheim Orange County Visitor and Convention Bureau: ☎(714) 765-8888 or ☎(888) 598-3200

The Block at Orange: ☎(714) 769-4000

Bolsa Chica Ecological Reserve: ☎(714) 846-1114

Bowers Museum of Cultural Art and Kidseum: ☎(714) 567-3600

California Adventure: ☎(714) 781-4565

Crystal Cathedral: ☎(714) 971-4000

Crystal Cove State Park: ☎(949) 494-3539

Disney Character Warehouse Outlet: ☎(714) 870-9363

Disneyland: ☎(714) 781-4565

Disneyland (TTY): ☎(714) 781-4569

Disneyland Guest Services: ☎(714) 781-4101

Disneyland Kennel: ☎(714) 781-4565

Disneyland Lost and Found: ☎(714) 817-2166

Disneyland Priority Seating: ☎(714) 781-3463

Disneyland Resort Express bus: ☎(714) 978-8855

Disneyland Resort Merchandise Services: ☎(800) 760-3566

Disneyland Tickets and Tour Reservations: ☎(714) 781-4400

Disneyland Weddings: ☎(714) 956-6527

Disney's California Adventure: ☎(714) 781-4565

Downtown Disney: ☎(714) 300-7800

Fashion Island: ☎(949) 721-2000

Festival de las Golondrinas: ☎(949) 493- 1976

Flight Deck Air Combat Center: ☎(714) 937-1511

Glen Ivy Hot Springs: ☎(888) 258-2683

The Grove of Anaheim: ☎(714) 712-2700

Hobby City Doll & Toy Museum: ☎(714) 527-2323

House Call Physicians: ☎(800) 362-7911

Huntington Beach Cruise of Lights: ☎(714) 840-7542

Huntington State Beach: ☎(714) 536-1454

International Surfing Museum: ☎(714) 960-3483

Joey & Maria's Comedy Italian Wedding: ☎(800) 944-5639

Knott's Southern California Resort: (714) 220-5200

Medieval Times Dinner & Tournament: (714) 521-4740
or (800) 899-6600

Mission San Juan Capistrano: (949) 234-1300

Newport Beach Harbor Parade: (949) 729-4400

Orange County Fair: (714) 708-1500

Orange County Marketplace: (949) 723-6616

Orange County Performing Arts Center: (714) 556-2787

Pageant of the Masters: (800) 487-3378

Pirate's Dinner Adventure: (714) 690-1497, (866) 439-2469

Richard Nixon Library and Birthplace: (714) 993-5075

Santa Ana Zoo: (714) 835-7484

Sawdust Art Festival: (949) 494-3030

South Coast Plaza: (800) 782-8888

Toshiba Tall Ships Festival: (949) 496-2274

U.S. Open of Surfing: (310) 473-0411

LOS ANGELES AND HOLLYWOOD

Aquarium of the Pacific: (562) 590-3100

Audiences Unlimited: (818) 753-3470

Beverly Hills Trolley Tour: (310) 285-2438

Bunny Museum: (626) 798-8848

Comedy & Magic Club, Hermosa Beach: (310) 372-1193

The Comedy Store: (323) 650-6268

Dodger Stadium: (866) 363-4377

George C. Page Museum at the La Brea Tar Pits: (323) 934-7243

Getty Center and Getty Villa: (310) 440-7330

Gibson Amphitheatre: (818) 622-4440

Griffith Park Observatory: (213) 473-0800

Guinness Book of World Records Museum: (323) 463-6433

Hollywood & Highland: (323) 467-6412

Hollywood Bowl: (323) 850-2000

Hollywood Forever Cemetery: ☎(323) 469-1181

Hollywood Heritage Museum: ☎(323) 874-4005

Hollywood Walk of Fame: ☎(323) 469-8311

Hollywood Wax Museum: ☎(323) 462-8860

The Improv: ☎(323) 651-2583

The Kodak Theatre: ☎(323) 308-6300

Laugh Factory: ☎(323) 656-1336

Los Angeles County Museum of Art: ☎(323) 857-6000

Los Angeles Fashion District: ☎(213) 488-1153

Los Angeles Zoo: ☎(323) 644-4200

Mann's Chinese Theater: ☎(323) 464-6266

Museum of Jurassic Technology: ☎(310) 836-6131

Museum of Neon Art: ☎(213) 489-9918

Musso and Frank Grill: ☎(323) 467-7788

NBC Studios Tour: ☎(818) 840-3537

Norton Simon Museum: ☎(626) 449-6840

Paramount Studios Tour: ☎(323) 956-1777

Petersen Automotive Museum: ☎(323) 930-2277

The *Queen Mary*: ☎(562) 435-3511

Ripley's Believe It or Not! Museum: ☎(323) 466-6335

Ronald Reagan Presidential Library: ☎(800) 410-8354

Santa Monica Pier: ☎(310) 458-8900

Six Flags Magic Mountain: ☎(661) 255-4100

Sony Pictures Studio Tour: ☎(323) 520-8687

Staples Center: ☎(877) 305-1111

Starline Tours: ☎(800) 959-3131

Universal Studios Hollywood: ☎(800) 864-8377

VIP Tours: ☎(800) 438-1814

Warner Bros. Studios Tour: ☎(818) 972-8687

SAN DIEGO

ARCO Olympic Training Center: (619) 656-1500

Balboa Park: (619) 239-0512

Belmont Park: (858) 228-9283

Birch Aquarium at Scripps: (858) 534-3774

Cabrillo National Monument: (619) 557-5450

Carlsbad Flower Fields: (760) 431-0352

Centro Cultural de la Raza: (619) 235-6135

Del Mar Fairgrounds: (858) 793-5555

Fashion Valley Shopping Center: (619) 297-3381

Gaslamp Quarter: (619) 233-5227

Hornblower Cruises: (888) 467-6256

Horton Plaza: (619) 239-8180

Japanese Friendship Garden: (619) 232-2721

LEGOLAND: (760) 438-5346

Marston House: (619) 298-3142

Mingei International Museum: (619) 239-0003

Mission San Diego de Alcala: (619) 281-8449

Mission Valley Center: (619) 296-6375

Museum of Photographic Arts: (619) 238-7559

Museum of San Diego History: (619) 232-6203

Old Town State Historical Park: (619) 220-5422

Palomar Observatory: (760) 742-2119

Petco Park (San Diego Padres): (619) 795-5000

Plaza del Pasado: (619) 297-3100

Quail Botanical Gardens: (760) 436-3036

Reuben H. Fleet Science Center: (619) 238-1233

San Diego Air & Space Museum: (619) 234-8291

San Diego Art Institute: (619) 236-0011

San Diego Automotive Museum: (619) 231-2886

San Diego Convention and Visitors Bureau: (619) 236-1212

San Diego Hall of Champions Sports Museum: ☎(619) 234-2544

San Diego Harbor Excursion: ☎(619) 234-4111, ☎(800) 442-7847

San Diego Maritime Museum: ☎(619) 234-9153

San Diego Model Railroad Museum: ☎(619) 696-0199

San Diego Museum of Art: ☎(619) 232-7931

San Diego Museum of Man: ☎(619) 239-2001

San Diego Natural History Museum: ☎(619) 232-3821

San Diego Trolley Tours: ☎(619) 298-8687

San Diego Wild Animal Park: ☎(619) 234-6541

San Diego Zoo: ☎(619) 234-3153

SeaWorld San Diego: ☎(619) 226-3815

Seal Tours: ☎(619) 298-8687

Seaport Village: ☎(619) 235-4014

Timken Museum of Art: ☎(619) 239-5548

USS *Midway*: ☎(619) 544-9600

Veterans Museum & Memorial Center: ☎(619) 239-2300

WorldBeat Center: ☎(619) 230-1190

Ride Overviews

Disneyland

Use this handy list to help prioritize your Disneyland activities.

DISNEYLAND RIDES

Ride	Notes	Description
Main Street, U.S.A.		
Disneyland Opera House		Daily shows: *The First 50 Magical Years* or Great Moments with Mr. Lincoln
Disneyland Railroad		The shortest boarding lines are on Main Street
Main Street Cinema		Six classic Mickey Mouse cartoons run simultaneously
Main Street Vehicles		Hitch a ride on a fire engine, a horse-drawn streetcar, or an omnibus
Adventureland		
Enchanted Tiki Room		"The birds sing songs and the flowers bloom" in an animated musical show

Ride	Notes	Description
Indiana Jones Adventure	FP, PC, 46 inches	Runaway railroad, a realistic setting and lots of turns, but no big drops
Tarzan's Treehouse		The fake tree is really a giant jungle gym, good for climbing
Critter Country		
Davy Crockett Explorer Canoes		Self-propelled way to see the Rivers of America; expect to paddle
The Many Adventures of Winnie the Pooh		Gentle ride through the Hundred Acre Wood, past scenes from the Winnie the Pooh stories
Splash Mountain	FP, SR, PC, 40 inches	Water ride based loosely on *The Song of the South*, with a 52-foot, splashing drop at the end
Fantasyland		
Alice in Wonderland		Gentle "dark" ride past scenes and characters from the story, ending with an exploding "unbirthday" cake
Casey Jr. Circus Train		Cute little circus train travels through Storybook Land
Dumbo the Flying Elephant		Vehicles shaped like Dumbo go in circles while riders control up-and-down
Disney Princess Fantasy Faire		Lots of things to do, princesses to greet, activities, and shows

Ride	Notes	Description
"it's a small world"		Gentle float past 300 Animatronic dolls singing the same song in different languages
King Arthur Carrousel		1876 antique carousel, a gentle trip for all ages
Mad Tea Party		Famous spinning teacups won't jerk and jostle but will make you dizzy
Matterhorn Bobsleds	PC, 35 inches	One of Disneyland's bigger thrills, a roller coaster disguised as a bobsled ride
Mr. Toad's Wild Ride		You'll want to revoke Mr. Toad's driver's license by the end, but it's a gentle ride with lots to see
Peter Pan's Flight		A dark ride with vehicles suspended to give a feeling of flying over London and Never Land
Pinocchio's Daring Journey		Scenes from the animated film and lots of fun special effects
Snow While's Scary Adventures		More charming than scary, a dark ride through the Seven Dwarfs' house and other scenes from the film
Storybook Land Canal Boats		Boat ride past miniature scenes from Disney films
Frontierland		
Big Thunder Mountain Railroad	FP, PC, 40 inches	Runaway railroad, a realistic setting and lots of turns, but no big drops

Ride	Notes	Description
Tom Sawyer Island		A good place for kids to work off some excess energy
Mark Twain Riverboat		Steamboat paddle wheeler, especially nice at night
Sailing Ship Columbia		Replica of the first American ship to circumnavigate the globe, seldom sails

Mickey's Toontown

Ride	Notes	Description
Chip 'n Dale's Treehouse		Kids can climb all around the chipmunks' house
Donald's Boat		Good place for kids to play, climb and pretend they're sailing
Gadget's Go Coaster	35 inches	Gentle roller coaster
Goofy's Playhouse		Kids can climb on the furniture and not get in trouble
Mickey's House		A cute house, but the main attraction is meeting Mickey on your way out
Minnie's House		Adults and kids alike think Minnie's House is the cutest
Roger Rabbit's Car Toon Spin	FP	A wild taxi ride where you control how much your vehicle spins

New Orleans Square

Ride	Notes	Description
Haunted Mansion		A Disneyland classic, home to 999 ghosts, cute decorations and fun special effects
Haunted Mansion Holiday	FP	Haunted Mansion takes on "Nightmare Before Christmas" décor for the holidays

Ride	Notes	Description
Pirates of the Caribbean		A float trip through the pirates' world as they attack a town, pillage, and plunder; new Animatronics added in 2006 make it more realistic

Tomorrowland

Ride	Notes	Description
Astro Orbitor		Similar to Dumbo but looks much cooler
Autopia	FP, PC, 52 inches to drive alone; minimum age is 12 months	Drive replica sports cars or off-road vehicles on a controlled track
Buzz Lightyear Astro Blasters	FP	Interactive game/ride based on *Toy Story*; noisy with flashing lights
Finding Nemo Submarine Voyage		New in 2007, a submarine ride with characters from the film swimming alongside
Innoventions		Explore the technology of the future
Space Mountain	FP, PC, 40 inches	Indoor dark roller coaster, Disneyland's fastest, like flying through space
Star Tours	PC, 40 inches	Simulator ride. A Star Tours Travel trip goes awry

FP = fastpass available. SR=Single Rider Line. PC = Physical considerations: not suitable for anyone who suffers from high blood pressure; heart, neck, or back problems; or other condition that the ride might aggravate. Those subject to motion sickness should take precautions before riding and pregnant women should not ride. Entries such as 46 inches define the minimum height requirement.

California Adventure

Use this handy list to help prioritize your California Adventure activities.

CALIFORNIA ADVENTURE RIDES

Ride	Notes	Description
"a bug's land"		
Flik's Flyers		Cute, gentle ride in a hot-air balloon made the bugs' way
Francis's Lady-bug Boogie		Spinning ride similar to Disneyland's teacups
Heimlich's Chew Chew Train		An easy train ride
Princess Dot Puddle Park		Water play area (bring dry clothes)
Tuck and Roll's Drive 'Em Buggies	PC, 36 inches	Gentle version of traditional bumper cars
Golden State		
Grizzly River Run	FP, SR, PC, 42 inches	Whitewater rafting, with a couple of drops
Redwood Creek Challenge Trail		Outdoor playground and obstacle course
Soarin' Over California	FP, SR, 40 inches	Simulated hang-gliding trip over California
Hollywood Pictures Backlot		
Monsters, Inc. Mike & Sulley to the Rescue!		Indoor ride based on the film features a race to save little Boo
Twilight Zone Tower of Terror	FP, PC, 40 inches	Wild ride in an out-of-order elevator, lots of fast ups-and-downs

Paradise Pier		
California Screamin'	FP, SR, PC, 48 inches	Goes from 0 to 55 mph in 4.7 seconds and includes a 360-degree loop
Golden Zephyr		Rotating swing ride in silver, rocket-shaped vehicles
Jumpin' Jellyfish	40 inches	Get lifted in the air, and come down in successively lower drops
King Triton's Carousel		Sea creatures replace the horses on this carousel
Maliboomer	SR, PC, 52 inches	Fly 180 feet in the air in 4 seconds, then bounce back down
Mulholland Madness	FP, SR, PC, 42 inches	Roller coaster with lots of sharp turns
Orange Stinger	48 inches	Rotating, tilting swing ride inside a giant orange
S.S. *rustworthy*		Water play area (bring dry clothes)
Sun Wheel		Ferris wheel with a twist: some of the cars slide and rock

FP = fastpass available. SR=Single Rider Line. PC = Physical considerations: not suitable for anyone who suffers from high blood pressure; heart, neck, or back problems; or other conditions that the ride might aggravate. Those subject to motion sickness should take precautions before riding and pregnant women should not ride. Entries such as 46 inches define the minimum height requirement.

Attraction Selection Worksheet

THE FOLLOWING WORKSHEETS will help you choose which rides, shows, and attractions you and your traveling companions will want to experience once you arrive at each of the Disney theme parks. Place a checkmark in the appropriate column next to each listed ride, show, or attraction.

Disneyland

Rides, shows, and attractions are listed in alphabetical order. Chapters 9 and 10 provide detailed information to help you prioritize.

Attraction Name	Must See	If Time Permits	No Interest
MAIN STREET, U.S.A.			
Disneyland Opera House	☐	☐	☐
Disneyland Railroad	☐	☐	☐
Main Street Cinema	☐	☐	☐
Main Street Vehicles	☐	☐	☐
Penny Arcade	☐	☐	☐
ADVENTURELAND			
Aladdin and Jasmine's StoryTale Adventures	☐	☐	☐
Enchanted Tiki Room	☐	☐	☐
Indiana Jones Adventure	☐	☐	☐

Jungle Cruise	☐	☐	☐
Tarzan's Treehouse	☐	☐	☐

CRITTER COUNTRY

Davy Crockett's Explorer Canoes	☐	☐	☐
The Many Adventures of Winnie the Pooh	☐	☐	☐
Splash Mountain	☐	☐	☐
Teddi Barra's Swinging Arcade	☐	☐	☐

FANTASYLAND

Alice in Wonderland	☐	☐	☐
Casey Jr. Circus Train	☐	☐	☐
Disney Princess Fantasy Faire	☐	☐	☐
Dumbo the Flying Elephant	☐	☐	☐
"it's a small world"	☐	☐	☐
King Arthur Carrousel	☐	☐	☐
Mad Tea Party	☐	☐	☐
Matterhorn Bobsleds	☐	☐	☐
Meet a Disney Princess	☐	☐	☐
Mr. Toad's Wild Ride	☐	☐	☐
Peter Pan's Flight	☐	☐	☐
Pinocchio's Daring Journey	☐	☐	☐
Snow White's Scary Adventure	☐	☐	☐
Storybook Land Canal Boats	☐	☐	☐
Sword in the Stone Ceremony	☐	☐	☐

FRONTIERLAND

Big Thunder Mountain Railroad	☐	☐	☐
Big Thunder Ranch	☐	☐	☐
Frontierland Shootin' Exposition	☐	☐	☐
Golden Horseshoe Stage	☐	☐	☐
Laughing Stock Co.	☐	☐	☐
Mark Twain Riverboat	☐	☐	☐
Sailing Ship *Columbia*	☐	☐	☐
Tom Sawyer Island	☐	☐	☐

MICKEY'S TOONTOWN

Chip 'n Dale Treehouse	☐	☐	☐
Donald's Boat	☐	☐	☐
Gadget's Go Coaster	☐	☐	☐
Goofy's Playhouse	☐	☐	☐
Jolly Trolley	☐	☐	☐
Mickey's House	☐	☐	☐
Minnie's House	☐	☐	☐
Roger Rabbit's Car Toon Spin	☐	☐	☐

NEW ORLEANS SQUARE

The Bilge Rats and the Bootstrappers	☐	☐	☐
The Disney Gallery	☐	☐	☐
Haunted Mansion	☐	☐	☐
Pirates of the Caribbean	☐	☐	☐

TOMORROWLAND

Astro Orbitor	☐	☐	☐
Autopia	☐	☐	☐
Buzz Lightyear Astro Blasters	☐	☐	☐
Finding Nemo Submarine Voyage	☐	☐	☐
"Honey, I Shrunk the Audience"	☐	☐	☐
Innoventions	☐	☐	☐
Space Mountain	☐	☐	☐
Starcade	☐	☐	☐
Star Tours	☐	☐	☐

SHOWS AND OTHER ATTRACTIONS

Believe: There's Magic in the Stars fireworks spectacular	☐	☐	☐
Disneyland Band	☐	☐	☐
Disneyland Monorail	☐	☐	☐
Disneyland Parade of the Stars	☐	☐	☐
Fantasmic!	☐	☐	☐
Walt Disney's Parade of Dreams	☐	☐	☐

	Must See	If Time Permits	No Interest
Character Greetings	☐	☐	☐
Character Meal	☐	☐	☐
Other:	☐	☐	☐
Other:	☐	☐	☐

Disney's California Adventure

Rides, shows, and attractions are listed in alphabetical order. Chapters 11 and 12 provide detailed information to help you prioritize.

Attraction Name	Must See	If Time Permits	No Interest
SUNSHINE PLAZA			
"A BUG'S LAND"			
Flik's Flyers	☐	☐	☐
Francis's Ladybug Boogie	☐	☐	☐
Heimlich's Chew Chew Train	☐	☐	☐
"It's Tough to Be a Bug!"	☐	☐	☐
Princess Dot Puddle Park	☐	☐	☐
Tuck and Roll's Drive 'Em Buggies	☐	☐	☐
GOLDEN STATE			
Boudin Bakery Tour	☐	☐	☐
Bountiful Valley Farm	☐	☐	☐
Golden Dreams	☐	☐	☐
Golden Vine Winery	☐	☐	☐
Grizzly River Run	☐	☐	☐
Mission Tortilla Factory	☐	☐	☐
Redwood Creek Challenge Trail	☐	☐	☐
Soarin' Over California	☐	☐	☐
HOLLYWOOD PICTURES BACKLOT			
Disney Animation	☐	☐	☐
Jim Henson's Muppet*Vision 3-D	☐	☐	☐
Monsters, Inc. Mike & Sulley to the Rescue!	☐	☐	☐

"Playhouse Disney—Live on Stage!"	☐	☐	☐
Turtle Talk with Crush	☐	☐	☐
Twilight Zone Tower of Terror	☐	☐	☐

PARADISE PIER

California Screamin'	☐	☐	☐
Games of the Boardwalk	☐	☐	☐
Golden Zephyr	☐	☐	☐
Jumpin' Jellyfish	☐	☐	☐
King Triton's Carousel	☐	☐	☐
Maliboomer	☐	☐	☐
Mulholland Madness	☐	☐	☐
Orange Stinger	☐	☐	☐
S.S. *rustworthy*	☐	☐	☐
Sun Wheel	☐	☐	☐

SHOWS AND OTHER ATTRACTIONS

Block Party Bash	☐	☐	☐
Disney's Electrical Parade	☐	☐	☐
Disney's Eureka! A California Parade	☐	☐	☐
High School Musical Pep Rally	☐	☐	☐
Hyperion Theater	☐	☐	☐
Monsters, Inc.	☐	☐	☐
Character Greetings	☐	☐	☐
Character Meal	☐	☐	☐
Other:	☐	☐	☐
Other:	☐	☐	☐
Other:	☐	☐	☐

Packing Checklist

THESE CHECKLISTS WILL HELP relieve your worries about forgetting something.

Travel Details

As you start to pack, take time to list all the things you're planning to do and be sure you've taken care of all the reservations you need. The following list and the daily itinerary in Appendix E will help you double-check.

Fill out the list and put it in your carry-on luggage. It will help you make sure you've done everything and that you have all your information at your fingertips.

Back Home
Pet sitter phone number: _____

House sitter phone number: _____

Neighbor's phone number: _____

Airline Information
Departing date: _____

Departing time: _____

Airline: _____

Airline phone number: _____

Reservation or e-ticket number: _____

Flight number(s)/connecting cities: _____

Departing airport: _____

Arriving airport: _____

Arrival time: _____

Seat assignment(s): _____

Returning date (to go home): _____

Departing time: _____

Airline: _____

Airline phone number: _____

Reservation or e-ticket number: _____

Flight number(s)/connecting cities: _____

Departing airport: _____

Arrival time (to home city): _____

Seat assignment(s): _____

Travel agency or Web site used: _____

Travel agent or Web site customer assistance phone number(s): ___

_____

Parking lot name/number at airport: _____

Location/aisle: _____

Airport and Ground Transportation

Getting to the airport

Taxi/limo service name: _____

Phone number: _____

Reservation number: _____

Pickup date/time: _____

Pickup location: _____

Getting from the airport to your destination

Taxi/limo service name: _____

Phone number: _____

Reservation number: _____

Pickup date/time: _____

Pickup location: _____

Getting from your destination back to the airport
Taxi/limo service name: _____
Phone number: _____
Reservation number: _____
Pickup date/time: _____
Pickup location: _____

Getting home from the airport
Taxi/limo service name: _____
Phone number: _____
Reservation number: _____
Pickup date/time: _____
Pickup location: _____

Rental Car Information
Rental car company: _____
Confirmation number: _____
Daily rate: _____
Pickup location: _____
Rental car company phone number: _____
Type of car reserved: _____
Have you researched your insurance options? See Chapter 3 for more information.

Accommodation Information
Hotel/resort name: _____
Phone number: _____
Reservation number: _____
Check-in date: _____
Checkout date: _____
Type of accommodations reserved: _____
Rate quoted: _____

Packing Checklist

If you are traveling by air, the items allowed past the security check-point or in a carryon taken on to an airplane change frequently. To find out the current regulations, check with the Transportation Safety Administration (TSA) *www.tsa.gov* or (866) 289-9673.

Packing for a theme park is a balance. Take everything that's essential but nothing that isn't. Remember, you'll have to lug every ounce of your gear around all day. Clean out your wallet or purse. Take out your library card, neighborhood video rental card, and all the other things you only need when you're at home. It will lighten your load, and you won't have to replace these items in case your bag is stolen.

Check these items off as you put them into your bags:

Paperwork, Tickets, and Confirmations

Having a single place to put all these items will make it easier to find them.

- ☐ Flight confirmation or tickets
- ☐ Hotel confirmation e-mail
- ☐ Car-rental or shuttle confirmation
- ☐ Disneyland tickets if you bought them online
- ☐ Other confirmations, tickets, or reservations
- ☐ List of credit card numbers and phone numbers to call in case of trouble. Don't pack this list in the same place as your credit cards.
- ☐ Identification for each person traveling (required if you're traveling by airplane)
- ☐ Driver's license for anyone driving a rental car
- ☐ Maps or driving directions
- ☐ RideMax itineraries
- ☐ Daily itinerary (Appendix E)

Toiletries and Comfort Items

- ☐ Prescription medicines (pack in carryon luggage if flying)
- ☐ Copies of prescriptions
- ☐ Waterproof sunscreen
- ☐ Motion sickness remedies (if needed)
- ☐ Earplugs

Clothing

Check the weather forecast at ✐*www.accuweather.com*. Is your clothing appropriate? Besides the normal things—clothing, underwear, and the like—do you have or need any of these items?

- ☐ Sunglasses
- ☐ Glasses case or strap
- ☐ Hats or sun visors
- ☐ Rain jackets (if rain is forecasted)
- ☐ Comfortable shoes
- ☐ Fanny pack or other bag

Ask yourself if your theme park clothing has pockets and if it dries easily (remember there are some attractions that will almost certainly get you wet).

Other Items

- ☐ Time-killers for standing in line
- ☐ Camera
- ☐ Film or digital media
- ☐ Batteries or charger

Use this space to list anything else you want to take along:

- ☐ _____
- ☐ _____
- ☐ _____
- ☐ _____
- ☐ _____

☐ _____
☐ _____
☐ _____
☐ _____
☐ _____
☐ _____
☐ _____
☐ _____

Daily Itinerary

YOU'VE JUST READ ABOUT the activities, theme parks, tourist attractions, and ways of spending your time in the Southern California area. Now that you know all that there is to see and do, a little planning before leaving on vacation will help you make the most of your time and stay within your allocated budget.

As you plan your itinerary, talk to everyone you'll be traveling with so you'll know what each person wants to do. Leave plenty of flexibility in each day's schedule and allow enough time to enjoy things. Otherwise, you'll be too worried about getting to the next activity to enjoy what you're doing.

If you're visiting some of the attractions in Orange County, San Diego, or Los Angeles, allow time in your schedule to get there and back. Southern California traffic is notoriously snarled, and you may need much more time than you think. Doubling the time you might expect given the distance is a good rule of thumb. Also, don't forget to allow time for meals, rest and relaxation, waiting in line, and so on.

Use this itinerary planning worksheet to help you get organized. Make a copy of the worksheet for each day of your vacation and use it as a guide for scheduling the things you (and the people you're traveling with) will most enjoy based on the time you have available.

DAY 1
Date:
Day of week:

Morning Activities

Time	Location	Activity	Description

Breakfast restaurant:
Reservation time:
Restaurant phone number:

Afternoon Activities

Time	Location	Activity	Description

Lunch restaurant:

Reservation time:

Restaurant phone number:

Evening/Nighttime Activities

Time	Location	Activity	Description

Dinner restaurant:

Reservation time:

Restaurant phone number:

Notes

_____

_____

_____

_____

_____

_____

_____

_____

_____

DAY 2
Date:
Day of week:

Morning Activities

Time	Location	Activity	Description

Breakfast restaurant:	
Reservation time:	
Restaurant phone number:	

Afternoon Activities

Time	Location	Activity	Description

Lunch restaurant:

Reservation time:

Restaurant phone number:

Evening/Nighttime Activities

Time	Location	Activity	Description

Dinner restaurant:

Reservation time:

Restaurant phone number:

Notes

DAY 3
Date:
Day of week:

Morning Activities

Time	Location	Activity	Description

Breakfast restaurant:
Reservation time:
Restaurant phone number:

Afternoon Activities

Time	Location	Activity	Description

Lunch restaurant:

Reservation time:

Restaurant phone number:

Evening/Nighttime Activities

Time	Location	Activity	Description

Dinner restaurant:

Reservation time:

Restaurant phone number:

Notes

DAY 4
Date:
Day of week:

Morning Activities

Time	Location	Activity	Description

Breakfast restaurant:
Reservation time:
Restaurant phone number:

Afternoon Activities

Time	Location	Activity	Description

Lunch restaurant:

Reservation time:

Restaurant phone number:

Evening/Nighttime Activities

Time	Location	Activity	Description

Dinner restaurant:

Reservation time:

Restaurant phone number:

Notes

_____

_____

_____

_____

_____

_____

_____

_____

_____

DAY 5			
Date:			
Day of week:			

Morning Activities

Time	Location	Activity	Description

Breakfast restaurant:	
Reservation time:	
Restaurant phone number:	

Afternoon Activities

Time	Location	Activity	Description

Lunch restaurant:

Reservation time:

Restaurant phone number:

Evening/Nighttime Activities

Time	Location	Activity	Description

Dinner restaurant:

Reservation time:

Restaurant phone number:

Notes

_____

_____

_____

_____

_____

_____

_____

_____

DAY 6			
Date:			
Day of week:			

Morning Activities

Time	Location	Activity	Description

Breakfast restaurant:	
Reservation time:	
Restaurant phone number:	

Afternoon Activities

Time	Location	Activity	Description

Lunch restaurant:

Reservation time:

Restaurant phone number:

Evening/Nighttime Activities

Time	Location	Activity	Description

Dinner restaurant:

Reservation time:

Restaurant phone number:

Notes

Index

Everything® You Need for a Family Vacation to Remember

The Everything® Family Guide to the Caribbean
ISBN 10: 1-59337-427-5
ISBN 13: 978-1-59337-427-3
$14.95

The Everything® Family Guide to Coastal Florida
ISBN 10: 1-59869-157-0
ISBN 13: 978-1-59869-157-3
$14.95

The Everything® Family Guide to Cruise Vacations
ISBN 10: 1-59337-428-3
ISBN 13: 978-1-59337-428-0
$14.95

The Everything® Family Guide to Hawaii
ISBN 10: 1-59337-054-7
ISBN 13: 978-1-59337-054-1
$14.95

The Everything® Family Guide to Las Vegas, 2nd Ed.
ISBN 10: 1-59337-359-7
ISBN 13: 978-1-59337-359-7
$14.95

The Everything® Family Guide to Mexico
ISBN 10: 1-59337-658-8
ISBN 13: 978-1-59337-658-1
$14.95

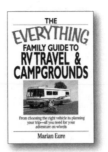